SQL Programmer's Guide

Umang Gupta
William Gietz

que
CORPORATION
LEADING COMPUTER KNOWLEDGE

SQL
Programmer's Guide

Copyright © 1989 by Que® Corporation

All rights reserved. Printed in the United States of America. No part of this book may be used or reproduced in any form or by any means, or stored in a database or retrieval system, without prior written permission of the publisher except in the case of brief quotations embodied in critical articles and reviews. Making copies of any part of this book for any purpose other than your own personal use is a violation of United States copyright laws. For information, address Que Corporation, 11711 N. College Ave., Carmel, IN 46032.

Library of Congress Catalog No.: 88-62184

ISBN 0-88022-390-1

This book is sold *as is*, without warranty of any kind, either express or implied, respecting the contents of this book, including but not limited to implied warranties for the book's quality, performance, merchantability, or fitness for any particular purpose. Neither Que Corporation nor its dealers or distributors shall be liable to the purchaser or any other person or entity with respect to any liability, loss, or damage caused or alleged to be caused directly or indirectly by this book.

92 91 90 89   7 6 5 4 3 2 1

Interpretation of the printing code: the rightmost double-digit number is the year of the book's printing; the rightmost single-digit number, the number of the book's printing. For example, a printing code of 89-1 shows that the first printing of the book occurred in 1989.

Specific examples in this book were developed using SQLBase Version 3.4.

Dedication

For Ruth and Trudy

Publishing Manager
   Allen L. Wyatt, Sr.

Technical Editor
   Sean Flynn

Editorial Assistant
   Ann K. Taylor

Illustrator
   Susan Moore

Index
   Brown Editorial Service

Keyboarding
   Lee Hubbard
   Type Connection; Indianapolis, IN

Cover Design
   Dan Armstrong

Book Design and Production
   Dan Armstrong
   Brad Chinn
   Cheryl English
   David Kline
   Lori A. Lyons
   Jennifer Matthews
   John Ogle

Composed in Garamond and OCRB
by Precision Printing

ABOUT THE AUTHORS

Umang Gupta

Umang Gupta is president and CEO of Gupta Technologies, Inc., a company that specializes in developing SQL database management software for PC local area networks. Before that Mr. Gupta spent three years as a senior executive with Oracle Corporation, where his last position was vice president and general manager of the Microcomputer Products Division. Before that he was the director of marketing for Magnuson Computers, a manufacturer of IBM plug-compatible mainframes. Mr. Gupta began his career in 1973 as a systems engineer in the data processing division of IBM Corporation. From there he held various sales and marketing management positions within IBM and was responsible for sales to some of IBM's largest corporate accounts. He holds an E.E. degree from the Indian Institute of Technology and an M.B.A. from Kent State University.

William Gietz

William Gietz has done a number of pieces of technical writing in the area of databases. He has a B.A. degree from Antioch College, and a Ph.D. in philosophy from the University of Rochester, and has taught at several universities. He is also the author (as William Getz) of a novel published both in the United States and abroad.

Contents at a Glance

Introduction 1

Part I   Using SQL Interactively

Chapter 1	Overview of a Relational Database	7
Chapter 2	Constructing a Table	19
Chapter 3	Getting the Data You Want: Queries	29
Chapter 4	Using Queries To Manipulate Data	45
Chapter 5	Arranging the Result	63
Chapter 6	Queries That Draw on More than One Table: Joins	77
Chapter 7	Queries in Other Statements	91
Chapter 8	Virtual Tables: Views	103
Chapter 9	Changing Tables and Data	115
Chapter 10	Using Indexes To Maximize Performance	125
Chapter 11	The System Catalog and Sharing a Database	131
Chapter 12	Database Utilities and Recovery	153

Part II   Programming with SQL

Chapter 13	SQL Programming Concepts	163
Chapter 14	Using a Function Call Interface	175
Chapter 15	Advanced Programming with a Function Call Interface	187
Chapter 16	Using a Precompiler Interface	199
Chapter 17	Using a COBOL SQL Precompiler	205
Chapter 18	Using a dBASE Interface	221

Part III   Looking Ahead

Chapter 19	Promising Developments and Extensions	233
Chapter 20	SQL: Where We Have Been and Where We Are Going	249
Appendix A	Sample C Program	257
Appendix B	SQLBase API Function Calls	263
Appendix C	Sample COBOL Programs	267
Appendix D	Sample Database	277
Appendix E	Sample dBASE Programs	283
Appendix F	Reserved Keywords	287

Glossary 289
Index 295

TABLE OF CONTENTS

Introduction 1
    About SQL and This Book 1

I   Using SQL Interactively

1   Overview of a Relational Database 7
    Columns and Rows 8
    Entities and the Primary Key 9
    Other Relational Features 12
    The SQL Language 15
    Other Database Objects 16
    Summary 16

2   Constructing a Table 19
    Creating a Table 19
    Identifiers and Attributes 20
    Data Types 21
    Inserting Data 24
    Summary 27

3   Getting the Data You Want: Queries 29
    Basic Elements of a Query: The SELECT and
      FROM Clauses 29
    Narrowing the Query: The WHERE Clause 34
      Relational Predicates 35
        Simple Relational Predicates 35
        Other Relational Predicates 38
      Connecting Several Predicates: AND and OR 42
    Summary 43

4   Using Queries To Manipulate Data 45
    Arithmetic Operators 46
    Functions 51
      Aggregate Functions 51
      Nonaggregate Functions 54
        String Functions 54

	Date or Time Functions............................	57
	Selecting Constants.................................	59
	Summary..	61
5	**Arranging the Result**.............................	**63**
	Grouping in Sets with the GROUP BY Clause...........	63
	Restricting Groupings with the HAVING Clause.........	70
	Sorting with the ORDER BY Clause....................	72
	Summary..	75
6	**Queries That Draw on More than One Table: Joins**.............................	**77**
	Equijoins...	79
	Outer Joins...	82
	Self Joins...	85
	Other Types of Joins................................	88
	Joins in Complex Queries............................	88
	Summary..	89
7	**Queries in Other Statements**.....................	**91**
	UNIONs of Queries..................................	91
	Simple Nested Queries...............................	94
	Compound Nested Queries...........................	98
	Correlated Subqueries...............................	99
	Using Queries To Insert Data........................	101
	Summary..	102
8	**Virtual Tables: Views**............................	**103**
	Replacing Complex Queries with Simpler Ones.........	103
	Queries Requiring a View............................	106
	Joins on Views......................................	107
	Security and Dropping a View........................	108
	Inserting Data into a View...........................	109
	Ensuring Data Integrity: The CHECK Option............	111
	Summary..	113
9	**Changing Tables and Data**.......................	**115**
	Changing the Data..................................	115
	Updating Data in a Row........................	116
	Deleting Rows................................	117
	Undoing and Saving Changes....................	118
	Changing a Table...................................	118
	Dropping a Column............................	119
	Adding a Column..............................	120
	Modifying a Column...........................	121

	Renaming a Table or Column	122
	Dropping a Table	122
	Summary	123
10	**Using Indexes To Maximize Performance**	**125**
	Using an Index	127
	Using a Unique Index	128
	Using a Concatenated Index	128
	Dropping an Index	129
	Summary	130
11	**The System Catalog and Sharing a Database**	**131**
	Tables, Views, and Indexes	132
	SYSTABLES	132
	SYSCOLUMNS	134
	SYSVIEWS	135
	SYSINDEXES	137
	SYSKEYS	138
	Authority Levels and Privileges	138
	Authority Levels	139
	Privileges	140
	Granting Authority and Privileges	140
	SYSUSERAUTH	142
	SYSTABAUTH	143
	SYSCOLAUTH	144
	Synonyms	147
	Granting Access to the System Catalog	146
	Revoking Authority and Privileges	148
	Changing a Password	150
	Summary	151
12	**Database Utilities and Recovery**	**153**
	The LOAD Command	154
	SQL Format	154
	ASCII Format	154
	DIF Format	154
	The UNLOAD Command	155
	The REORGANIZE Command	156
	Journaling	157
	Automatic Recovery	157
	Summary	159

II Programming with SQL

13 SQL Programming Concepts 163
Why Embedded SQL.. 163
Row-at-a-Time Processing 164
Substituting for Variables................................ 165
Error Handling... 166
Phases of Processing SQL Statements 167
    The Compile Phase 168
    The Execute Phase................................... 169
    The Fetch Phase..................................... 171
    Cursors... 172
Connecting and Disconnecting............................. 172
Programming Options 173
Summary.. 174

14 Using a Function Call Interface 175
Before We Begin.. 175
    Notes About the Sample Code........................ 175
    Special Files....................................... 176
    Getting Information................................. 176
    Errors.. 177
The API Database Access Cycle 178
    CONNECT.. 179
    COMPILE.. 180
    BIND DATA.. 181
    SET OUTPUT BUFFERS 183
    EXECUTE.. 184
    FETCH.. 184
    COMMIT... 185
    DISCONNECT... 185
Summary.. 186

15 Advanced Programming with a Function Call Interface 187
Manipulating LONG VARCHAR Columns 187
    Querying LONG Data 188
    Writing LONG Data.................................. 189
Using Multiple Handles 190
Result Set Operations.................................... 191
Using Result Sets.. 192
Data Consistency and Multiple Users 193
    Locking 193
    Isolation Levels.................................... 194

		Read Repeatability	195
		Cursor Stability	195
		Read Only	196
	Deadlocks		196
	More on Rollbacks and Locking		196
	Summary		197

16 Using a Precompiler Interface ... 199

    What Is a Precompiler? ... 199
    Advantages of Precompilers ... 201
    Limitations of Precompilers ... 203
    Summary ... 204

17 Using a COBOL SQL Precompiler ... 205

    Syntax of Precompiler Statements ... 205
    Connecting to a Database ... 207
    SELECT Statements that Return Multiple Rows ... 208
        The WHENEVER Statement ... 210
        The SQL Communication Area ... 211
        Fetching ... 213
    The SELECT INTO Statement ... 215
    Host Variables ... 216
    COBOL Host Structures ... 218
    Declaring Table and View Definitions ... 219
    Summary ... 220

18 Using a dBASE Interface ... 221

    Invisible and Embedded SQL ... 223
        Invisible SQL ... 224
        Embedded SQL ... 226
    Cursor Operations ... 228
    Summary ... 230

III Looking Ahead

19 Promising Developments and Extensions ... 233

    The DEFAULT Clause ... 233
    The CHECK Constraint ... 234
    Integrity Constraints ... 236
    Referential Integrity Constraints ... 237
    Scroll Cursors ... 238
    The CONNECT BY Clause ... 240
    The COMPUTE Clause ... 243
    Summary ... 247

20	**SQL: Where We've Been and Where We're Going**	**249**
	The Origins of SQL	250
	A Universal SQL?	252
	Prospects	253
	Summing Up	254
A	**Sample C Program**	**257**
	SAMPLE.C	257
	SAMPLE.TXT	261
B	**SQLBase API Function Calls**	**263**
C	**Sample COBOL Programs**	**267**
	Program for a Function Call Interface	267
	Program for Precompiler	273
D	**Sample Database**	**277**
E	**Sample dBASE Programs**	**283**
	Sample Program 1	283
	Sample Program 2	285
F	**Reserved Keywords**	**287**
	Glossary	**289**
	Index	**295**

Trademark Acknowledgments

Que Corporation has made every attempt to supply trademark information about company names, products, and services mentioned in this book. Trademarks indicated below were derived from various sources. Que Corporation cannot attest to the accuracy of this information.

UNIX is a trademark of AT&T.

SQLBase is a registered trademark of Gupta Technologies, Inc. SQLWindows is a trademark of Gupta Technologies, Inc.

OS/2 is a registered trademark of International Business Machines Corporation. SQL/DS is a trademark of International Business Machines Corporation.

dBXL and Quicksilver are trademarks of WordTech Systems, Inc.

ACKNOWLEDGMENTS

This book could not have been written without the help of many people who generously contributed information and advice and were cheerfully there when we needed them. Our particular thanks go out to Dave Isherwood, who not only provided the sample COBOL programs and other material that became the basis of the chapters on using a precompiler, but who also reviewed the entire finished manuscript. Other people we want to thank are Shelly Dimmick, Rich Heaps, Michael Lee, Trudy Rucker, Bruce Scott, Liz Stevenson, Frances Thomas, and Kevin Watts. Any shortcomings the book may have are our fault, not theirs.

Introduction

About SQL and This Book

A database is like an electronic filing cabinet. It is used for the same purpose as any other filing cabinet—to store records. The only difference is that, with a database, the records are stored electronically.

To get at the records we have stored, or even to store them in the first place, we need a system for managing the database. This database management system is what enables us to perform operations—"Bring me this file," "Update this record"—on the contents of the "cabinet."

Various types of database management system (DBMS) exist, representing different approaches to the tasks of furnishing access to information in a database, preserving the data's integrity, keeping track of users, and providing security. For our purposes, though, we can classify all of the systems into two kinds: relational and nonrelational. By and large, all the newer systems on the market are relational.

In a relational system, data is stored and represented exclusively in tables. There is never any need to negotiate some other structure—such as a hierarchical tree—to get at data. We talk at length in the first chapter of this book about the significance of this: briefly, it enables relational systems to offer a new measure of flexibility and convenience in manipulating data.

The SQL language—the name is an acronym for "Structured Query Language" and is pronounced both "sequel" and "s-q-l"—is a language for managing a relational database system. It is not the only such language, but it is increasingly the most popular and has pretty well become the standard. It consists of a certain more or less agreed-upon set of types of statements that let us perform various operations.

We have to say "more or less agreed-upon" here because, although a standard SQL has been defined by the American National Standards Institute (ANSI), every proprietary implementation of SQL customizes the language in various ways. These implementations both supplement the standard set with additional useful types of statements or expressions and also sometimes tailor the standard statements to meet particular needs.

For example, each SQL implementation has its own command interface, with its own set of features that go beyond standard SQL. These features that are not part of standard SQL are called *extensions* of the standard SQL. Because they offer different sets of extensions and implement them in different ways, all implementations of SQL are not the same.

As a result, any detailed look at how to use SQL is inevitably to some extent a look at how to use somebody or other's particular brand. We can't confine ourselves to looking just at features that are shared or standard because that approach would cause us to leave out too much important information relating to how SQL is actually used.

Fortunately, the variations among implementations are not particularly significant from a standpoint of familiarizing ourselves with the basic language. For the most part, the discussions in this book are generic, and we indicate where they are not.

For screen displays and in other instances where we need examples that are at least representative if not generic, we will use Gupta Technologies' SQLBase implementation of a SQL-based database management system. Besides being a system for which we have a perhaps understandable personal fondness, SQLBase offers the advantage that it stays particularly close to standard SQL.

SQL is used in two ways. It is embedded in application programs, and it is also used by issuing SQL statements directly to the system from the keyboard. SQL used in the latter way is often referred to as *interactive* SQL; SQL used in applications is called *embedded* SQL. In itself, though, SQL is neither an interactive language nor a programming language. To use SQL in either way, we need to work through an interface belonging to one of the proprietary SQL implementations. In the first chapter of Part II we explain at length why.

Reflecting the two basic ways SQL is used, we have devoted Part I of *SQL Programmer's Guide* to interactive SQL and Part II to embedded SQL.

In Part I we explain the basic types of SQL statement, their components, and the various kinds of database objects to be met with in a relational DBMS. Part I closes with a look at some commonly available database utilities and a discussion of the options for enabling recovery in the event of a system crash. For the screens and examples in Part I, we use the Gupta Technologies SQLTalk interactive interface to SQLBase. For all intents and purposes, this interface is transparent to the user: no special syntax or other requirements are imposed that would detract from the universality of the examples.

In Part II we explain in what ways SQL is not a programming language and why SQL has to be embedded. We also show how to build database applications by embedding SQL in programs written in a language that *is* a programming language. We discuss both coding for a function call interface and coding for a precompiler, giving as examples excerpts of programs written in the C language and in COBOL. We also include a chapter on using SQL with the new dBASE interfaces. Complete sample C, COBOL, and dBASE programs are included for reference in appendixes at the end of the book.

In Part III, we cover some interesting extensions and some new features that have just been added to the standard and have only begun to appear in actual implementations. Then, in the concluding chapter, we give a capsule history of SQL and venture an assessment of where SQL seems to be headed.

A word about notational conventions: names of tables, columns, indexes, and so forth, as well as special keywords (for example, "SELECT") of SQL statements and commands are entered in uppercase in this book, in keeping with the general practice in writings about database systems. Also, we take some liberties with quotation marks: where the meaning is clear from the context, we often let a word's being in all uppercase or italics serve as a substitute for putting it in quotation marks, though quotation marks may strictly speaking be required. Again for clarity, we will customarily leave periods and commas outside the quotation marks unless we actually mean to quote them.

Readers who have a SQL DBMS are encouraged to try the examples appearing in Part I, or variations on them, for themselves. As an aid to doing this, we include in an appendix the data for the five main tables used in these examples, as well as SQL statements to create the tables and insert the data into them.

Readers owning Gupta Technologies' SQLBase can re-create the SPA database used in the examples by entering these SQL statements, with data, from SQLTalk. Readers working with some other vendor's SQL-based DBMS can do the same thing through their own interactive interface rather than through SQLTalk, although small syntactical changes in the SQL statements may be necessary, depending on their system.

Readers working through the examples should note, though, that the results they get will be exactly the same as what they see in this book only if their database is in the identical state that ours was in when we issued the same statement. In other words, the same tables and views must exist, with the same rows; the same users must be connected; and so on. Sometimes in this book we do something— an update, for instance—in the examples that we subsequently undo without particularly advertising the fact; so readers should not be surprised if their results are only similar but not identical to ours.

Part I

Using SQL Interactively

CHAPTER 1

Overview of a Relational Database

Relational systems mark a big advance in the storing and managing of quantities of data. The main reason for this is that in a relational system it is possible to greatly reduce the storage of redundant data. Ideally, in fact, in a system set up in strict accord with certain theoretical principles of relational design, there would be no redundancy. No relationship between two items of data (that a certain person has a certain address, for instance) would appear in more than one place in a database.

In practice, actual systems only more or less approach this ideal, for various reasons, and often enough contain some of the same data in several places. But even in a relational system that only approaches the ideal, minimizing redundancy of data has two major benefits. First, data can be rearranged and combined more easily in new relationships: it is not locked into certain relationships as a result of the way it is stored. Second, minimizing redundancy permits greater ease of updating. Fewer instances of data need to be updated, and this reduces the likelihood of errors arising from failure to update all instances.

All data in a relational system is stored and displayed in *tables*. Spreadsheet programs and nonrelational database systems also use tables, so there is nothing distinctive about the fact that relational systems use them too. But there is something distinctive about the *way* that relational systems use them. This distinction derives from setting up and using the database according to certain theoretical principles of relational design. These principles are outlined in this chapter.

Columns and Rows

All information is information *about* something, and perhaps the first principle of relational design is that all the information in a particular table should always be information about examples of some *one kind of thing*. This principle underlies everything that is distinctive about the relational use of tables.

For example, the following table GUESTS contains information about the guests of an exclusive, chic, and imaginary health facility called La Bamba Spa (see fig. 1.1):

Fig. 1.1. GUESTS.

NAME	SEX	BUILD	HEIGHT
BETTE MIDRIFF	F	M	66
MARCELLO HISTRIONI	M	M	66
JEAN-PAUL ROTUNDO	M	L	70
MICHAEL JOHNSON	M	L	71
CLINT WESTWOOD	M	M	73
JOANNIE RIVULETS	F	S	65
WARREN AMOROSO	M	M	70
MARLON SPANDEX	M	M	71
OLYMPIA WELCH	F	L	70
HEATHER STARLETTE	F	M	66
DOLLY BRISKET	F	S	61
JOAN TONIC	F	M	62
MEL GIMLET	M	M	70
DON JACKSON	M	M	70
ROBERT DINERO	M	L	69
JANE FYUNDAI	F	L	65
DYAN HOWITZER	F	S	68
BIANCA JOGGER	F	S	61
ENGLEBERT HUMPTYDUMPTY	M	L	72
SHIRLEY O'SHADE	F	M	64
SHARE	F	S	71
STELLA SHIELDS	F	M	65
SEAN PENCIL	M	S	65
HETAERA	F	S	63

The table contains four columns—NAME, SEX, BUILD, and HEIGHT—and has 24 rows.

The table is *about* the spa's guests; each vertical column contains information about a different characteristic or *attribute* of the guests. The attributes we are interested in are each guest's name, sex, build, and height, so a column is devoted to each.

This is the function of the vertical *columns* in a table: to give information about the *attributes* of the entities that the table is *about*.

Each horizontal *row* in table GUEST lists information about all attributes tracked in the table for *one guest in particular*. Thus, whereas column NAME shows the name of every guest in the table, and column SEX shows the sex of every guest, and so on for the other columns, the row on which Bette Midriff's name appears shows information only about the attributes of the guest whose name is Bette Midriff.

All the information in a *row*, in other words, is information about the attributes of one particular entity.

How this conception of the roles of rows and columns distinguishes the relational approach to tables becomes clearer in the next section, in which we explain some implications of this conception and introduce a new relational concept: the primary key.

Entities and the Primary Key

In the real world, you would have a variety of reasons for wanting to be able to tell the guests at La Bamba Spa apart: if you cannot tell them apart, you cannot make satisfactory room assignments, design customized fitness programs, prepare correct invoices, and so on. For the same reasons, you want to be able to tell the guests apart in the database, too. Practically speaking, this means that you want to differentiate the rows in a table. If you can't tell the row for Bette Midriff from the row for Jean-Paul Rotundo, the database is not useful for making satisfactory room assignments, designing customized fitness programs, preparing correct invoices, and so on.

For a row to be distinguishable from other rows, it needs to be different in some way. It needs to have a defining characteristic that sets it apart. In a relational system, this defining characteristic is not allowed to be an extraneous feature such as the row's position with regard to other rows; it must be a feature of the row itself. Because a row by itself consists only of items of data, you must look at the row's data for the defining characteristic that enables you to pick out that row.

You must look, in other words, for a column (or group of columns) that contains different data for every row—data that is not *duplicated* in any two rows. Then you can use this unique feature to identify the row just as you use a name to identify a person.

Refer again to table GUESTS (see fig. 1.1). Notice that not all the attributes, or columns, are equally useful in helping you to pick out particular rows. For example, it is not much help to know only the sex of a guest you want to identify if that attribute applies to half your guests. Similarly, knowing a guest's build may narrow the field but does not allow you to pick out any one guest in particular.

The problem is that columns SEX and BUILD contain duplicate values. When two rows list the same attribute, that attribute cannot be used to choose between the rows.

Plainly, the only column you can use as an *identifying attribute* is column NAME. Because NAME contains no duplicate values, the information in this column is enough by itself to let you pick out a guest's row in the table.

We have drawn, in effect, a distinction between two kinds of columns. One kind of column is based on a *defining* or *uniquely identifying* attribute of a row. The other kind of column is based on *descriptive* attributes that give information, but not enough to identify a row or entity.

The column (or group of columns) based on a defining attribute of a row is called the *key*, or *primary key*. A table's key lets you identify particular rows; it also defines the entities that the table is about.

This last becomes clearer in a few paragraphs. For now, just remember that in a relational database every table should have a key that makes each row distinct.

As we have said, sometimes a key consists of more than one column. In table GUEST_ROSTER, for instance, you cannot pick out individual rows using only one column (see fig. 1.2). Two columns are required to do the job:

The GUEST_ROSTER columns list the names of all guests who have come or gone in the period June 14 though June 27, 1988, which we shall imagine to be the current period. The columns also list the arrival date of each guest, the departure date when known, the room and trainer assigned to each guest, and the discount, if a discount is given.

No single column will work as a key because all columns, including column NAME, contain duplicate values: Sean Pencil and Hetaera both made more than one visit to the spa during the two-week period and so are listed twice. To establish a key for this table, then, you need to consider using two or more columns in conjunction. A key of this sort, based on two or more columns, is called a *composite key*, or a *composite primary key*.

The best candidate for a composite key for table GUEST_ROSTER are the two columns NAME and ARRIVAL, for a couple of reasons. First, NAME and ARRIVAL taken together let you identify individual rows. If you know just the values for NAME and ARRIVAL, you can distinguish any given row from all others: these values are not the same for any two rows.

At present, other groupings of columns—NAME and ROOM, for instance—may also let you uniquely identify rows. But if they do, it is an accident and a feature liable to let you down in the future: a guest could return for a second visit in the current period and take the same room. NAME and ARRIVAL are a better choice because only in a very contrived case can we imagine them failing as a key (namely,

***Fig. 1.2.** GUEST_ROSTER.*

```
SELECT NAME, ROOM, TRAINER, ARRIVAL, DEPARTURE, DISCOUNT
FROM GUEST_ROSTER;
NAME                         ROOM TRAINER    ARRIVAL     DEPARTURE    DISCOUNT
=========================    ==== ========   ==========  ===========  ==========
JEAN-PAUL ROTUNDO             3   JULIO      15-JUN-1988 17-JUN-1988       .2
MARCELLO HISTRIONI            2   TODD       26-JUN-1988                   .1
BETTE MIDRIFF                 1   MICHAEL    14-JUN-1988 16-JUN-1988
MICHAEL JOHNSON               4   JULIO      15-JUN-1988 19-JUN-1988
CLINT WESTWOOD                5   MICHAEL    25-JUN-1988                   .15
SEAN PENCIL                   6   TODD       15-JUN-1988 20-JUN-1988       .05
HETAERA                       7   SERENA     24-JUN-1988
JOANNIE RIVULETS              8   SERENA     25-JUN-1988                   .15
WARREN AMOROSO                9   TODD       16-JUN-1988 23-JUN-1988       .2
MARLON SPANDEX               10   JULIO      16-JUN-1988 23-JUN-1988       .05
OLYMPIA WELCH                11   MICHAEL    22-JUN-1988 27-JUN-1988       .1
HEATHER STARLETTE            12   SERENA     22-JUN-1988                   .05
DOLLY BRISKET                13   SERENA     22-JUN-1988
JOAN TONIC                   14   MICHAEL    23-JUN-1988                   .05
SEAN PENCIL                   9   TODD       23-JUN-1988                   .1
MEL GIMLET                   15   YVETTE     17-JUN-1988 24-JUN-1988
DON JACKSON                  16   TODD       17-JUN-1988 25-JUN-1988       .1
HETAERA                      10   SERENA     14-JUN-1988 20-JUN-1988       .2
ROBERT DINERO                17   YVETTE     18-JUN-1988 25-JUN-1988       .1
JANE FYUNDAI                 18   MICHAEL    19-JUN-1988 26-JUN-1988       .1
DYAN HOWITZER                19   YVETTE     19-JUN-1988 26-JUN-1988
BIANCA JOGGER                20   TODD       20-JUN-1988 27-JUN-1988       .15
```

in the case of someone arriving, departing, and then arriving again all on the same day). And this is a case you could take steps to rule out.

But a more important reason for favoring NAME and ARRIVAL as the key is that this grouping, more than any other, reflects what the table is *about*. What, after all, are the entities that the attributes of the table describe? Or, to ask the question another way, what are the attributes of the table really attributes *of*? They are attributes of the guests' *stays* or *visits*—that is, of the entities defined by the two attributes guest name plus an arrival date. That is why you use a different row for a guest every time he or she visits—a different row for each visit, not for each guest.

To sum up: you need to be able to identify particular rows (or entities), and to do this you need to be able to tell the rows apart. The attribute (or attributes) that lets you tell rows apart is the key. Every table should have a key. The key, in essence, defines the entities that the table is about—that is, the entities that all the attributes describe.

It follows that if a table has a primary key, the table does *not* have duplicate rows—rows exactly the same in every column. For a primary key lets you pick out individual rows, and if the table contains duplicate rows, then it contains rows you cannot tell apart; so evidently a table with duplicate rows does not have a primary key.

In other words, from the rule that a table should have a primary key, it follows that a table should not have duplicate rows.

Other Relational Features

In addition to sharing the conception of columns and rows and the rule that every table should have a primary key, all relational systems have three other features in common. You are permitted to select data from certain *columns* without having to select from all columns; you are permitted to select data from certain *rows* without having to select from all rows; and you are permitted to select data from more than one table at a time.

We remarked in the preceding section that the identifying characteristic of a row must not be something extraneous, such as the row's position in relation to other rows; it should be a feature of the row itself. In fact, a row should not depend on positioning for any of its information. A similar rule applies to columns: in a relational system, neither a column nor a row should depend for its meaning on the order in which it appears among other columns or rows.

The two tables GUEST and GUEST_ROSTER both follow this rule. For example, the way you interpret the data in table GUESTS is not affected if the order in which the columns appear is rearranged, as shown:

```
BUILD SEX     HEIGHT NAME
===== ===  ========== ======================
  M    F          66  BETTE MIDRIFF
  M    M          66  MARCELLO HISTRIONI
  L    M          70  JEAN-PAUL ROTUNDO
  I    M          71  MICHAEL JOHNSON
  M    M          73  CLINT WESTWOOD
  S    F          65  JOANNIE RIVULETS
  M    M          70  WARREN AMOROSO
  M    M          71  MARLON SPANDEX
                   .
                   .
                   .
```

Nor would the information be affected if you rearranged the rows.

On the other hand, in a table in which the columns represent the order of the weighings, the order of the columns is important:

Chapter 1: Overview of a Relational Database **13**

```
       DAILY WEIGHINGS
       ===================================
GUEST  WEIGHT WEIGHT WEIGHT WEIGHT WEIGHT
=====  ====== ====== ====== ====== ======
BETTE  150    148.5  148    149    150
```

The WEIGHT columns could not be reordered without affecting your ability to use the data: you would lose information about the sequence of the weighings.

The following table shows another way you might organize the same data—by putting each day's weight in a different row:

```
DAILY WEIGHINGS
===============
GUEST WEIGHT
===== ======
BETTE 150
BETTE 148.5
BETTE 148
BETTE 149
BETTE 150
```

If this table represents a sequential record, with each row appearing in the order in which the respective weight was recorded, then the information in this table depends on maintaining the order of the rows, just as the information in the previous table depended on maintaining the order of the columns. You cannot change the order of the rows without losing information.

Notice, incidentally, that the table also breaks another rule of relational design: the first and last rows are duplicates: they have no distinct identity. In this table, it is impossible to tell rows apart just on the basis of their data, for the table has no key. Duplicate rows are always likely in tables in which the ordering of the rows matters.

We might put the point of these examples this way: as much as possible, organization of the data in a relational system should always be *modular* so that the data loses nothing by being detached from its original context.

This way of storing data permits items of data to be readily used in new combinations. Nothing in a relational system actually prevents you from building tables in which, for instance, the order of the rows is important; but if you do build such tables, you in effect deny yourself two of the most advantageous features of relational systems. One is the ability to retrieve data from only certain columns without having to retrieve from all columns:

```
NAME                        HEIGHT
=========================   ==========
BETTE MIDRIFF                   66
MARCELLO HISTRIONI              66
JEAN-PAUL ROTUNDO               70
MICHAEL JOHNSON                 71
CLINT WESTWOOD                  73
JOANNIE RIVULETS                65
                              .
                              .
                              .
24 ROWS SELECTED
```

The other feature is the ability to retrieve data just from certain rows without having to retrieve from all rows:

```
NAME                        HEIGHT
=========================   ==========
BETTE MIDRIFF                   66
MEL GIMLET                      70
2 ROWS SELECTED
```

If you have built your tables so that the information in a given row or column is meaningless out of its original context, or if you cannot even identify particular items of information apart from their context in the table because the table contains duplicate rows, then you have no use for either of these two features.

Finally, there is a third important feature of any relational system. It is always possible in a relational system to perform a *join*—that is, to retrieve rows from more than one table simultaneously. This operation is called a join because the rows retrieved from the different tables are *joined* on one or more columns of data that appear in two of the tables. The following table, for instance, shows data returned from several columns of the two tables GUESTS and GUEST_ROSTER, joined on the similar NAME column in each table:

```
NAME                        HEIGHT  TRAINER  ARRIVAL
=========================   ======  =======  ===========
JEAN-PAUL ROTUNDO              70   JULIO    15-JUN-1988
MARCELLO HISTRIONI             66   TODD     26-JUN-1988
BETTE MIDRIFF                  66   MICHAEL  14-JUN-1988
MICHAEL JOHNSON                71   JULIO    15-JUN-1988
CLINT WESTWOOD                 73   MICHAEL  25-JUN-1988
SEAN PENCIL                    65   TODD     15-JUN-1988
                              .
                              .
                              .
22 ROWS SELECTED
```

In the following chapters, we describe how to perform each of these operations—selecting data from certain columns only, for certain rows only, and from more than one table at a time—as well as a host of other operations. But now we need to describe where SQL comes into play.

The SQL Language

SQL is a language for performing relational operations such as those discussed in the preceding section. It is, in short, a language for managing a relational system. Data is retrieved, updated, or deleted with SQL statements; columns are modified, tables are created or dropped, and any other changes to the structure of a database are made with SQL statements.

SQL statements can be sorted into four general categories: queries, data-definition statements, data-manipulation statements, and data-control statements.

Queries retrieve data from the tables in a database. Queries are also called SELECT statements, after the operative keyword ("SELECT") in a query.

In a query, you identify the tables, columns, and, if you want, the rows from which you want to select data. The database then furnishes the data matching your specifications in a *result table*, or *result*, like those displayed in this chapter.

Data-definition statements define the structure of the database. In this category are those SQL statements that create, alter, or drop structural components—that is, such database objects as tables, views, and indexes. Examples are the statements CREATE TABLE, CREATE VIEW, CREATE INDEX, ALTER TABLE, and the various forms of the DROP statement for dropping a table, view, or index.

Data-manipulation statements change the data in a database by inserting new data, updating existing data, or deleting rows. The SQL statements INSERT, UPDATE, and DELETE accomplish these operations.

Data-control statements create other users or determine authority levels and privileges on tables and views in the database. Two examples of statements in this category are GRANT (Database Authority) and GRANT (Table Privileges). The privileges granted with these statements range from the ability simply to log on to the database and do nothing more, to the ability to create and drop tables and to grant and revoke privileges oneself.

The syntax of SQL statements was designed to approximate English syntax. Without going so far as to say that SQL statements are always easy to understand (English, after all, can be tricky too), or even always very English-like, their generally English-like syntax is a help. For example, the following query, which selects the data in columns NAME and HEIGHT from table GUESTS, is easy to understand:

```
SELECT NAME, HEIGHT
FROM GUESTS;
```

By the way, we refer to queries and other types of SQL statements as *statements* in this book even though from a grammatical standpoint they actually look more like commands. This is the conventional way to refer to them. Following this practice enables us to reserve the word *command* for command structures that have been added to SQL by particular implementations and are not strictly part of SQL.

Other Database Objects

In the preceding section, we mentioned (besides tables) two types of database objects—indexes and views—that we have not mentioned before. We will round off our overview of a relational database by saying a few words about each of these and also about the system catalog and synonyms. Indexes, views, the system catalog, and synonyms are all more fully discussed in later chapters.

Indexes, which the user creates on one or more columns of a table, enable the system to find particular rows by looking up their location in the index instead of having to search for them through all rows in a table. In this respect, an index on a table works like an index in a book. Indexes are created with the CREATE INDEX statement and are automatically maintained by the system as rows are added, updated, or deleted. They can significantly speed performance, particularly in queries in which individual rows are sought.

Views are not created *on* tables but rather *from* them. A view is the result table of a query, preserved with the CREATE VIEW statement. After a result table is preserved as a view, it can be treated in many respects like a base table (that is, like a table created with a CREATE TABLE statement): it has a name, it can be queried, and in many cases it can even be updated, with all changes being passed on to the base table underneath.

The *system catalog* is a group of tables maintained by the system. These tables automatically keep track of information about the database. Thus, if you want to see a list of all the tables, views, or indexes in the database, or if you want to find information about various users and their privileges, you can look up this information in the tables in the system catalog.

A *synonym* is a user's own name for a table created by another user. Synonyms are a convenient shorthand that saves having to prefix the name of the table with the other user's name every time you refer to it, as you would otherwise have to do. All synonyms created by any user are also kept track of in the system catalog.

Summary

All data in a relational database is stored and displayed in tables, each of which contains information about one kind of thing, or entity. The columns of a table give information about the attributes of these entities; each row gives information about the attributes of one entity in particular.

Each table should have a primary key. This is a column (or group of columns) based on a defining attribute of a row. The purpose of the key is to let you pick out individual rows in a table.

Relational systems have three important features in common. You are permitted to select data from certain columns without having to select from all columns; you are permitted to select data from certain rows without having to select from all rows; and you are permitted to select data from more than one table at a time.

SQL is a language for performing these and other relational operations. It is a language for managing a relational system.

CHAPTER 2

Constructing a Table

Suppose that you want to build a database for the imaginary La Bamba Spa. Suppose, too, that you have already taken the first step of creating a brand new database and logging on, or *connecting*, to it, to use the database term. How to do this is not important at this point, and the details vary anyway, depending on the system you use, so we do not go into them. What you want to do now is to populate the database with some tables.

Creating a Table

You use a CREATE TABLE statement to create a table.

The next two statements create the two tables GUESTS and GUEST_ROSTER referred to in Chapter 1, "Overview of a Relational Database." Table GUESTS contains vital statistics on all past and present guests of La Bamba Spa. Table GUEST_ROSTER keeps track of arrivals, departures, room assignments, and so on for all visits to the spa over the two-week period June 14 through June 27, 1988.

You saw in Chapter 1 what these tables, with data, look like. Note that the following statements merely *create* the tables, however. Getting data into them requires a separate operation, one described later in this chapter:

```
CREATE TABLE GUESTS (NAME VARCHAR(25) NOT NULL, SEX VARCHAR(1),
BUILD VARCHAR(1), HEIGHT INTEGER);

TABLE CREATED

CREATE TABLE GUEST_ROSTER (NAME VARCHAR(25) NOT NULL,
ROOM VARCHAR(3), TRAINER VARCHAR(8), ARRIVAL DATE NOT NULL,
DEPARTURE DATE, DISCOUNT DECIMAL(2,2));

TABLE CREATED
```

Tables GUESTS and GUEST_ROSTER now exist, though without any data in them. Table GUESTS consists of the four columns NAME, SEX, BUILD, and HEIGHT; table GUEST_ROSTER consists of the six columns NAME, ROOM, TRAINER, ARRIVAL, DEPARTURE, and DISCOUNT.

Notice that both CREATE TABLE statements end with a semicolon (;). This is a mark of termination, marking the end of the statement. Though termination marks are not actually a feature of SQL, every interactive implementation of SQL requires one at the end of a SQL statement so that the system can tell where a SQL statement ends.

SQLTalk, the interactive interface we are using, offers a choice of two ways to terminate statements. One way is to enter a semicolon followed by a carriage return at the end of the last line of the statement, as we have done; the other way is to enter on the line *following* the last line a slash (/) and then a carriage return, as follows:

```
SELECT NAME, HEIGHT
FROM GUESTS;
```

or

```
SELECT NAME, HEIGHT
FROM GUESTS
/
```

Both these methods are widely used by other implementations. In this book we customarily terminate with the semicolon.

A SQL statement can be any number of lines, by the way. We could have entered each statement all on one line, space permitting, or broken the statements with carriage returns in other places than we did. The placement of carriage returns and the number of spaces separating elements of a SQL statement are not critical. Termination with a semicolon or slash is required only at the end of the last line of the statement.

Identifiers and Attributes

Notice the underscore character (_) between the two parts of the name of table GUEST_ROSTER. The underscore is the conventional way of representing a space in table names and column names that contain more than one part. The underscore character ties together the two or more parts of a name so that they make up only one character string and can thus be recognized as parts of a single name.

Names of users, columns, tables, and indexes are also called *identifiers*. We could have used a space rather than an underscore to tie together the two parts of the name GUEST_ROSTER, but then every time we used it in a SQL statement we would have to put the name in double quotation marks (" ") to show that the two words "GUEST" and "ROSTER" were part of a single name. You must also always put double quotation marks around any name that starts with a digit and around any reserved keyword ("SELECT", for instance) that you want to use as a name. Names that require quotation marks in this fashion are called *delimited identifiers*: they are delimited by the quotes.

Following the table name in each CREATE TABLE statement are *column definitions*. These definitions are enclosed together in parentheses and separated from one another by commas. They list the attributes that define the columns. In each column definition, the name of the column appears first, then its *data type*, and then, if the data type has one, a *length attribute* consisting of one or more numbers in parentheses. This attribute specifies the maximum length for data in the column, that is, how many characters or digits a value in the specified column can have.

We will have more to say about data types and length attributes shortly.

Besides a column name, a data type specification, and perhaps a length attribute, a column definition can also contain certain special keywords that put constraints on the column.

For example, declaring a column to be NOT NULL, as we did for column NAME of GUESTS and for NAME and ARRIVAL of GUEST_ROSTER, prevents the column from containing a null value—that is, a value of "unknown" or "not applicable," not to be confused with a blank or a zero. All columns, regardless of data type, accept null values unless explicitly defined not to.

We defined certain columns in the CREATE TABLE statements to be NOT NULL because these columns make up the primary keys of the tables, as you may recall from Chapter 1, "Overview of a Relational Database." To allow nulls in a key would defeat the key's purpose. The key contains the attributes that uniquely identify particular rows. To accept a value of "unknown" or "not applicable" would amount to accepting the possibility of rows having unknown defining characteristics—that is, rows we could not uniquely identify. We do not want that, so we specify NOT NULL for the columns in the key.

We turn now to data types.

Data Types

ANSI-standard SQL recognizes two general kinds of data, character string and numeric, and provides several specific data types with different characteristics to accommodate the needs of particular columns. These data types include CHAR (or CHARACTER) for character string data and the data types NUMERIC, DECIMAL, INTEGER, SMALLINT, FLOAT, REAL, and DOUBLE PRECISION for numeric data.

CHAR is a fixed-length data type. Every value in a CHAR column is stored as having the full length specified by the column's length attribute. If, for example, column NAME in table GUESTS were CHAR(25), then all names in the column, regardless of their actual length, would be stored as having 25 bytes. Blanks would be added to pad any names not already 25 bytes long.

Another character-string data type, VARCHAR, is not recognized by ANSI but is universally implemented. VARCHAR is a variable-length character-string data type. In VARCHAR columns, only actual data is stored, making for more economical use of disk space. If, for example, a name uses only 15 of a possible 25 bytes, then the name is stored in 15 bytes; any trailing blanks are dropped. The length attribute of a VARCHAR column represents a maximum length for data in the column, not an invariable actual length as it does for CHAR columns.

In most implementations, CHAR and VARCHAR data can have a length attribute as large as 254.

When a column has a numeric data type, the length attribute often has two components, a precision and a scale. The *precision* specifies the overall maximum number of digits accepted by the column. The *scale* indicates how many of the digits are to the right of the decimal point.

For example, column DISCOUNT is defined as DECIMAL(2,2). The first 2 is the precision, and the second 2 is the scale. The column can contain as many as two digits, both appearing to the right of the decimal point. In a column defined as DECIMAL(8,2), to give another example, 8 is the precision and 2 is the scale. This column can contain as many as eight digits, with two of the eight digits appearing to the right of the decimal.

There are widely implemented data types for two additional kinds of data. One of these is date and time data, represented in SQLBase by the data types DATE, TIME, and TIMESTAMP; the other is the LONG VARCHAR or LONG data type, a catchall data type that can store data of any kind, including binary. In SQLBase, LONG data can be of virtually any length (billions of bytes); in other implementations, the limit is commonly 64 kilobytes.

SQLBase offers the following data types:

Character-String Data Types

CHAR stores fixed-length character strings consisting of letters, special characters, or digits, with the length not to exceed 254 bytes. The maximum length (up to 255 bytes) that a column will accept is defined when the column is created and a length attribute is specified. All data in the column is stored with the length specified when the column was defined. In standard SQL, when a particular value is less than that length, it is padded with blanks. In SQLBase, CHAR behaves the same as VARCHAR.

VARCHAR stores variable-length character strings consisting of letters, special characters, or digits, with length not to exceed 254 bytes. The maximum length (up to 255 bytes) that a column will accept is defined when the column is created and a length attribute is specified. This data type differs from CHAR in that the length defined for a column of this type represents only a maximum. Particular values are stored in their original or actual length; they are not padded. In fact, any trailing blanks are stripped for more economical storage.

LONG VARCHAR (also called LONG) stores data of considerable length—in particular, longer than 254 bytes—and accepts text or binary data. Columns of this type do not take a length attribute. Various implementation-specific restrictions apply to operations on columns of this data type.

Numeric Data Types

NUMBER stores numbers from $1.0E-100$ to $1.0E+100$, with as many as 22 decimal digits of precision. NUMBER columns are not defined to have a precision or scale.

DECIMAL stores numbers from $1.0E-100$ to $1.0E+100$, with as many as 22 decimal digits of precision, but unlike NUMBER columns, DECIMAL columns must be defined to have a precision and scale.

INTEGER stores a number with 10 or fewer digits of precision. No fractional digits are accepted; digits to the right of the decimal point are truncated.

SMALLINT stores a number with five or fewer digits of precision. As with INTEGER, no fractional digits are accepted; digits to the right of the decimal point are truncated.

FLOAT stores a floating point decimal in either single-precision or double-precision format, depending on the size of the length specification.

Date and Time Values

DATE stores date values, which can be entered and displayed in a variety of formats.

TIME stores time values, with resolution to microseconds. Values can be entered and displayed in a variety of formats.

TIMESTAMP is used for columns intended to maintain both date and time information. This is a combination of DATE and TIME data type formats, with values having both date and time components.

These are the principal conventional formats for representing dates (see table 2.1):

Table 2.1. Date Formats

Name	Date Format	Example
International Standards Organization (ISO)	yyyy-mm-dd	1988-10-30
IBM USA standard (USA)	mm/dd/yyyy	10/30/1988
IBM European standard (EUR)	dd.mm.yyyy	30.10.1988
Japanese Industrial Standard (JIS)	yyyy-mm-dd	1988-10-30

SQLBase also accepts a number of other formats, including the dd-mon-yyyy format (for example, 30-OCT-1988) used throughout this book.

The major conventional time formats are as follows (see table 2.2):

Table 2.2. Time Formats

Name	Time Format	Example
International Standards Organization (ISO)	hh.mm.ss	15.30.05
IBM USA standard (USA)	hh:mm AM or PM	3:30 PM
IBM European standard (EUR)	hh.mm.ss	15.30.05
Japanese Industrial Standard (JIS)	hh:mm:ss	15:30:05

Inserting Data

The CREATE TABLE statement at the beginning of the chapter only *created* tables GUESTS and GUEST_ROSTER; it did not put any data in them. To insert data, you use a different statement or command.

In standard SQL, the only way to insert data is with an INSERT statement, and ordinarily, this statement inserts only a single row. The statement can be used to insert multiple rows, but only by including in it a query that retrieves the data to be inserted from another table. We are not ready to talk about queries yet, and we have no other tables, so we postpone discussing this method until Chapter 7, "Queries in Other Statements."

Fortunately, every implementation of SQL supplies commands that extend SQL to let you load data in bulk. Chapter 12, "Database Utilities and Recovery," discusses a SQLTalk command that does this and is fairly representative; Part II, "Programming with SQL," which covers using SQL in programs, explains another method, one that uses program variables. In the real world, in other words, inserting multiple rows is not hard to do; there is just not much provision for it in standard interactive SQL.

The following SQL statement illustrates a single-row INSERT. The statement inserts one row of data into table GUEST_ROSTER. The row consists of six items of data, separated by commas—one item for each of the six columns of GUEST_ROSTER. The first item of data is inserted into the first column of the table, the second item in the second column, and so on, as follows:

```
INSERT INTO GUEST_ROSTER (NAME, ROOM, TRAINER, ARRIVAL,
    DEPARTURE, DISCOUNT)
VALUES ('JEAN-PAUL ROTUNDO','3','JULIO',15-JUN-1988,
17-JUN-1988,.2);

1 ROW INSERTED
```

Because we are inserting data into all columns of table GUEST_ROSTER, in this instance we could have omitted the list of column names that appears after the table name. Such a list is necessary only when you are inserting data into certain columns only and not into other columns, in which case you must name the columns you want to receive the data. We name all columns in this example only to make it easier to analyze the statement.

Notice that data for columns NAME, ROOM, and TRAINER is enclosed in single quotation marks. This is because the data type of these three columns is VARCHAR. When CHAR and VARCHAR character-string data is used in a SQL statement, it must be enclosed in single quotation marks. To include a single quotation mark in a character string, you enter it twice—for example, 'O''BRIEN'.

CHAR and VARCHAR data is stored in the table in the case in which it is entered. Thus, in Chapter 1, "Overview of a Relational Database," data in the NAME column of table GUESTS is all in uppercase because the data was entered that way. We could have entered it in lowercase, or in uppercase and lowercase, in which case the table would look like

```
NAME                       SEX BUILD      HEIGHT
========================== === ========== ======
Bette Midriff               F   M           66
Marcello Histrioni          M   M           66
Jean-Paul Rotundo           M   L           70
Michael Johnson             M   L           71
Clint Westwood              M   M           73
Joannie Rivulets            F   S           65
                             .
                             .
                             .
24 ROWS SELECTED
```

Generally, it is better to insert string data all in uppercase or all lowercase. Entering the data this way is easier and makes using the data more straightforward. Because string data is case-sensitive, any SQL statement must refer to particular strings exactly as they are stored or they will not be found. For instance, if Bette Midriff's name is stored in table GUESTS in the form 'Bette Midriff', a SQL statement looking for 'BETTE MIDRIFF' will not find the row. You are less likely to encounter this sort of problem if string data is stored in a uniform format.

All other elements of a SQL statement are case-insensitive, however. In other words, we could equally well have issued the INSERT statement this way:

```
insert into guest_roster (name, room, trainer, arrival,
departure, discount)
values ('JEAN-PAUL ROTUNDO','3','JULIO',15-jun-1988,
17-jun-1988,.2);
```

Unlike CHAR and VARCHAR, the data types DATE and TIME and the various numeric data types do not require single quotation marks, although single quotation marks are accepted.

DATE and TIME data may be entered in any of the formats mentioned in the preceding section. Numeric data can be entered in either decimal or scientific notation.

If you do not have data for every column, you can insert data in columns selectively. To do this, you list in the INSERT statement just the columns into which you want to insert data. The remaining, unlisted columns (or *fields*, as these places are also called) in any row you insert receive a null value in the table.

Because columns receive data in the order in which the columns are listed in the INSERT statement, you can insert items of data into a table in any order. Just be sure that the order in which columns and data are listed in the INSERT statement is the same.

In the following INSERT statement, because we do not know the departure date for Marcello Histrioni, we list only the columns for which we do have data—the other five. In the table, a null is automatically assigned for DEPARTURE, the column we do not mention, in the new row for Marcello.

For demonstration, we list in the INSERT statement the columns (and data) in the reverse order in which they appear in the table, as follows:

```
INSERT INTO GUEST_ROSTER (DISCOUNT, ARRIVAL, TRAINER, ROOM, NAME)
VALUES (.1, 26-JUN-1988, 'TODD','2','MARCELLO HISTRIONI');

1 ROW INSERTED
```

Another way to insert data selectively is to specify nulls in the list of values to be inserted. You do this by using the NULL keyword for any column for which you do not have data. For example, we could have written the preceding INSERT statement as follows:

```
INSERT INTO GUEST_ROSTER (DISCOUNT, DEPARTURE, ARRIVAL,
TRAINER, ROOM, NAME)
VALUES (.1,NULL,26-JUN-1988,'TODD','2','MARCELLO HISTRIONI');
```

This statement differs from the preceding one in two respects: column name DEPARTURE is included in the list of columns, and the NULL keyword marks the place of the null in the list of values to be inserted.

Now, having created some tables and inserted data into them, you are ready to learn various ways to combine and retrieve your data by using queries. Queries are discussed in the next chapter.

Summary

In this chapter, we introduced the two SQL statements CREATE TABLE and INSERT. The CREATE TABLE statement creates database tables, and the INSERT statement inserts data into these tables. We also discussed a representative selection of data types available in implementations of SQL and described the typographical conventions for entering data of various data types into a SQL statement.

CHAPTER 3

Getting the Data You Want: Queries

The query is the means by which you fetch data from tables in a database. In this chapter, we explore the basic elements of the query, including the two essential clauses every query must have and a third clause that lets you specify particular rows containing data you want.

Basic Elements of a Query: The SELECT and FROM Clauses

At its most basic, a query has just two components, a SELECT clause and a FROM clause. In a simple query, the SELECT clause lists the names of the columns containing the data you want, and the FROM clause specifies the tables in which these columns are located.

The simplest query selects all data in all columns of one table. You can narrow the SELECT clause, however, to select data only from particular columns, and you can narrow the selection in other ways by attaching various qualifications. You can also name in the SELECT clause columns from more than one table. And you can specify various operations to be performed on the data and display the results of these operations.

The *result* of a query is displayed in table form and is sometimes called the *result table*. The rows in the result represent the data that meets the conditions or has undergone the operations specified in the query. If no data qualifies, zero rows are selected.

30   Part I: Using SQL Interactively

What becomes of a result depends on whether it is generated by a SQL statement embedded in an application or by a SQL statement entered through an interactive interface such as SQLTalk. In the former case, it is likely assigned to a variable and used by the application. In the latter case, it is displayed on the monitor screen, like the examples in this book.

These examples, by the way, were assembled with the help of a feature of SQLTalk offered in some form by all SQL implementations. This feature, called *spooling*, automatically records in a file the SQL statements you have issued and any result tables or other responses from the database. After spooling is turned on, any change to the screen, initiated by you or the system, is appended to the *spool file* until spooling is turned off. The spool file, which is an ordinary text file, can then be edited or printed.

Let's look at an example of a query and its result. The following query asks for all rows of data from all columns of table GUEST_ROSTER. No qualifications are attached, so all the data in these columns—that is, all the data in the table—is in the result. (You saw this result in Chapter 1, "Overview of a Relational Database.") When a row in the result displays no data in a particular field, as in several cases for DEPARTURE and DISCOUNT, the value of that field is null.

```
SELECT NAME, ROOM, TRAINER, ARRIVAL, DEPARTURE, DISCOUNT
FROM GUEST_ROSTER;

NAME                        ROOM  TRAINER   ARRIVAL      DEPARTURE    DISCOUNT
==========================  ====  ========  ===========  ===========  ========
JEAN-PAUL ROTUNDO             3   JULIO     15-JUN-1988  17-JUN-1988       .2
MARCELLO HISTRIONI            2   TODD      26-JUN-1988                    .1
BETTE MIDRIFF                 1   MICHAEL   14-JUN-1988  16-JUN-1988
MICHAEL JOHNSON               4   JULIO     15-JUN-1988  19-JUN-1988
CLINT WESTWOOD                5   MICHAEL   25-JUN-1988                   .15
SEAN PENCIL                   6   TODD      15-JUN-1988  20-JUN-1988      .05
HETAERA                       7   SERENA    24-JUN-1988
JOANNIE RIVULETS              8   SERENA    25-JUN-1988                   .15
WARREN AMOROSO                9   TODD      16-JUN-1988  23-JUN-1988       .2
MARLON SPANDEX               10   JULIO     16-JUN-1988  23-JUN-1988      .05
OLYMPIA WELCH                11   MICHAEL   22-JUN-1988  27-JUN-1988       .1
HEATHER STARLETTE            12   SERENA    22-JUN-1988                   .05
DOLLY BRISKET                13   SERENA    22-JUN-1988
JOAN TONIC                   14   MICHAEL   23-JUN-1988                   .05
SEAN PENCIL                   9   TODD      23-JUN-1988                    .1
MEL GIMLET                   15   YVETTE    17-JUN-1988  24-JUN-1988
DON JACKSON                  16   TODD      17-JUN-1988  25-JUN-1988       .1
HETAERA                      10   SERENA    14-JUN-1988  20-JUN-1988       .2
ROBERT DINERO                17   YVETTE    18-JUN-1988  25-JUN-1988       .1
JANE FYUNDAI                 18   MICHAEL   19-JUN-1988  26-JUN-1988       .1
DYAN HOWITZER                19   YVETTE    19-JUN-1988  26-JUN-1988
BIANCA JOGGER                20   TODD      20-JUN-1988  27-JUN-1988      .15

22 ROWS SELECTED
```

Often enough, only column names appear in the SELECT clause, as in the preceding query. But column names are just one of several kinds of things that can appear there. More generally, the SELECT clause specifies *expressions to be evaluated* for each qualifying row. The FROM clause specifies the tables used in evaluating these expressions.

An *expression* is a word or phrase that yields a value. Thus, a column name is an expression, in the context of the SELECT clause, because it yields a value for each row of the table to which the column belongs. For instance, the NAME column in the preceding query yields the name of a guest for each row of the table.

As you will see, there are several kinds of expressions besides column names, and so there are several kinds of things that can appear in the SELECT clause.

The result table contains a column for each expression listed in the SELECT clause. This column displays the value of the expression for each row of the specified table. In the last example, the expressions are all column names and appear in the same order in which they occur in the table being queried, so the result table of the query is identical to table GUEST_ROSTER itself.

In brief, then, a query consisting of only a SELECT clause and a FROM clause essentially says

For all rows,
SELECT the value of these expressions
FROM these tables

The types of expressions in a SELECT clause can be broadly classified into two kinds: those that simply yield the value of a column in each qualifying row, and those that yield the value of operations *performed on* a column or columns. These operations are again, broadly speaking, of two kinds: arithmetic operations and functions. For now, we deal with column-name expressions in the SELECT clause; we discuss other kinds of expressions that can appear in a SELECT clause in the next chapter.

Incidentally, in queries you can use an asterisk (*) rather than column names in the SELECT clause. The asterisk is a wild-card operator that means "the values of all columns." Using the asterisk is the same as naming all columns of a table or tables in their original order. Thus, instead of typing all the column names as we did in the preceding query, we could have obtained the same result by entering the query this way:

```
SELECT *
FROM GUEST_ROSTER;

NAME                      ROOM  TRAINER    ARRIVAL      DEPARTURE    DISCOUNT
========================  ====  =========  ===========  ===========  ========
JEAN-PAUL ROTUNDO         3     JULIO      15-JUN-1988  17-JUN-1988       .2
MARCELLO HISTRIONI        2     TODD       26-JUN-1988                    .1
BETTE MIDRIFF             1     MICHAEL    14-JUN-1988  16-JUN-1988
MICHAEL JOHNSON           4     JULIO      15-JUN-1988  19-JUN-1988
CLINT WESTWOOD            5     MICHAEL    25-JUN-1988                   .15
SEAN PENCIL               6     TODD       15-JUN-1988  20-JUN-1988      .05
                               .
                               .
                               .
22 ROWS SELECTED
```

You can also select data from certain columns only and omit others. The next query draws data just from column NAME:

```
SELECT NAME
FROM GUEST_ROSTER;

NAME
==========================
JEAN-PAUL ROTUNDO
MARCELLO HISTRIONI
BETTE MIDRIFF
MICHAEL JOHNSON
CLINT WESTWOOD
SEAN PENCIL
HETAERA
JOANNIE RIVULETS
WARREN AMOROSO
MARLON SPANDEX
OLYMPIA WELCH
HEATHER STARLETTE
DOLLY BRISKET
JOAN TONIC
SEAN PENCIL
MEL GIMLET
DON JACKSON
HETAERA
ROBERT DINERO
JANE FYUNDAI
DYAN HOWITZER
BIANCA JOGGER

22 ROWS SELECTED
```

Notice that column NAME contains some duplicates: there are two entries apiece for Hetaera and Sean Pencil. You can use the special keyword DISTINCT immediately after the word "SELECT" in the SELECT clause to suppress duplicate rows in the result—that is, rows having the same values for each expression listed in the SELECT list as some other row. In the following example, the DISTINCT keyword is added to the preceding query. Note that this time the result does not contain any duplicate rows:

```
SELECT DISTINCT NAME
FROM GUEST_ROSTER;

NAME
=========================
BETTE MIDRIFF
BIANCA JOGGER
CLINT WESTWOOD
DOLLY BRISKET
DON JACKSON
DYAN HOWITZER
HEATHER STARLETTE
HETAERA
JANE FYUNDAI
JEAN-PAUL ROTUNDO
JOAN TONIC
JOANNIE RIVULETS
MARCELLO HISTRIONI
MARLON SPANDEX
MEL GIMLET
MICHAEL JOHNSON
OLYMPIA WELCH
ROBERT DINERO
SEAN PENCIL
WARREN AMOROSO

20 ROWS SELECTED
```

The DISTINCT keyword suppresses only *duplicate rows* in the result, not duplicate values. In the following query, the duplicate values in column NAME are back, but each is paired with a different value in ROOM, so the rows themselves are not duplicates. Consequently, no rows are suppressed:

```
SELECT DISTINCT NAME, ROOM
FROM GUEST_ROSTER;

NAME                      ROOM
========================= ====
BETTE MIDRIFF             1
BIANCA JOGGER             20
CLINT WESTWOOD            5
DOLLY BRISKET             13
DON JACKSON               16
DYAN HOWITZER             19
HEATHER STARLETTE         12
HETAERA                   10
HETAERA                   7
JANE FYUNDAI              18
JEAN-PAUL ROTUNDO         3
JOAN TONIC                14
JOANNIE RIVULETS          8
```

```
MARCELLO HISTRIONI        2
MARLON SPANDEX            10
MEL GIMLET                15
MICHAEL JOHNSON           4
OLYMPIA WELCH             11
ROBERT DINERO             17
SEAN PENCIL               6
SEAN PENCIL               9
WARREN AMOROSO            9
22 ROWS SELECTED
```

Another keyword, ALL, is used in the same way as DISTINCT and has the effect of *including* any duplicate rows. If neither DISTINCT nor ALL is used, duplicate rows are included as if you had used the ALL keyword.

Narrowing the Query: The WHERE Clause

The WHERE clause narrows the scope of the query by focusing on only certain rows. Instead of returning the values of the expressions in the SELECT clause *for all rows*, a query with a WHERE clause returns values only for rows that meet the conditions specified in the WHERE clause.

In other words, a query containing a WHERE clause essentially says

SELECT the value of these expressions
FROM these tables
in just the rows WHERE these conditions are met.

The conditions in the WHERE clause are called *search conditions*.

For instance, the next query selects data in columns NAME and TRAINER of GUEST_ROSTER in just those rows *where the trainer is Todd*. In other words, the query lists the name (and trainer) of everyone whose trainer is Todd:

```
SELECT NAME, TRAINER
FROM GUEST_ROSTER
WHERE TRAINER = 'TODD';

NAME                      TRAINER
========================  ========
MARCELLO HISTRIONI        TODD
SEAN PENCIL               TODD
WARREN AMOROSO            TODD
SEAN PENCIL               TODD
DON JACKSON               TODD
BIANCA JOGGER             TODD

6 ROWS SELECTED
```

The single quotation marks surrounding TODD in the query are necessary because TODD is a character string. Also, the name must be entered all in uppercase because that is the way the name appears in the table. If you were to specify

'Todd' instead, the query would return zero rows because there is no value 'Todd' in column TRAINER.

You are not restricted in the WHERE clause to using only columns that appear in the SELECT clause. The preceding query works just as well if you drop TRAINER from the SELECT clause:

```
SELECT NAME
FROM GUEST_ROSTER
WHERE TRAINER = 'TODD';

NAME
========================
MARCELLO HISTRIONI
SEAN PENCIL
WARREN AMOROSO
SEAN PENCIL
DON JACKSON
BIANCA JOGGER

6 ROWS SELECTED
```

In the following sections, you will see how to include in the WHERE clause multiple search conditions specifying a considerable range of requirements.

Relational Predicates

In the preceding example, TRAINER = 'TODD' is a *relational predicate*. The equal sign (=) in the middle is a *simple relational operator*.

There are nine simple relational operators. These can be used to form nine types of simple relational predicates for use in search conditions. Five additional types of relational predicates can also be formed. We discuss the various types of relational predicates in the following two sections.

Simple Relational Predicates

The query used in the last example is

```
SELECT NAME
FROM GUEST_ROSTER
WHERE TRAINER = 'TODD';
```

As we said, the query contains a simple relational operator, the equal sign. The query means

```
SELECT the value of NAME and TRAINER
FROM table GUEST_ROSTER
in just the rows WHERE the value of TRAINER is identical to 'TODD'.
```

There are nine simple relational operators:

=	is equal/identical to
!=	is not equal/identical to
<>	is not equal/identical to
>	is greater than
!>	is not greater than
<	is less than
!<	is not less than
>=	is greater than or equal to
<=	is less than or equal to

Each of these can be used in search conditions to form relational predicates such as the one in the preceding query.

For example, the following query selects the name, trainer, and arrival date of everyone whose trainer is *not* Todd:

```
SELECT NAME, TRAINER, ARRIVAL
FROM GUEST_ROSTER
WHERE TRAINER != 'TODD';
```

NAME	TRAINER	ARRIVAL
JEAN-PAUL ROTUNDO	JULIO	15-JUN-1988
BETTE MIDRIFF	MICHAEL	14-JUN-1988
MICHAEL JOHNSON	JULIO	15-JUN-1988
CLINT WESTWOOD	MICHAEL	25-JUN-1988
HETAERA	SERENA	24-JUN-1988
JOANNIE RIVULETS	SERENA	25-JUN-1988
MARLON SPANDEX	JULIO	16-JUN-1988
OLYMPIA WELCH	MICHAEL	22-JUN-1988
HEATHER STARLETTE	SERENA	22-JUN-1988
DOLLY BRISKET	SERENA	22-JUN-1988
JOAN TONIC	MICHAEL	23-JUN-1988
MEL GIMLET	YVETTE	17-JUN-1988
HETAERA	SERENA	14-JUN-1988
ROBERT DINERO	YVETTE	18-JUN-1988
JANE FYUNDAI	MICHAEL	19-JUN-1988
DYAN HOWITZER	YVETTE	19-JUN-1988

16 ROWS SELECTED

The operators work with numeric data as well as with character strings:

```
SELECT NAME, DISCOUNT
FROM GUEST_ROSTER
WHERE DISCOUNT = .1;
```

NAME	DISCOUNT
MARCELLO HISTRIONI	.1
OLYMPIA WELCH	.1
SEAN PENCIL	.1

```
DON JACKSON                            .1
ROBERT DINERO                          .1
JANE FYUNDAI                           .1

6 ROWS SELECTED
```

The .1 does not have to be surrounded by single quotation marks because it is numeric data, not string data.

The following query makes a selection that is *not* based on an equality. The query selects the name and discount of everyone who receives a discount greater than 15 percent:

```
SELECT NAME, DISCOUNT
FROM GUEST_ROSTER
WHERE DISCOUNT > .15;

NAME                            DISCOUNT
=========================       ==========
JEAN-PAUL ROTUNDO                      .2
WARREN AMOROSO                         .2
HETAERA                                .2

3 ROWS SELECTED
```

The operators also work with date fields. This query selects the name and departure date of every guest who departed after June 23, 1988:

```
SELECT NAME, DEPARTURE
FROM GUEST_ROSTER
WHERE DEPARTURE > 23-JUN-1988;

NAME                            DEPARTURE
=========================       ===========
OLYMPIA WELCH                   27-JUN-1988
MEL GIMLET                      24-JUN-1988
DON JACKSON                     25-JUN-1988
ROBERT DINERO                   25-JUN-1988
JANE FYUNDAI                    26-JUN-1988
DYAN HOWITZER                   26-JUN-1988
BIANCA JOGGER                   27-JUN-1988

7 ROWS SELECTED
```

In this query, 23-JUN-1988 is a date constant. Date and time constants are neither strings nor numbers and are calendar based. Thus, the following query, which asks for the name and departure date of everyone who left after February 29, 1987, results in an error because the system knows that there is no date February 29, 1987.

```
SELECT NAME, DEPARTURE
FROM GUEST_ROSTER
WHERE DEPARTURE > 29-FEB-87;

SELECT NAME, DEPARTURE
FROM GUEST_ROSTER
WHERE DEPARTURE > 29-FEB-87
                  ^
Error: invalid date
```

Now we substitute a date that does exist. Notice that the system accepts the date even though it is entered in a variant format:

```
SELECT NAME, DEPARTURE
FROM GUEST_ROSTER
WHERE DEPARTURE > 2/29/88;

NAME                      DEPARTURE
========================= ===========
JEAN-PAUL ROTUNDO         17-JUN-1988
BETTE MIDRIFF             16-JUN-1988
MICHAEL JOHNSON           19-JUN-1988
SEAN PENCIL               20-JUN-1988
WARREN AMOROSO            23-JUN-1988
MARLON SPANDEX            23-JUN-1988
OLYMPIA WELCH             27-JUN-1988
MEL GIMLET                24-JUN-1988
DON JACKSON               25-JUN-1988
HETAERA                   20-JUN-1988
ROBERT DINERO             25-JUN-1988
JANE FYUNDAI              26-JUN-1988
DYAN HOWITZER             26-JUN-1988
BIANCA JOGGER             27-JUN-1988

14 ROWS SELECTED
```

Other Relational Predicates

Besides the simple operators just discussed, there are five other relational operators that can be used to form relational predicates. These additional relational operators are

```
BETWEEN...AND
IS NULL
EXISTS
LIKE
IN
```

The BETWEEN operator specifies data in a certain range. This operator works with both numbers and dates. For instance, you can ask for the name and discount of everyone receiving a discount between 10 percent and 20 percent, inclusive, as follows:

```
SELECT NAME, DISCOUNT
FROM GUEST_ROSTER
WHERE DISCOUNT BETWEEN .10 AND .20;

NAME                      DISCOUNT
========================= ==========
JEAN-PAUL ROTUNDO              .2
MARCELLO HISTRIONI             .1
CLINT WESTWOOD                 .15
JOANNIE RIVULETS               .15
WARREN AMOROSO                 .2
```

```
OLYMPIA WELCH                          .1
SEAN PENCIL                            .1
DON JACKSON                            .1
HETAERA                                .2
ROBERT DINERO                          .1
JANE FYUNDAI                           .1
BIANCA JOGGER                          .15

12 ROWS SELECTED
```

You can also ask for the name and date of departure of everyone who left between June 19 and June 24:

```
SELECT NAME, DEPARTURE
FROM GUEST_ROSTER
WHERE DEPARTURE BETWEEN 19-JUN-1988 AND 24-JUN-1988;

NAME                         DEPARTURE
==========================   ===========
MICHAEL JOHNSON              19 JUN 1988
SEAN PENCIL                  20-JUN-1988
WARREN AMOROSO               23-JUN-1988
MARLON SPANDEX               23-JUN-1988
MEL GIMLET                   24-JUN-1988
HETAERA                      20-JUN-1988

6 ROWS SELECTED
```

The IS NULL operator lets you select from rows where the value of a particular field is unknown. For example, several guests have no value entered for DEPARTURE. You can select the names of those guests by using the IS NULL operator:

```
SELECT NAME, DEPARTURE
FROM GUEST_ROSTER
WHERE DEPARTURE IS NULL;

NAME                         DEPARTURE
==========================   ===========
MARCELLO HISTRIONI
CLINT WESTWOOD
HETAERA
JOANNIE RIVULETS
HEATHER STARLETTE
DOLLY BRISKET
JOAN TONIC
SEAN PENCIL

8 ROWS SELECTED
```

We explain the EXISTS operator in Chapter 7, "Queries in Other Statements," in which we discuss nesting queries in other queries. This operator can be used only with nested queries.

The LIKE operator lets you use wild-card pattern-matching characters to match data in a search condition. Instead of the data having to be *identical* to thus-and-such, you can specify that it just be *like* thus-and-such to a certain degree.

You can use the following two wild-card characters with LIKE:

__ (underscore)   Matches any single character
% (percent)   Matches any string

In the context of a LIKE predicate, the underscore character functions analogously to the MS-DOS question mark (?) wild-card character in file names; the percent character functions analogously to the MS-DOS asterisk (*).

The following query uses LIKE and a wild-card character to select every name that begins with the string 'JOAN', regardless of what other characters follow.

```
SELECT NAME
FROM GUEST_ROSTER
WHERE NAME LIKE 'JOAN%';

NAME
=========================
JOANNIE RIVULETS
JOAN TONIC

2 ROWS SELECTED
```

The next query selects every name with *J* in the first position and *N* in the fourth, whatever characters are between or follow:

```
SELECT NAME
FROM GUEST_ROSTER
WHERE NAME LIKE 'J__N%';

NAME
=========================
JEAN-PAUL ROTUNDO
JOANNIE RIVULETS
JOAN TONIC

3 ROWS SELECTED
```

One more example:

```
SELECT NAME
FROM GUEST_ROSTER
WHERE NAME LIKE '_AR__N%';

NAME
=========================
WARREN AMOROSO
MARLON SPANDEX

2 ROWS SELECTED
```

To treat a percent or underscore character in a LIKE predicate as a regular character—that is, not as a special pattern-matching character—you precede the percent or underscore with a backslash (\). This disables the character's pattern-matching ability. For example, the predicate

```
LIKE '50\%'
```

matches only the value 50% but not the value 50123; without the backslash, the predicate would match both values.

The last operator discussed in this chapter is the IN operator. This operator lets you select data that matches other data in a specified collection or list of values. The values can be listed explicitly in the statement, as in the following examples, or they can be the result of a subquery, as you will see in Chapter 7, "Queries in Other Statements."

The next query selects the name, trainer, and room assignment of every guest whose trainer's name appears in the list 'MICHAEL', 'TODD':

```
SELECT NAME, TRAINER, ROOM
FROM GUEST_ROSTER
WHERE TRAINER IN ('MICHAEL', 'TODD');

NAME                        TRAINER   ROOM
-------------------------   --------  ----
MARCELLO HISTRIONI          TODD      2
BETTE MIDRIFF               MICHAEL   1
CLINT WESTWOOD              MICHAEL   5
SEAN PENCIL                 TODD      6
WARREN AMOROSO              TODD      9
OLYMPIA WELCH               MICHAEL   11
JOAN TONIC                  MICHAEL   14
SEAN PENCIL                 TODD      9
DON JACKSON                 TODD      16
JANE FYUNDAI                MICHAEL   18
BIANCA JOGGER               TODD      20

11 ROWS SELECTED
```

Each of the relational operators also works with NOT. In the next query, we select the name, trainer, and accommodation of every guest whose trainer's name does *not* appear in the list:

```
SELECT NAME, TRAINER, ROOM
FROM GUEST_ROSTER
WHERE TRAINER NOT IN ('MICHAEL', 'TODD');

NAME                        TRAINER   ROOM
=========================   ========  ====
JEAN PAUL ROTUNDO           JULIO     3
MICHAEL JOHNSON             JULIO     4
HETAERA                     SERENA    7
JOANNIE RIVULETS            SERENA    8
MARLON SPANDEX              JULIO     10
HEATHER STARLETTE           SERENA    12
DOLLY BRISKET               SERENA    13
MEL GIMLET                  YVETTE    15
HETAERA                     SERENA    10
ROBERT DINERO               YVETTE    17
DYAN HOWITZER               YVETTE    19

11 ROWS SELECTED
```

The following query selects the name and departure date of every guest having a departure date:

```
SELECT NAME, DEPARTURE
FROM GUEST_ROSTER
WHERE DEPARTURE IS NOT NULL;
```

NAME	DEPARTURE
JEAN-PAUL ROTUNDO	17-JUN-1988
BETTE MIDRIFF	16-JUN-1988
MICHAEL JOHNSON	19-JUN-1988
SEAN PENCIL	20-JUN-1988
WARREN AMOROSO	23-JUN-1988
MARLON SPANDEX	23-JUN-1988
OLYMPIA WELCH	27-JUN-1988
MEL GIMLET	24-JUN-1988
DON JACKSON	25-JUN-1988
HETAERA	20-JUN-1988
ROBERT DINERO	25-JUN-1988
JANE FYUNDAI	26-JUN-1988
DYAN HOWITZER	26-JUN-1988
BIANCA JOGGER	27-JUN-1988

14 ROWS SELECTED

Connecting Several Predicates: AND and OR

By using a WHERE clause with more than one search condition, you can further narrow the selection of rows. You attach additional search conditions by using the operators AND and OR.

In the next query, we select the name, trainer, and discount of every guest who has not left yet and whose trainer is Serena:

```
SELECT NAME, TRAINER, DISCOUNT
FROM GUEST_ROSTER
WHERE DEPARTURE IS NULL
AND TRAINER = 'SERENA';
```

NAME	TRAINER	DISCOUNT
HETAERA	SERENA	
JOANNIE RIVULETS	SERENA	.15
HEATHER STARLETTE	SERENA	.05
DOLLY BRISKET	SERENA	

4 ROWS SELECTED

You can add numerous components to the WHERE clause using AND and OR. The next query adds several:

```
SELECT NAME, ROOM, TRAINER, ARRIVAL, DEPARTURE
FROM GUEST_ROSTER
WHERE DEPARTURE IS NOT NULL
```

```
AND TRAINER = 'YVETTE'
AND ROOM > 16
AND ARRIVAL < 20-JUN-1988;

NAME                         ROOM TRAINER    ARRIVAL     DEPARTURE
=========================    ==== ========   ==========  ==========
ROBERT DINERO                17   YVETTE     18-JUN-1988 25-JUN-1988
DYAN HOWITZER                19   YVETTE     19-JUN-1988 26-JUN-1988

2 ROWS SELECTED
```

The predicates you add can themselves be compound. The following example selects the name, trainer, and arrival date of every guest whose departure date is known and whose trainer is Serena or who arrived after June 25. The AND clause contains a compound predicate. The components are enclosed in parentheses to represent them as part of the same predicate:

```
SELECT NAME, TRAINER, ARRIVAL
FROM GUEST_ROSTER
WHERE DEPARTURE IS NOT NULL
AND (TRAINER = 'SERENA' OR ARRIVAL > 21-JUN-1988);

NAME                         TRAINER    ARRIVAL
=========================    ========   ==========
OLYMPIA WELCH                MICHAEL    14-JUN-1988
HETAERA                      SERENA     22-JUN-1988

2 ROWS SELECTED
```

Summary

This chapter discussed how to use the SQL SELECT statement, or query, to retrieve data from the database.

A basic query consists of a SELECT clause and a FROM clause; you can narrow the focus of a query by adding a WHERE clause specifying one or more search conditions. These consist of relational predicates, of which there are 14 types: 9 built around the 9 simple relational operators, and 5 others. Multiple search conditions in a WHERE clause are connected by means of the conjunctions AND and OR.

CHAPTER 4

Using Queries To Manipulate Data

With SQL you are not confined to selecting data in the form in which it appears in the tables. As we mentioned at the beginning of Chapter 3, "Getting the Data You Want: Queries," you can also use queries to select the results of performing various operations on the data.

In this chapter, we describe three devices for performing operations on data in a query. These are

- Arithmetic operators
- Aggregate functions
- Nonaggregate functions

In each case, the operator or function is used with constants, column names, and so on to form a new expression. This expression is then used in the same way as column names: in the SELECT list of a query or in a search condition. Just as with column name expressions, using the expression in the SELECT list generates a column in the result table for the value of the expression.

We begin by looking at the kinds of expressions that can be formed using arithmetic operators.

Arithmetic Operators

Four arithmetic operators can be used to form expressions:

+   addition
−   subtraction
*   multiplication
/   division

These operators can be used with constants, column names, functions, special keywords, more complex expressions, and program variables (discussed in Part II, "Programming with SQL"). We show how to use them with column names and constants first.

In the following query, we use the addition operator to add .05 (a constant) to the current value in DISCOUNT in Marcello Histrioni's row. The SELECT clause contains two expressions: NAME and the expression formed with the arithmetic operator, DISCOUNT + .05. The result table thus contains two columns, one for each:

```
SELECT NAME, DISCOUNT + .05
FROM GUEST_ROSTER
WHERE NAME = 'MARCELLO HISTRIONI';

NAME                         DISCOUNT + .05
==========================   ==============
MARCELLO HISTRIONI                      .15

1 ROW SELECTED
```

The query directs that a value be returned for the two expressions NAME and DISCOUNT + .05 for each row of GUEST_ROSTER where the value of NAME is MARCELLO HISTRIONI.

There is one row for Marcello in GUEST_ROSTER; getting the value for NAME in that row is straightforward. To get the value for the expression DISCOUNT + .05, the value for DISCOUNT is fetched, the specified operation (adding .05) is performed on this value, and then the result is displayed.

In GUEST_ROSTER itself, Marcello's discount remains unchanged: it is still .1. *No SELECT statement ever changes data* in a base table, no matter what operations are performed on the data before it is displayed in the result. All that happens is that values of expressions in the SELECT list are returned in the result table for each qualifying row of the base table queried. Data in a base table itself can be changed only by using such SQL statements as UPDATE and DELETE or by dropping a column or table altogether. We discuss how to perform these operations in Chapter 9, "Changing Tables and Data."

You can use arithmetic operators on more complex expressions, too. The next query shows the result of dividing by 2 the increased discount that Marcello might receive. (To save typing, we identify him using the LIKE predicate in the WHERE clause.) The expression as a whole is (DISCOUNT + .05) / 2, and that is the expression for which a column appears in the result:

```
SELECT NAME, (DISCOUNT + .05) / 2
FROM GUEST_ROSTER
WHERE NAME LIKE 'MARC%';

NAME                          (DISCOUNT + .05) / 2
==========================    ====================
MARCELLO HISTRIONI                            .075

1 ROW SELECTED
```

Arithmetic operators can be used with the name of any column having a numeric data type, including groups of columns whose numeric data types are not the same. For example, DECIMAL data can be added to INTEGER data, and so forth. This is possible because all types of numeric data are transformed into a common internal format before being stored. The exact mechanics of this vary with the SQL implementation, so there are apt to be differences in, for instance, the way rounding takes place; but numeric data of various types can be operated on in one expression.

In SQLBase, although not in all other implementations, you can also use arithmetic operators with character string data if that data consists of digits. For instance, column ROOM in GUEST_ROSTER, like column NAME, is of character string data type VARCHAR; because all the data in ROOM consists of digits, you can use arithmetic operators with ROOM, though you cannot with NAME:

```
SELECT ROOM + 5
FROM GUEST_ROSTER;

  ROOM + 5
==========
         8
         7
         6
         9
        10
        11
        12
         .
         .
         .

22 ROWS SELECTED

SELECT NAME + 5
FROM GUEST_ROSTER;

Error: data is not numeric
```

It is important to note that string digits do not behave like true numeric data in all contexts. How they behave differently is discussed later in this chapter in the section "String Functions."

Although the rules vary with the implementation, some implementations also allow use of arithmetic operators with date and time data. In SQLBase, for instance, the following query can be used to determine length of stay for those guests who have departed. The figure is arrived at by subtracting the guests' arrival date from their date of departure. Similar, though not identical, queries can be used in a number of implementations.

```
SELECT NAME, DEPARTURE - ARRIVAL
FROM GUEST_ROSTER;

NAME                          DEPARTURE - ARRIVAL
============================  ====================
JEAN-PAUL ROTUNDO                               2
MARCELLO HISTRIONI
BETTE MIDRIFF                                   2
MICHAEL JOHNSON                                 4
CLINT WESTWOOD
SEAN PENCIL                                     5
HETAERA
JOANNIE RIVULETS
WARREN AMOROSO                                  7
MARLON SPANDEX                                  7
                                .
                                .
                                .

22 ROWS SELECTED
```

The DEPARTURE − ARRIVAL field is blank (that is, null or unknown), for those guests such as Clint and Marcello who have not yet departed. For the other guests, the length of stay is given in days.

In SQLBase, you can also use arithmetic operators to project the date a given number of days in the past or future. For instance, suppose that Don Jackson wants to make a reservation for 63 days from his date of departure. What date is that?

```
SELECT NAME, DEPARTURE, DEPARTURE + 63
FROM GUEST_ROSTER
WHERE NAME LIKE 'DON%';

NAME                          DEPARTURE    DEPARTURE + 63
============================  ===========  ==============
DON JACKSON                   25-JUN-1988  27-AUG-1988

1 ROW SELECTED
```

SQLBase automatically interprets the 63 to mean days because no type of interval was specified.

Most SQL implementations offer special keyword constants that return the current date or time or both, although different implementations name and handle the mechanics of using this type of keyword a bit differently.

For instance, the three SQLBase keywords SYSDATETIME, SYSDATE, and SYSTIME function similarly to the DB2 keyword constants CURRENT TIMESTAMP or (equivalently) CURRENT DATETIME, CURRENT DATE, and CURRENT TIME. Oracle, too, has a SYSDATE keyword, which essentially combines the functions of the three SQLBase or DB2 keywords. The Oracle SYSDATE keyword returns the current date, current time, or both, depending on special formatting parameters specified when the keyword is used.

The special keyword constants, which can be used in arithmetic operations on date and time data, use the system date or time that applies at the beginning of the execution of a statement containing keywords.

For example, suppose that Joannie Rivulets is about to depart and wants to make a return reservation for exactly one week from today. We can project that date as follows:

```
SELECT NAME, SYSDATE + 7
FROM GUEST_ROSTER
WHERE NAME LIKE 'JOANNIE%';

NAME                        SYSDATE + 7
==========================  ===========
JOANNIE RIVULETS            23-OCT-1988

1 ROW SELECTED
```

To give another example, the following query uses SYSDATE to determine the length of stay, from date of arrival to the present, of all guests not already listed as departed. The query subtracts the date in ARRIVAL from the current date, SYSDATE, and states the difference in number of days. Because SYSDATE always represents the current date, this identical query, like the preceding query, gives a unique result for each day on which it is run.

```
SELECT NAME, ARRIVAL, SYSDATE - ARRIVAL
FROM GUEST_ROSTER
WHERE DEPARTURE IS NULL;

NAME                        ARRIVAL      SYSDATE - ARRIVAL
==========================  ===========  =================
MARCELLO HISTRIONI          26-JUN-1988                112
CLINT WESTWOOD              25-JUN-1988                113
HETAERA                     24-JUN-1988                114
JOANNIE RIVULETS            25-JUN-1988                113
HEATHER STARLETTE           22-JUN-1988                116
DOLLY BRISKET               22-JUN-1988                116
JOAN TONIC                  23-JUN-1988                115
SEAN PENCIL                 23-JUN-1988                115

8 ROWS SELECTED
```

Keywords SYSTIME and SYSDATETIME can be used similarly: SYSTIME with time data, and SYSDATETIME with data that has both a date and a time component.

Also available in some implementations, although less universally, are constants representing various date and time intervals for use in arithmetic operations involving date and time data. SQLBase, for instance, offers YEAR[S], MONTH[S], DAY[S], HOUR[S], MINUTE[S], SECOND[S], MICROSECOND[S]. These may be used in either singular or plural form for closer assimilation to English usage.

For example, here is a variation on the query we used earlier to project the date of Don Jackson's next reservation. This query uses the special keyword MONTHS:

```
SELECT NAME, DEPARTURE, DEPARTURE + 63 MONTHS
FROM GUEST_ROSTER
WHERE NAME LIKE 'DON%';

NAME                        DEPARTURE    DEPARTURE + 63 MONTHS
==========================  ===========  =====================
DON JACKSON                 25-JUN-1988  25-SEP-1993

1 ROW SELECTED
```

Expressions using arithmetic operators can appear in the WHERE clause, too, whether or not the same expression appears in the SELECT list. Whether we put an arithmetic expression in the SELECT clause or in a WHERE clause depends on what we want to do with it. If we want the value of the expression to be *stated* in the result (for all rows satisfying the WHERE clause, if any), we will put the expression in the SELECT list. If we want to *use* the expression in a search condition to narrow the selection of rows for which values of expressions in the SELECT list are returned, we put the arithmetic expression in the WHERE clause.

In the following query, we want both: We want to *state* the value of ARRIVAL − 36 HOURS, but we want to state it only for certain rows—namely, for just those rows in which ARRIVAL − 36 HOURS does not fall before June 14, 1988.

```
SELECT NAME, ARRIVAL - 36 HOURS
FROM GUEST_ROSTER
WHERE ARRIVAL - 36 HOURS !< 14-JUN-1988;

NAME                        ARRIVAL - 36 HOURS
==========================  ==================
MARCELLO HISTRIONI          24-JUN-1988
CLINT WESTWOOD              23-JUN-1988
HETAERA                     22-JUN-1988
JOANNIE RIVULETS            23-JUN-1988
WARREN AMOROSO              14-JUN-1988
MARLON SPANDEX              14-JUN-1988
OLYMPIA WELCH               20-JUN-1988
                     .
                     .
                     .
17 ROWS SELECTED
```

Functions

Functions provide another means of using queries to perform manipulations on the data in base tables.

A function returns a value by performing a certain operation on the function's *argument* (or arguments). A function, with its argument, yields a value and is thus an expression.

The argument of a function is also an expression. Depending on the function, an argument may be either a constant (string, numeric, or date or time), returning a single value, or an expression containing a column name and capable of returning different values for different rows. The expression @PROPER('BETTE MIDRIFF') is an example of a function (namely, @PROPER) taking a constant as its argument; the expression @PROPER(NAME) shows the same function taking column name NAME as its argument. Most functions have only one argument.

In the following sections, we discuss two types of functions: aggregate functions and nonaggregate functions. Of these, only the aggregate functions are strictly a part of SQL; the nonaggregate functions are extensions, and the offerings of these vary considerably with the particular implementation. We discuss examples of these functions anyway because every implementation has some.

Aggregate Functions

The distinctive feature of aggregate functions is that they compute a single value from an entire column of data. Thus, where every other type of expression returns a value *for each row* specified by a query, aggregate functions return a value that represents a single *aggregate* of the values in *a number of* rows. For this reason, aggregate functions are also sometimes called column functions.

There are five aggregate functions:

AVG(argument)	Returns the average of the values in the argument
MAX(argument)	Returns the maximum value in the argument
MIN(argument)	Returns the minimum value in the argument
SUM(argument)	Returns the sum of the values of the argument
COUNT(argument)	Returns the number of rows in the argument

Aggregate functions most often take as their argument either a column name by itself or an expression having a column name as a component—for example, DISCOUNT + 5—but you can use them with any numeric or date expression. In the case of AVG and SUM, the argument *must* be a column name or numeric or date expression; it cannot be a string. MAX, MIN, and COUNT, however, also accept strings.

COUNT, unlike the other aggregate functions, can also take as its argument an asterisk wild-card character signifying in this context "all rows": for example, COUNT(*). Used with the asterisk, COUNT returns the number of rows in the result set; used with a column name or expression rather than an asterisk, COUNT returns the number of rows having a nonnull value in the column or expression.

All the functions ignore null values.

Two keywords, DISTINCT and ALL, may be used with aggregate functions. The keywords are placed preceding the argument inside the parentheses: for example, COUNT(DISTINCT NAME). These keywords have a function analogous to that of the DISTINCT and ALL keywords that can be used immediately after the word "SELECT" in the SELECT clause: the DISTINCT keyword causes duplicate values to be ignored; ALL takes account of them. In any aggregate function where neither keyword is used, duplicates are handled as if ALL were specified.

We turn now to some examples.

The following query operates on all values in the DISCOUNT column to compute the average, maximum, and minimum discounts received by La Bamba's guests. Because AVG, MAX, MIN, and SUM ignore null values, the AVG figure is actually the average discount just of those guests who receive some discount:

```
SELECT AVG(DISCOUNT), MAX(DISCOUNT), MIN(DISCOUNT)
FROM GUEST_ROSTER;

AVG(DISCOUNT) MAX(DISCOUNT) MIN(DISCOUNT)
============= ============= =============
     .115625            .2           .05

1 ROW SELECTED
```

The next query shows aggregate functions used with arithmetic operators. The query multiplies the minimum discount given to any of Serena's guests by the average length of stay of Serena's guests. Note that this query contains a WHERE clause restricting the rows over which the aggregate functions operate:

```
SELECT MIN(DISCOUNT) * AVG(DEPARTURE - ARRIVAL)
FROM GUEST_ROSTER
WHERE TRAINER = 'SERENA';

MIN(DISCOUNT) * AVG(DEPARTURE - ARRIVAL)
========================================
                                      .3

1 ROW SELECTED
```

Aggregate functions cannot themselves appear in a WHERE clause, however, as the following query demonstrates. This query asks for the names of all guests whose length of stay is the same as the average length of stay. The aggregate function in the search condition causes the query to generate an error:

```
SELECT NAME
FROM GUEST_ROSTER
WHERE DEPARTURE - ARRIVAL = MAX(DEPARTURE - ARRIVAL);

SELECT NAME
FROM GUEST_ROSTER
WHERE DEPARTURE - ARRIVAL = MAX(DEPARTURE - ARRIVAL)
                            ^
Error: set function not allowed here
```

Fortunately, there is, in effect, a way around this prohibition against including an aggregate function in a search condition. We will discuss it when we take up the subject of *views* in Chapter 8, "Virtual Tables: Views."

The next query illustrates COUNT. In this query, COUNT(*) counts all rows in the table, COUNT(DEPARTURE) and COUNT(NAME) count the rows that contain data in columns DEPARTURE and NAME, and COUNT(DISTINCT NAME) uses the keyword DISTINCT to suppress duplicates and count only the rows in column NAME that contain unique data:

```
SELECT COUNT(*), COUNT(DEPARTURE), COUNT(NAME), COUNT(DISTINCT NAME)
FROM GUEST_ROSTER;

  COUNT(*) COUNT(DEPARTURE) COUNT(NAME) COUNT(DISTINCT NAME)
========== ================ =========== ====================
        22               14          22                   20

1 ROW SELECTED
```

The DEPARTURE column contains nulls, which COUNT ignored. This is why COUNT(*) and COUNT(DEPARTURE) returned different values. COUNT(*) handles nulls by counting all rows that have at least one data field containing data.

The result column COUNT(NAME) shows a different result from column COUNT(DISTINCT NAME) because in the latter column the DISTINCT keyword caused duplicate values to be ignored, that is, not counted.

An aggregate function can contain another aggregate function, too. We give an example of this when we discuss the GROUP BY clause in the next chapter. Aggregate functions containing another aggregate function require a GROUP BY clause.

In fact, whenever a SELECT clause containing aggregate functions also contains anything that is *not* an aggregate function, the query requires a GROUP BY clause. The following query violates this rule by including in the SELECT clause an aggregate function and a column name. The query generates an error. We explain why when we discuss the GROUP BY clause.

```
SELECT NAME, AVG(DEPARTURE - ARRIVAL)
FROM GUEST_ROSTER;

SELECT NAME, AVG(DEPARTURE - ARRIVAL)
       ^
Error: not a single value set function
```

Nonaggregate Functions

Nonaggregate functions differ from aggregate functions in that they do *not* compute a single value from an entire column of data. Instead, nonaggregate functions, like all other expressions we have discussed (except aggregate functions), return a value for *each row*.

In SQLBase, nonaggregate functions are always prefixed with an "@" character, but this convention is peculiar to SQLBase. In other respects, the syntax of nonaggregate functions is like the syntax of aggregate functions: the function is followed by its argument entered in parentheses, for example, @PROPER('BETTE MIDRIFF'). When the argument is a string, as opposed to a number or a date, the argument must be enclosed in single quotes as in other contexts when you enter character strings in a SQL statement.

Like aggregate functions, nonaggregate functions can be nested in other nonaggregate functions such that the output of the inner function is used as an argument by the outer function. For example, in the nested function

```
@PROPER(@LEFT('BETTE MIDRIFF',5))
```

@LEFT returns the first five characters of the string "BETTE MIDRIFF" (namely, "BETTE"), and this smaller string then becomes the argument for @PROPER. Function @PROPER makes the first letter of each word in its argument uppercase and all other letters lowercase, as for representing proper names. In this instance, @PROPER thus converts "BETTE" to "Bette".

Nonaggregate functions can take either a constant (for example, any of the following types of values: BETTE MIDRIFF, 25, 29-JUN-1988, or SYSDATE) or a column name (for example, NAME) as an argument. If a column name is specified, then, for each row, the function takes as its argument the value of the column in that row.

Unlike aggregate functions, nonaggregate functions can be used in the WHERE clause as well as in the SELECT list.

The next two sections show how nonaggregate functions are used. We sort the functions into two categories, string functions and date and time functions, but this classification is simply one of convenience, based solely on the type of data that particular nonaggregate functions take as an argument. There happen to be few nonaggregate functions that take numeric data.

String Functions

Because nonaggregate functions vary so much from one SQL implementation to another, it falls outside the scope of this book to examine any one assortment in too much detail. In this and the following section, we look at a few representative examples offered by SQLBase.

The following example uses the function @LENGTH(*string*). We put "string" in parentheses here to signify that the argument this function takes is a string. Function @LENGTH returns the number of characters in its argument. In this instance, we use the function to return the number of characters in each name in NAME in GUEST_ROSTER:

```
SELECT NAME, @LENGTH(NAME)
FROM GUEST_ROSTER;

NAME                        @LENGTH(NAME)
==========================  =============
JEAN-PAUL ROTUNDO                      17
MARCELLO HISTRIONI                     18
BETTE MIDRIFF                          13
MICHAEL JOHNSON                        15
CLINT WESTWOOD                         14
SEAN PENCIL                            11
           .
           .
           .

22 ROWS SELECTED
```

In the preceding section, we mentioned functions @PROPER(*string*) and @LEFT(*string,length*) when we remarked that functions can be nested. The next example nests these two functions in a query. The argument of @LEFT has two components: a string, and a number specifying how many characters of the string, counting from the left, that we want the function to return. In the example, specifying column NAME as the first component of the argument of @LEFT causes the function to use the values of NAME for strings:

```
SELECT NAME, @PROPER(@LEFT(NAME,5))
FROM GUEST_ROSTER;

NAME                        @PROPER(@LEFT(NAME,5))
==========================  ==========================
JEAN-PAUL ROTUNDO           Jean-
MARCELLO HISTRIONI          Marce
BETTE MIDRIFF               Bette
MICHAEL JOHNSON             Micha
CLINT WESTWOOD              Clint
SEAN PENCIL                 Sean
HETAERA                     Hetae
JOANNIE RIVULETS            Joann
WARREN AMOROSO              Warre
MARLON SPANDEX              Marlo
OLYMPIA WELCH               Olymp
HEATHER STARLETTE           Heath
           .
           .
           .

22 ROWS SELECTED
```

We can reverse the order of the nesting, too:
```
SELECT NAME, @LEFT(@PROPER(NAME),5)
FROM GUEST_ROSTER;

NAME                      @LEFT(@PROPER(NAME),5)
========================  ==========================
JEAN-PAUL ROTUNDO         Jean-
MARCELLO HISTRIONI        Marce
BETTE MIDRIFF             Bette
MICHAEL JOHNSON           Micha
CLINT WESTWOOD            Clint
SEAN PENCIL               Sean
HETAERA                   Hetae
            .
            .
            .
22 ROWS SELECTED
```

To give one more example, function @VALUE(*string*) converts a character string of digits into the number represented by that string. This makes possible sorts and arithmetic operations that would not otherwise yield correct results.

For instance, the ROOM column in GUEST_ROSTER lists room assignments. Although the values in this column are digits, the data type of the column is VARCHAR, and the data is character string data. Consequently, data in this column is sorted from the leftmost character, the way we sort to alphabetize, and no attention is paid to the number of decimal places. As a result, 1 is regarded as the smallest value and 9 as the largest, even though the results we would expect arithmetically are the values 1 and 20:

```
SELECT MIN(ROOM), MAX(ROOM)
FROM GUEST_ROSTER;

MIN(ROOM) MAX(ROOM)
========= =========
1         9

1 ROW SELECTED
```

We can use @VALUE to treat the data in ROOM like numeric data—as if the data type of the column were INTEGER, for instance. This enables us to get a correct numeric sorting:

```
SELECT MIN(@VALUE(ROOM)), MAX(@VALUE(ROOM))
FROM GUEST_ROSTER;

MIN(@VALUE(ROOM)) MAX(@VALUE(ROOM))
================= =================
                1                20

1 ROW SELECTED
```

Chapter 4: Using Queries To Manipulate Data

One last thing we will mention before leaving this section is the *concatenate* operator, represented by two bar characters (||). The syntax for using this operator is

string||string

where the arguments can be either string constants or column names. The operator concatenates the arguments, that is, juxtaposes them, in the result. For instance, the following query concatenates the strings in NAME with the string " has not yet departed" for all guests who have not given a departure date:

```
SELECT NAME||' has not yet departed'
FROM GUEST_ROSTER
WHERE DEPARTURE IS NULL;

NAME||' HAS NOT YET DEPARTED'
==================================================
MARCELLO HISTRIONI has not yet departed
CLINT WESTWOOD has not yet departed
HETAERA has not yet departed
JOANNIE RIVULETS has not yet departed
HEATHER STARLETTE has not yet departed
DOLLY BRISKET has not yet departed
JOAN TONIC has not yet departed
SEAN PENCIL has not yet departed

8 ROWS SELECTED
```

The concatenate operator is discussed some more later in this chapter in the section "Selecting Constants."

Date or Time Functions

Date and time functions are nonaggregate functions that either return information about a column of date or time data type or generate results of date or time type.

Date function @DAY(*date*), for instance, selects just the day of the month from DATE data:

```
SELECT NAME, ARRIVAL, @DAY(ARRIVAL)
FROM GUEST_ROSTER;

NAME                      ARRIVAL      @DAY(ARRIVAL)
========================  ===========  =============
JEAN-PAUL ROTUNDO         15-JUN-1988             15
MARCELLO HISTRIONI        26-JUN-1988             26
BETTE MIDRIFF             14-JUN-1988             14
MICHAEL JOHNSON           15-JUN-1988             15
CLINT WESTWOOD            25-JUN-1988             25
SEAN PENCIL               15-JUN-1988             15
                              .
                              .
                              .

22 ROWS SELECTED
```

Similar queries can be constructed using @MONTH, @YEAR, @HOUR, @MINUTE, and @SECOND.

The system also computes for you the day of the week on which a date falls. Here we use @WEEKDAY(*date*) to yield a number from 0 to 6 for the weekdays represented by the dates in ARRIVAL. Saturday is "0":

```
SELECT NAME, @WEEKDAY(ARRIVAL)
FROM GUEST_ROSTER;

NAME                        @WEEKDAY(ARRIVAL)
=========================   =================
JEAN-PAUL ROTUNDO                           4
MARCELLO HISTRIONI                          1
BETTE MIDRIFF                               3
MICHAEL JOHNSON                             4
CLINT WESTWOOD                              0
SEAN PENCIL                                 4
         .
         .
         .
22 ROWS SELECTED
```

Using arithmetic operators works too:

```
SELECT NAME, @WEEKDAY(ARRIVAL + 4)
FROM GUEST_ROSTER;

NAME                        @WEEKDAY(ARRIVAL + 4)
=========================   =====================
JEAN-PAUL ROTUNDO                               1
MARCELLO HISTRIONI                              5
BETTE MIDRIFF                                   0
MICHAEL JOHNSON                                 1
CLINT WESTWOOD                                  4
SEAN PENCIL                                     1
         .
         .
         .
22 ROWS SELECTED
```

Function @QUARTER works similarly.

Other SQLBase functions—@WEEKBEG, @MONTHBEG, @QUARTERBEG, @YEARBEG—return the date of the beginning of the week, month, quarter, or year that the date used as the argument of the respective function falls in. Different implementations offer their own selections of nonaggregate functions tailored to a variety of special purposes.

Selecting Constants

We said at the beginning of Chapter 3, "Getting the Data You Want: Queries," that the types of expressions that can appear in a SELECT clause are, broadly speaking, of two kinds: those that yield the value of a column, and those that yield the value of operations *performed on* a column or columns by means of arithmetic operators and functions.

We round out this chapter with a look at a topic we have skirted until now, namely, what happens when an expression in the SELECT clause is a constant or other type of expression that makes no reference to any column name. Using such expressions in the SELECT clause can produce what may seem to be odd results.

Constants are of three kinds: string, numeric, and date or time. The string 'GEORGE' is an example of a string constant, 252 is a numeric constant, and 5-JAN 1988 and the keyword SYSDATE are date constants.

Plainly, each of these yields a value—namely, the current date in the case of SYSDATE, and the constant itself in each of the other cases—and so qualifies as an expression. But constants yield a value without reference to any column. Similarly with the expression 2 + 2. Consequently, because all data in a table occurs in columns, we might expect that a query containing only a constant or an expression such as 2 + 2 in its SELECT clause would return no rows in the result. Actually, the reverse is true, as the following query shows:

```
SELECT 2 + 2
FROM GUEST_ROSTER;
     2 + 2
==========
         4
         4
         4
         4
         4
         4
         4
         4
         4
         4
         .
         .
         .

22 ROWS SELECTED
```

A value is returned for *every* row.

Here is another example:

```
SELECT 'GEORGE'
FROM GUEST_ROSTER
WHERE NAME = 'BETTE MIDRIFF';
```

```
'GEORGE'
========
GEORGE

1 ROW SELECTED
```

A value is returned for only one row because only one row in GUEST_ROSTER satisfies the search condition.

Next, we select the value of the date function @WEEKDAY applied to a constant rather than to a column name:

```
SELECT NAME, @WEEKDAY(20-JUN-1988)
FROM GUEST_ROSTER;

NAME                      @WEEKDAY(20-JUN-1988)
========================= =====================
JEAN-PAUL ROTUNDO                             2
MARCELLO HISTRIONI                            2
BETTE MIDRIFF                                 2
MICHAEL JOHNSON                               2
CLINT WESTWOOD                                2
SEAN PENCIL                                   2
HETAERA                                       2
JOANNIE RIVULETS                              2
WARREN AMOROSO                                2
                    .
                    .
                    .
22 ROWS SELECTED
```

As we said earlier, the result table contains a column for each expression listed in the SELECT clause. This column displays the value of the expression for each qualifying row of the specified table.

If the expression is a constant or other expression (for example, arithmetic) that evaluates without reference to any column, then that value is returned for every (specified) row. The rationale is that if the value holds or is true absolutely, without reference to any context, then it holds or is true in any given row; hence, it is returned for that row.

This curious feature of the way queries work can be useful at times. Without advertising this aspect of what we were doing, we have already given one example of selecting a constant when we introduced the concatenate operator. In the following similar example, the string 'Mr/Mrs ' is a constant; its value is returned for every row:

```
SELECT 'Mr/Mrs '||NAME
FROM GUEST_ROSTER;
```

```
'MR/MRS '||NAME
==================================
Mr/Mrs JEAN-PAUL ROTUNDO
Mr/Mrs MARCELLO HISTRIONI
Mr/Mrs BETTE MIDRIFF
Mr/Mrs MICHAEL JOHNSON
Mr/Mrs CLINT WESTWOOD
Mr/Mrs SEAN PENCIL
Mr/Mrs HETAERA
Mr/Mrs JOANNIE RIVULETS
Mr/Mrs WARREN AMOROSO
Mr/Mrs MARLON SPANDEX
                .
                .
                .

22 ROWS SELECTED
```

Here is a last example, this time using some of the special keyword constants we mentioned a few sections ago. Keyword SYSTIME, you recall, returns the current time. The example also demonstrates several of the keyword constants for particular time intervals, used in combination:

```
SELECT (SYSTIME + 3 HOURS) + 5 MINUTES
FROM GUEST_ROSTER;

(SYSTIME + 3 HOURS) + 5 MINUTES
================================
           17:55:00
           17:55:00
           17:55:00
           17:55:00
           17:55:00
           17:55:00
                .
                .
                .

22 ROWS SELECTED
```

Summary

The expressions given in the SELECT list determine the columns in the result table. This chapter discussed the kinds of expressions the SELECT list can contain besides column names. These include arithmetic expressions and two general classes of functions, aggregate and nonaggregate. These other types of expressions return the result of manipulations on the data contained in database tables instead of returning just the data itself. All of these entities except aggregate functions can occur in a WHERE clause as well.

The chapter closed with a look at the special case of selecting constants.

CHAPTER 5

Arranging the Result

Chapters 3 and 4 illustrated various ways of using queries to get information from the database. This chapter introduces three clauses that can be appended to a query to let you organize the result in various ways.

The most important of the three clauses is the GROUP BY clause. This clause allows you to group rows in the result and also allows you to construct queries you could not otherwise construct.

Another clause, the HAVING clause, lets you apply search conditions to the rows yielded by the GROUP BY clause. The third clause, ORDER BY, lets you sort result rows in various ways.

Grouping in Sets with the GROUP BY Clause

The GROUP BY clause groups distinct result rows of a query in sets according to the columns, called *grouping columns*, named in the GROUP BY clause. The rows are "grouped" in two different ways, or respects.

The following query illustrates the first way in which rows are grouped, namely, that all rows having the same value in the primary grouping column are placed together in the result. In this query, the primary grouping column is TRAINER. All rows having the same value in TRAINER are placed together.

```
SELECT TRAINER, NAME
FROM GUEST_ROSTER
GROUP BY TRAINER, NAME;
```

```
TRAINER   NAME
========  =========================
JULIO     JEAN-PAUL ROTUNDO
JULIO     MARLON SPANDEX
JULIO     MICHAEL JOHNSON
MICHAEL   BETTE MIDRIFF
MICHAEL   CLINT WESTWOOD
MICHAEL   JANE FYUNDAI
MICHAEL   JOAN TONIC
MICHAEL   OLYMPIA WELCH
SERENA    DOLLY BRISKET
SERENA    HEATHER STARLETTE
SERENA    HETAERA
SERENA    JOANNIE RIVULETS
TODD      BIANCA JOGGER
TODD      DON JACKSON
TODD      MARCELLO HISTRIONI
TODD      SEAN PENCIL
TODD      WARREN AMOROSO
YVETTE    DYAN HOWITZER
YVETTE    MEL GIMLET
YVETTE    ROBERT DINERO

20 ROWS SELECTED
```

Any rows listing guests not assigned a trainer, that is, with a null value for TRAINER, would also have been placed together. And rows are similarly grouped within each subsequent grouping column, although that is not apparent here where there are only two.

Notice that column NAME was listed in the GROUP BY clause along with TRAINER in the preceding query. Except for aggregate functions, all expressions in the SELECT clause must appear as grouping columns in the GROUP BY clause. The order in which these expressions are listed in the GROUP BY clause determines the order in which the columns are grouped.

Compare, for instance, the results of the two following queries. In the first query, TRAINER is the primary grouping column. The values in ARRIVAL are grouped subordinate to the primary sets of rows with identical values for TRAINER. In the second query, this grouping order is reversed:

```
SELECT TRAINER, ARRIVAL, NAME
FROM GUEST_ROSTER
GROUP BY TRAINER, ARRIVAL, NAME;

TRAINER    ARRIVAL      NAME
========  ===========  =========================
JULIO      15-JUN-1988  JEAN-PAUL ROTUNDO
JULIO      15-JUN-1988  MICHAEL JOHNSON
JULIO      16-JUN-1988  MARLON SPANDEX
MICHAEL    14-JUN-1988  BETTE MIDRIFF
MICHAEL    19-JUN-1988  JANE FYUNDAI
MICHAEL    22-JUN-1988  OLYMPIA WELCH
MICHAEL    23-JUN-1988  JOAN TONIC
```

```
MICHAEL  25-JUN-1988  CLINT WESTWOOD
SERENA   14-JUN-1988  HETAERA
SERENA   22-JUN-1988  DOLLY BRISKET
SERENA   22-JUN-1988  HEATHER STARLETTE
                .
                .
                .

22 ROWS SELECTED

SELECT TRAINER, ARRIVAL, NAME
FROM GUEST_ROSTER
GROUP BY ARRIVAL, TRAINER, NAME;

TRAINER   ARRIVAL      NAME
========  ===========  ==========================
MICHAEL   14-JUN-1988  BETTE MIDRIFF
SERENA    14-JUN-1988  HETAERA
JULIO     15-JUN-1988  JEAN-PAUL ROTUNDO
JULIO     15-JUN-1988  MICHAEL JOHNSON
TODD      15-JUN-1988  SEAN PENCIL
JULIO     16-JUN-1988  MARLON SPANDEX
TODD      16-JUN-1988  WARREN AMOROSO
TODD      17-JUN-1988  DON JACKSON
YVETTE    17-JUN-1988  MEL GIMLET
YVETTE    18-JUN-1988  ROBERT DINERO
MICHAEL   19-JUN-1988  JANE FYUNDAI
YVETTE    19-JUN-1988  DYAN HOWITZER
TODD      20-JUN-1988  BIANCA JOGGER
MICHAEL   22-JUN-1988  OLYMPIA WELCH
SERENA    22-JUN-1988  DOLLY BRISKET
SERENA    22-JUN-1988  HEATHER STARLETTE
                .
                .
                .

22 ROWS SELECTED
```

Aggregate functions—AVG, SUM, MAX, MIN, and COUNT—are not allowed in the GROUP BY clause because they yield only a single value and are thus impossible to group by.

The GROUP BY clause can also be used in queries containing a WHERE clause. The GROUP BY is appended after the WHERE clause, if there is one. For example, the next query shows the number of guests who arrived after June 15 who are assigned to each trainer.

```
SELECT TRAINER, NAME
FROM GUEST_ROSTER
WHERE ARRIVAL > 15-JUN-1988
GROUP BY TRAINER, NAME;

TRAINER   NAME
========  ==========================
JULIO     MARLON SPANDEX
MICHAEL   CLINT WESTWOOD
MICHAEL   JANE FYUNDAI
```

```
MICHAEL   JOAN TONIC
MICHAEL   OLYMPIA WELCH
SERENA    DOLLY BRISKET
SERENA    HEATHER STARLETTE
SERENA    HETAERA
SERENA    JOANNIE RIVULETS
TODD      BIANCA JOGGER
TODD      DON JACKSON
TODD      MARCELLO HISTRIONI
TODD      SEAN PENCIL
TODD      WARREN AMOROSO
YVETTE    DYAN HOWITZER
YVETTE    MEL GIMLET
YVETTE    ROBERT DINERO

17 ROWS SELECTED
```

As we said, a GROUP BY clause must contain every item in the SELECT clause except aggregate functions. If, however, an item is anything but a column name—if it is a function or an arithmetic expression, for instance—then you cannot designate it by name in the GROUP BY clause. You must refer to it in the GROUP BY clause with a *number* that indicates its position in the SELECT clause.

For example, the following query groups results first by trainer and then by length of stay. For each trainer, the result lists the various lengths of stay of that trainer's guests. The expression DEPARTURE − ARRIVAL appears second in the SELECT clause, so it is referred to by "2" in the GROUP BY clause:

```
SELECT TRAINER, DEPARTURE - ARRIVAL
FROM GUEST_ROSTER
GROUP BY TRAINER, 2;

TRAINER   DEPARTURE - ARRIVAL
========  ====================
JULIO                        2
JULIO                        4
JULIO                        7
MICHAEL
MICHAEL                      2
MICHAEL                      5
MICHAEL                      7
SERENA
SERENA                       6
TODD
TODD                         5
TODD                         7
TODD                         8
YVETTE                       7

14 ROWS SELECTED
```

Where no length of stay is displayed, the guests in question have not given a departure date, so the expression DEPARTURE − ARRIVAL yields a null. Only distinct rows are given: where more than one guest has the same trainer and the same length of stay, the duplicate rows are suppressed and only one row is listed.

Incidentally, numbers can be used as a shorthand in the GROUP BY clause to pick out any item in the SELECT clause: you are not confined to using them only with expressions. Nor do you need to use them in any special order.

```
SELECT DEPARTURE - ARRIVAL, TRAINER
FROM GUEST_ROSTER
GROUP BY 2, 1;

DEPARTURE - ARRIVAL TRAINER
=================== ========
                  2 JULIO
                  4 JULIO
                  7 JULIO
                    MICHAEL
                  2 MICHAEL
                  5 MICHAEL
                  7 MICHAEL
                    SERENA
                  6 SERENA
                    TODD
                  5 TODD
                  7 TODD
                  8 TODD
                  7 YVETTE
```

14 ROWS SELECTED

We turn now to the second and more significant way that rows are grouped by GROUP BY. The first way is that, for each grouping column, rows with the same values are placed together in the result. The second way is that rows that are duplicates with respect to *all* the grouping columns are counted as a group by aggregate functions, and the duplicate rows are suppressed.

The following queries illustrate the suppression of duplicate rows by GROUP BY.

```
SELECT TRAINER
FROM GUEST_ROSTER;

TRAINER
========
JULIO
TODD
MICHAEL
JULIO
MICHAEL
TODD
SERENA
SERENA
TODD
JULIO
MICHAEL
SERENA
SERENA
MICHAEL
TODD
YVETTE
```

```
TODD
SERENA
YVETTE
MICHAEL
YVETTE
TODD

22 ROWS SELECTED

SELECT TRAINER
FROM GUEST_ROSTER
GROUP BY TRAINER;

TRAINER
========
JULIO
MICHAEL
SERENA
TODD
YVETTE

5 ROWS SELECTED
```

In the preceding chapter, we mentioned that any query with both an aggregate function and something that is *not* an aggregate function in the SELECT clause requires a GROUP BY clause. The following query, for example, violates this rule and consequently does not work.

```
SELECT TRAINER, COUNT(NAME)
FROM GUEST_ROSTER;
SELECT TRAINER, COUNT(NAME)
                ^
Error: not a single value set function
```

The query does not work because its syntax is incoherent: for NAME we are asked to select a value for *each row*, and for COUNT(NAME) we are asked for a *single value* derived from all rows taken together.

The GROUP BY clause enables us to avoid this situation by parceling the rows of the result into groups, such that an aggregate function no longer returns only a single value for all rows in the table, but instead returns a value for each group. By "group" in this instance we mean the second kind of grouping performed by GROUP BY, such that each row of (non-aggregate) grouping column values in the result, together with any suppressed duplicates of that row, constitutes a group.

In the following query, for example, rows are grouped first by TRAINER, then by NAME, such that the names of all guests having the same trainer appear in a "group" (the first kind). The aggregate function COUNT(NAME), however, regards just those rows that are duplicates with respect to their values for TRAINER and NAME as making a distinct group (the second kind). In each case, it is the number of rows in this second kind of group that is represented in the COUNT(NAME) column.

```
SELECT TRAINER, NAME, COUNT(NAME)
FROM GUEST_ROSTER
GROUP BY TRAINER, NAME;

TRAINER   NAME                        COUNT(NAME)
========  ==========================  ===========
JULIO     JEAN-PAUL ROTUNDO                     1
JULIO     MARLON SPANDEX                        1
JULIO     MICHAEL JOHNSON                       1
MICHAEL   BETTE MIDRIFF                         1
MICHAEL   CLINT WESTWOOD                        1
MICHAEL   JANE FYUNDAI                          1
MICHAEL   JOAN TONIC                            1
MICHAEL   OLYMPIA WELCH                         1
SERENA    DOLLY BRISKET                         1
SERENA    HEATHER STARLETTE                     1
SERENA    HETAERA                               2
SERENA    JOANNIE RIVULETS                      1
TODD      BIANCA JOGGER                         1
TODD      DON JACKSON                           1
TODD      MARCELLO HISTRIONI                    1
TODD      SEAN PENCIL                           2
TODD      WARREN AMOROSO                        1
YVETTE    DYAN HOWITZER                         1
YVETTE    MEL GIMLET                            1
YVETTE    ROBERT DINERO                         1

20 ROWS SELECTED
```

The following example may make it easier to see the usefulness of GROUP BY with aggregate functions. The query contains only one grouping column, TRAINER. The query selects the number of guests assigned to each trainer. To try at the same time to list these guests would result in the preceding query.

```
SELECT TRAINER, COUNT(NAME)
FROM GUEST_ROSTER
GROUP BY TRAINER;

TRAINER   COUNT(NAME)
========  ===========
JULIO               3
MICHAEL             5
SERENA              5
TODD                6
YVETTE              3

5 ROWS SELECTED
```

A final word on the subject of aggregate functions: We mentioned in Chapter 4, "Using Queries to Manipulate Data," that aggregate functions can be nested in other aggregate functions, but we deferred showing how because such aggregates require a GROUP BY clause. Now we can give an example.

Aggregate functions can contain one subsidiary level of aggregate functions. The following query uses nested aggregate functions to ask for the largest number of guests assigned to any trainer. Notice that TRAINER appears in the GROUP BY clause even though it does not appear in the SELECT clause:

```
SELECT MAX(COUNT(NAME))
FROM GUEST_ROSTER
GROUP BY TRAINER;

MAX(COUNT(NAME))
================
               6

1 ROW SELECTED
```

Aggregates containing another aggregate require a GROUP BY clause because without one the inner aggregate function would produce only a single value, and there would thus be no plurality of values for the exterior aggregate function to operate on.

At the same time, we cannot in this instance put TRAINER in the SELECT clause along with MAX(COUNT(NAME)) because, again, we would then be including a multiple-value function (TRAINER) in the SELECT clause with a single-value function (the outer aggregate function MAX).

Restricting Groupings with the HAVING Clause

The HAVING clause lets you narrow the focus of a GROUP BY clause similarly to the way that the WHERE clause lets you narrow the focus of the SELECT clause, namely, by applying a search condition.

Unlike the WHERE clause, though, the HAVING clause *can* contain aggregates.

A new table, GUEST_WT, will help us at this point. The table is created with the following CREATE TABLE statement. The table is designed to contain La Bamba's records of periodic weighings of the guests.

```
CREATE TABLE GUEST_WT (GUEST VARCHAR(25) NOT NULL, WEIGHT DECIMAL(4,1),
WHEN DATE);

TABLE CREATED
```

The DATE-type column is called WHEN because "DATE" is a reserved keyword. A reserved keyword cannot be used as a column name or other identifier unless it is enclosed in quotation marks (see Chapter 2, "Constructing a Table").

After data is inserted, table GUEST_WT looks like this:

```
SELECT * FROM GUEST_WT;

GUEST                      WEIGHT     WHEN
========================= ========== ===========
BETTE MIDRIFF                  150   14-JUN-1988
HETAERA                        130   14-JUN-1988
```

```
JEAN-PAUL ROTUNDO           190  15-JUN-1988
MICHAEL JOHNSON             186  15-JUN-1988
SEAN PENCIL                 148  15-JUN-1988
BETTE MIDRIFF             148.5  16-JUN-1988
WARREN AMOROSO              168  16-JUN-1988
MARLON SPANDEX              171  16-JUN-1988
JEAN-PAUL ROTUNDO           189  17-JUN-1988
MEL GIMLET                  166  17-JUN-1988
DON JACKSON                 165  17-JUN-1988
ROBERT DINERO               195  18-JUN-1988
MICHAEL JOHNSON             183  19-JUN-1988
DYAN HOWITZER               125  19-JUN-1988
JANE FYUNDAI                165  19-JUN-1988
SEAN PENCIL                 150  20-JUN-1988
                             .
                             .
                             .
44 ROWS SELECTED
```

The table contains two weight records for each visit: one from the arrival date, one from the date of departure. The following query lists those guests having a difference greater than three between their minimum and maximum weights. Notice the aggregate functions in the HAVING clause.

```
SELECT GUEST, MIN(WEIGHT), MAX(WEIGHT), MAX(WEIGHT) - MIN(WEIGHT)
FROM GUEST_WT
GROUP BY GUEST
HAVING MAX(WEIGHT) - MIN(WEIGHT) > 3;

GUEST                    MIN(WEIGHT) MAX(WEIGHT) MAX(WEIGHT) - MIN(WEIGHT)
======================== =========== =========== =========================
BIANCA JOGGER                    109         113                         4
DON JACKSON                      159         165                         6
HEATHER STARLETTE                143         147                         4
JANE FYUNDAI                     160         165                         5
MARLON SPANDEX                   165         171                         6
OLYMPIA WELCH                    159         165                         6
ROBERT DINERO                    185         195                        10
SEAN PENCIL                      148         152                         4
WARREN AMOROSO                 162.5         168                       5.5

9 ROWS SELECTED
```

All items except GUEST in the SELECT list are aggregate functions, so only GUEST needs to appear in the GROUP BY clause. By using GROUP BY, we confine the scope of the aggregate functions to just those rows with identical values in the grouping column GUEST. The HAVING clause contains aggregate functions appearing in an arithmetic expression.

Here is another example. This query asks for the number of guests assigned to each trainer who has more than three guests.

```
SELECT TRAINER, COUNT(NAME)
FROM GUEST_ROSTER
GROUP BY TRAINER
HAVING COUNT(NAME) > 3;

TRAINER   COUNT(NAME)
=======   ===========
MICHAEL            5
SERENA             5
TODD               6

3 ROWS SELECTED
```

A GROUP BY clause can contain any number of columns and expressions, and a HAVING clause can contain any number of conditions. There are just two restrictions: column names that do not also appear in the GROUP BY cannot be used as terms of search conditions in the HAVING clause, and neither can grouping columns in the GROUP BY that are expressions.

The latter restriction refers to those grouping columns that must be listed in the GROUP BY as numbers. Aggregate functions do not appear in the GROUP BY and can, as we have seen, occur in the HAVING clause.

Sorting with the ORDER BY Clause

The ORDER BY clause lets you sort rows in the result alphabetically and numerically in either ascending or descending order. Ascending order is the default. The ORDER BY clause is always the last clause appended to a query.

In the following example, we cause the guests' names to be sorted in descending order by placing DESC in the ORDER BY clause after the result column we want sorted this way. We use the DISTINCT keyword (discussed in Chapter 3, "Getting the Data You Want: Queries") to suppress duplicate rows:

```
SELECT DISTINCT NAME
FROM GUEST_ROSTER
ORDER BY NAME DESC;

NAME
=========================
WARREN AMOROSO
SEAN PENCIL
ROBERT DINERO
OLYMPIA WELCH
MICHAEL JOHNSON
MEL GIMLET
         .
         .
         .
```

```
DOLLY BRISKET
CLINT WESTWOOD
BIANCA JOGGER
BETTE MIDRIFF

20 ROWS SELECTED
```

Sorts are performed in ascending order by default in any column in the ORDER BY clause whose name is not followed by the keyword DESC. Ascending order may also be explicitly specified, however, for a particular column by using the keyword ASC after the name in the ORDER BY clause.

Any number of columns of the result table can be sorted. The major sort is on the first column specified in the ORDER BY clause, with minor sorts on subsequent columns, taken in the order in which they appear. Rows with identical values in the first column sorted are placed together, as are rows within each subgroup of the minor sorts. The next query selects three columns—TRAINER, DEPARTURE, and NAME—sorting first by trainer and then by departure date:

```
SELECT TRAINER, DEPARTURE, NAME
FROM GUEST_ROSTER
ORDER BY TRAINER, DEPARTURE;

TRAINER   DEPARTURE    NAME
========  ===========  ==========================
JULIO     17-JUN-1988  JEAN-PAUL ROTUNDO
JULIO     19-JUN-1988  MICHAEL JOHNSON
JULIO     23-JUN-1988  MARLON SPANDEX
MICHAEL                CLINT WESTWOOD
MICHAEL                JOAN TONIC
MICHAEL   16-JUN-1988  BETTE MIDRIFF
MICHAEL   26-JUN-1988  JANE FYUNDAI
MICHAEL   27-JUN-1988  OLYMPIA WELCH
SERENA                 HETAERA
SERENA                 JOANNIE RIVULETS
SERENA                 HEATHER STARLETTE
SERENA                 DOLLY BRISKET
SERENA    20-JUN-1988  HETAERA
TODD                   MARCELLO HISTRIONI
TODD                   SEAN PENCIL
TODD      20-JUN-1988  SEAN PENCIL
TODD      23-JUN-1988  WARREN AMOROSO
TODD      25-JUN-1988  DON JACKSON
TODD      27-JUN-1988  BIANCA JOGGER
YVETTE    24-JUN-1988  MEL GIMLET
YVETTE    25-JUN-1988  ROBERT DINERO
YVETTE    26-JUN-1988  DYAN HOWITZER

22 ROWS SELECTED
```

In SQLBase, nulls in a column being sorted are displayed first when that column is sorted. The DEPARTURE column contains nulls, so, for each trainer, these null values were placed at the top of that trainer's list of departure dates.

Following is the same query again; but instead of ordering first by trainer and then by departure date, this time we order by DEPARTURE first.

Notice that this time all null departure dates for all trainers appear first in a group, instead of appearing piecemeal at the top of each trainer's own list. This is because the DEPARTURE column is sorted first in this query:

```
SELECT TRAINER, DEPARTURE, NAME
FROM GUEST_ROSTER
ORDER BY DEPARTURE, TRAINER ;

TRAINER    DEPARTURE     NAME
========   ===========   =========================
MICHAEL                  CLINT WESTWOOD
MICHAEL                  JOAN TONIC
SERENA                   HETAERA
SERENA                   JOANNIE RIVULETS
SERENA                   HEATHER STARLETTE
SERENA                   DOLLY BRISKET
TODD                     MARCELLO HISTRIONI
TODD                     SEAN PENCIL
MICHAEL    16-JUN-1988   BETTE MIDRIFF
JULIO      17-JUN-1988   JEAN-PAUL ROTUNDO
JULIO      19-JUN-1988   MICHAEL JOHNSON
SERENA     20-JUN-1988   HETAERA
TODD       20-JUN-1988   SEAN PENCIL
JULIO      23-JUN-1988   MARLON SPANDEX
TODD       23-JUN-1988   WARREN AMOROSO
YVETTE     24-JUN-1988   MEL GIMLET
TODD       25-JUN-1988   DON JACKSON
YVETTE     25-JUN-1988   ROBERT DINERO
MICHAEL    26-JUN-1988   JANE FYUNDAI
YVETTE     26-JUN-1988   DYAN HOWITZER
MICHAEL    27-JUN-1988   OLYMPIA WELCH
TODD       27-JUN-1988   BIANCA JOGGER

22 ROWS SELECTED
```

To order by an expression or a function, you must pick out the expression or function with a number identifying its relative place in the SELECT clause, similarly to the way you must use a number with expressions in a GROUP BY clause. Again, you may use such numbers all the time in preference to naming the columns:

```
SELECT DEPARTURE - ARRIVAL, NAME
FROM GUEST_ROSTER
ORDER BY 1, 2;

DEPARTURE - ARRIVAL   NAME
===================   =========================
                      CLINT WESTWOOD
                      DOLLY BRISKET
                      HEATHER STARLETTE
                      HETAERA
                      JOAN TONIC
                      JOANNIE RIVULETS
                      MARCELLO HISTRIONI
```

```
            SEAN PENCIL
          2 BETTE MIDRIFF
          2 JEAN-PAUL ROTUNDO
          4 MICHAEL JOHNSON
          5 OLYMPIA WELCH
          5 SEAN PENCIL
          6 HETAERA
            .
            .
            .

22 ROWS SELECTED
```

ORDER BY can also be used when there is a GROUP BY clause, as the following two queries show:

```
SELECT TRAINER, COUNT(NAME)
FROM GUEST_ROSTER
GROUP BY 1
ORDER BY 1 DESC;

TRAINER   COUNT(NAME)
========  ===========
YVETTE          3
TODD            6
SERENA          5
MICHAEL         5
JULIO           3

5 ROWS SELECTED

SELECT TRAINER, COUNT(NAME)
FROM GUEST_ROSTER
GROUP BY 1
ORDER BY 2 DESC;

TRAINER   COUNT(NAME)
========  ===========
TODD            6
MICHAEL         5
SERENA          5
JULIO           3
YVETTE          3

5 ROWS SELECTED
```

Summary

Three clauses can be appended to a query to further narrow the focus of the query and organize the result: a GROUP BY clause, a HAVING clause, and an ORDER BY clause.

The GROUP BY clause groups rows in two ways: (1) It groups rows with similar values in the specified grouping columns. (2) The clause suppresses rows that are duplicates with respect to all grouping columns, counting each set of duplicate rows as a group.

By parceling the rows of the result table into groups such that aggregate functions in the SELECT list return a value for each group rather than for all rows as a whole, the GROUP BY clause makes it possible to include aggregate functions in a SELECT list containing entries that are not aggregate functions.

The HAVING clause can be used to confine the scope of a GROUP BY clause in much the same way that a WHERE clause can be used to narrow the focus of a SELECT clause, namely, by specifying search conditions.

Rows in the result can be sorted alphabetically and numerically, in ascending or descending order, with an ORDER BY clause.

CHAPTER 6

Queries That Draw on More than One Table: Joins

Many times the data you want will not always be in one table. For instance, to find out Mel Gimlet's height and who his trainer is, we have to go to two different tables. His trainer is listed in table GUEST_ROSTER, but his height is listed only in table GUESTS. This table, which you may recall from earlier chapters, looks like this:

```
SELECT * FROM GUESTS;
NAME                     SEX BUILD  HEIGHT
========================  === =====  ==========
BETTE MIDRIFF             F    M        66
MARCELLO HISTRIONI        M    M        66
JEAN-PAUL ROTUNDO         M    L        70
MICHAEL JOHNSON           M    L        71
CLINT WESTWOOD            M    M        73
JOANNIE RIVULETS          F    S        65
WARREN AMOROSO            M    M        70
MARLON SPANDEX            M    M        71
OLYMPIA WELCH             F    L        70
HEATHER STARLETTE         F    M        66
DOLLY BRISKET             F    S        61
JOAN TONIC                F    M        62
MEL GIMLET                M    M        70
DON JACKSON               M    M        70
ROBERT DINERO             M    L        69
JANE FYUNDAI              F    L        65
DYAN HOWITZER             F    S        68
BIANCA JOGGER             F    S        61
ENGLEBERT HUMPTYDUMPTY    M    L        72
SHIRLEY O'SHADE           F    M        64
```

```
SHARE                         F    S         71
STELLA SHIELDS                F    M         65
SEAN PENCIL                   M    S         65
HETAERA                       F    S         63
24 ROWS SELECTED
```

The following query draws Mel Gimlet's height from table GUESTS:

```
SELECT NAME, HEIGHT
FROM GUESTS
WHERE NAME = 'MEL GIMLET';

NAME                           HEIGHT
==========================  ==========
MEL GIMLET                       70

1 ROW SELECTED
```

The next query gives us his trainer from GUEST_ROSTER:

```
SELECT NAME, TRAINER
FROM GUEST_ROSTER
WHERE NAME = 'MEL GIMLET';

NAME                         TRAINER
==========================  ========
MEL GIMLET                   YVETTE

1 ROW SELECTED
```

We can, however, get this information in one fell swoop by using a query called a *join*. A join is a query that draws data from more than one table at once, pivoting on a *join condition* in the WHERE clause. Here is a join that gives us the height and trainer of every guest:

```
SELECT GUESTS.NAME, HEIGHT, TRAINER
FROM GUESTS, GUEST_ROSTER
WHERE GUESTS.NAME = GUEST_ROSTER.NAME;

GUESTS.NAME                  HEIGHT   TRAINER
==========================  ========  ========
JEAN-PAUL ROTUNDO              70     JULIO
MARCELLO HISTRIONI             66     TODD
BETTE MIDRIFF                  66     MICHAEL
MICHAEL JOHNSON                71     JULIO
CLINT WESTWOOD                 73     MICHAEL
SEAN PENCIL                    65     TODD
HETAERA                        63     SERENA
JOANNIE RIVULETS               65     SERENA
WARREN AMOROSO                 70     TODD
MARLON SPANDEX                 71     JULIO
OLYMPIA WELCH                  70     MICHAEL
HEATHER STARLETTE              66     SERENA
DOLLY BRISKET                  61     SERENA
JOAN TONIC                     62     MICHAEL
SEAN PENCIL                    65     TODD
MEL GIMLET                     70     YVETTE
```

```
DON JACKSON           70  TODD
HETAERA               63  SERENA
ROBERT DINERO         69  YVETTE
JANE FYUNDAI          65  MICHAEL
DYAN HOWITZER         68  YVETTE
BIANCA JOGGER         61  TODD

22 ROWS SELECTED
```

The query says, in effect, "For all rows in GUESTS and GUEST_ROSTER where the value of GUESTS.NAME is the same as the value of GUEST_ROSTER.NAME, return the respective values of NAME and HEIGHT from GUESTS and of TRAINER from GUEST_ROSTER."

The join condition in the WHERE clause is a search condition like those already discussed. It is built around a relational predicate like any other search condition. The only difference is that the expressions related in the join condition refer to more than one table.

To avoid ambiguity, two of the column names are prefixed with the name of their respective tables, as follows: GUESTS.NAME, GUEST_ROSTER.NAME. As we said in Chapter 2, "Constructing a Table," a name is also called an *identifier*; a name explicitly qualified with a prefix—for example, "GUESTS.NAME"—is called a *qualified identifier*.

The prefixes are necessary only because the two column names are the same. Prefixes are not ordinarily necessary except to avoid this sort of ambiguity. For instance, HEIGHT and TRAINER occur only in one table apiece, so they do not require prefixes. In the queries that follow, however, column names are often qualified even when they do not have to be, to advertise the table they derive from.

The join condition itself is necessary unless we want to match *every* row of TRAINER in GUEST_ROSTER with the values for NAME and HEIGHT in *each* row of GUESTS. This type of result, called the Cartesian product of the tables, is generally not desired. It would in this instance yield 22 rows (from GUEST_ROSTER) multiplied by 24 rows (from GUESTS), or 528 rows.

Equijoins

The previous query is an example of an *equijoin*. This is simply a join embodying a join condition based on an equality. Other types of relational predicates can be used to form other types of join conditions, and we will look at some samples shortly; but perhaps the most common type of join condition is the equijoin.

We now introduce another table, ROOMS, to use in a slightly different example. This table gives particulars about the accommodations in La Bamba Spa and is created with the following statement:

80 Part I: Using SQL Interactively

```
CREATE TABLE ROOMS (ROOM VARCHAR(3), NAME VARCHAR(15),
RATE FLOAT, DESCRIPTION LONG VARCHAR);
TABLE CREATED
```

The table, minus the LONG column and with data inserted, looks like this:

```
SELECT ROOM, NAME, RATE
FROM ROOMS;
```

ROOM	NAME	RATE
1	ANNATTO RM	300
2	CARMINE RM	300
3	CERISE RM	250
4	CHERRY RM	250
5	MAROON RM	250
7	PEACH RM	250
8	MARIGOLD SUITE	325
9	GOLD RM	250
10	AMBER RM	250
11	BEIGE RM	250
12	SAND RM	250
13	JADE SUITE	325
14	MYRTLE SUITE	325
15	TURQUOISE RM	250
18	DAHLIA SUITE	325
19	OLIVE SUITE	375
20	PEARL SUITE	425
6	PUCE RM	250
16	MARINE RM	250
17	INDIGO RM	250

20 ROWS SELECTED

Here is our example. In this query, for purposes of demonstration, the equijoin is in an AND clause. Notice, too, that neither of the two joined columns, ROOM from table ROOMS and ROOM from table GUEST_ROSTER, has to appear in the SELECT list.

```
SELECT GUEST_ROSTER.NAME, ROOMS.NAME, ROOMS.RATE, GUEST_ROSTER.DISCOUNT
FROM ROOMS, GUEST_ROSTER
WHERE GUEST_ROSTER.NAME = 'JANE FYUNDAI'
AND ROOMS.ROOM = GUEST_ROSTER.ROOM;
```

GUEST_ROSTER.NAME	ROOMS.NAME	ROOMS.RATE	GUEST_ROSTER.DISCOUNT
JANE FYUNDAI	DAHLIA SUITE	325	.1

1 ROW SELECTED

A query may require more than one join condition, depending on how many columns you need to join on. To illustrate this, we introduce another new table, WEIGHT_CHART, which gives minimum and maximum acceptable weights for males and females of small, medium, or large build and a specified height in inches. The statement that creates this table is

Chapter 6: Queries That Draw on More than One Table: Joins

```
CREATE TABLE WEIGHT_CHART (HEIGHT INTEGER, SEX CHAR(1),
BUILD CHAR(1),MIN_WT DECIMAL(3,0), MAX_WT DECIMAL(3,0));
TABLE CREATED
```

Here is an excerpt to show what the table with its data (inserted separately) looks like:

```
SELECT * FROM WEIGHT_CHART;
    HEIGHT SEX BUILD    MIN_WT     MAX_WT
    ====== === =====    ======     ======
        61 M   S           123        129
        62 M   S           125        131
        63 M   S           127        133
                   .
                   .
                   .
        73 M   M           159        173
        74 M   M           162        177
        75 M   M           166        182
        61 M   L           133        145
        62 M   L           135        148
        63 M   L           137        151
                   .
                   .
        68 F   S           126        139
        69 F   S           129        142
        70 F   S           132        145
        71 F   S           135        148
        57 F   M           106        117
        58 F   M           108        120
        59 F   M           110        123
                   .
                   .
        68 F   L           146        167
        69 F   L           149        170
        70 F   L           152        173
        71 F   L           155        176
  90 ROWS SELECTED
```

Here is our query. It returns all rows in NAME from table GUESTS and in MIN_WT and MAX_WT from table WEIGHT_CHART where the respective columns SEX, BUILD, and HEIGHT in the two tables contain the same values. In other words, the tables GUESTS and WEIGHT_CHART are joined on three columns to give the acceptable weight range for each guest, given each guest's sex, build, and height.

```
SELECT GUESTS.NAME, WEIGHT_CHART.MIN_WT, WEIGHT_CHART.MAX_WT
FROM GUESTS, WEIGHT_CHART
WHERE GUESTS.SEX = WEIGHT_CHART.SEX
AND GUESTS.BUILD = WEIGHT_CHART.BUILD
AND GUESTS.HEIGHT = WEIGHT_CHART.HEIGHT;
```

GUESTS.NAME	WEIGHT_CHART.MIN_WT	WEIGHT_CHART.MAX_WT
BETTE MIDRIFF	130	143
MARCELLO HISTRIONI	137	149
JEAN-PAUL ROTUNDO	156	179
MICHAEL JOHNSON	159	183
CLINT WESTWOOD	159	173
JOANNIE RIVULETS	117	130
WARREN AMOROSO	149	161
MARLON SPANDEX	152	165
.		
.		
.		

24 ROWS SELECTED

Outer Joins

Suppose that we want to know the name, sex, build, height, and trainer of each of our guests. Trainers are assigned in table GUEST_ROSTER, which contains information about current guests; the other information is in table GUESTS, which contains records on all guests, past and present.

We can use the following query, a straightforward equijoin:

```
SELECT GUESTS.NAME, SEX, BUILD, HEIGHT, TRAINER
FROM GUESTS, GUEST_ROSTER
WHERE GUESTS.NAME = GUEST_ROSTER.NAME;
```

GUESTS.NAME	SEX	BUILD	HEIGHT	TRAINER
JEAN-PAUL ROTUNDO	M	L	70	JULIO
MARCELLO HISTRIONI	M	M	66	TODD
BETTE MIDRIFF	F	M	66	MICHAEL
MICHAEL JOHNSON	M	L	71	JULIO
CLINT WESTWOOD	M	M	73	MICHAEL
SEAN PENCIL	M	S	65	TODD
.				
.				
.				

22 ROWS SELECTED

The query works fine as far as it goes, but notice this feature about the two columns used in the join condition: the column of names in GUESTS has four more entries than the similar column in GUEST_ROSTER, which lists only *current guests*. Because no rows exist in table GUEST_ROSTER for the four extra names, these four rows in GUESTS cannot be matched according to the join condition. Consequently, no entries appear for these four names in the result.

An outer join lets us join on columns with unequal numbers of rows without the unmatched rows being dropped. Rather, the unmatched rows are listed, too, with nulls appearing in any column from the table where those rows do not exist.

Chapter 6: Queries That Draw on More than One Table: Joins

The capability to perform outer joins is presently found in only a couple of implementations of SQL. Nevertheless, because this is an important feature and one likely to be more widely implemented in the future, we will look at how this type of join is handled in SQLBase.

The SQLBase syntax for converting our example to an outer join to include the four unmatched rows from GUESTS is simple: we have only to add a plus sign (+) to the column in the join condition that lacks the matching rows, that is, to the column where we want to add nulls in the result. In our example, that column is GUEST_ROSTER.NAME. Adding the plus sign ensures that all names from GUESTS are listed, whether or not these names appear in GUEST_ROSTER.

```
SELECT GUESTS.NAME, GUESTS.SEX, GUEST_ROSTER.TRAINER
FROM GUESTS, GUEST_ROSTER
WHERE GUESTS.NAME = GUEST_ROSTER.NAME(+);

GUESTS.NAME              GUESTS.SEX  GUEST_ROSTER.TRAINER
==========================  ==========  ====================
BETTE MIDRIFF            F           MICHAEL
MARCELLO HISTRIONI       M           TODD
JEAN-PAUL ROTUNDO        M           JULIO
           .
           .
           .
JANE FYUNDAI             F           MICHAEL
DYAN HOWITZER            F           YVETTE
BIANCA JOGGER            F           TODD
ENGLEBERT HUMPTYDUMPTY   M
SHIRLEY O'SHADE          F
SHARE                    F
STELLA SHIELDS           F
SEAN PENCIL              M           TODD
SEAN PENCIL              M           TODD
HETAERA                  F           SERENA
HETAERA                  F           SERENA

26 ROWS SELECTED
```

This time the four names ENGLEBERT HUMPTYDUMPTY, SHIRLEY O'SHADE, SHARE, and STELLA SHIELDS appear, even though no rows for these names exist in table GUEST_ROSTER. Nulls appear opposite these names in the TRAINER column, which derives from table GUEST_ROSTER.

Here is another example. Suppose that we want to know the names and room assignments of all the guests who arrived before June 20. This information is in table GUEST_ROSTER. Suppose, too, that we also want the *name* of the room or suite assigned to each guest. The names of the rooms are listed in table ROOMS.

We can get the information we want with a join on the two tables GUEST_ROSTER and ROOMS:

```
SELECT GUEST_ROSTER.NAME, GUEST_ROSTER.ROOM, ROOMS.NAME
FROM GUEST_ROSTER, ROOMS
WHERE GUEST_ROSTER.ROOM = ROOMS.ROOM
AND ARRIVAL < 20-JUN-1988;

GUEST_ROSTER.NAME          GUEST_ROSTER.ROOM  ROOMS.NAME
=========================  =================  ==========
JEAN-PAUL ROTUNDO          3                  CERISE RM
BETTE MIDRIFF              1                  ANNATTO RM
MICHAEL JOHNSON            4                  CHERRY RM
SEAN PENCIL                6                  PUCE RM
WARREN AMOROSO             9                  GOLD RM
MARLON SPANDEX             10                 AMBER RM
MEL GIMLET                 15                 TURQUOISE RM
DON JACKSON                16                 MARINE RM
HETAERA                    10                 AMBER RM
ROBERT DINERO              17                 INDIGO RM
JANE FYUNDAI               18                 DAHLIA SUITE
DYAN HOWITZER              19                 OLIVE SUITE

12 ROWS SELECTED
```

Suppose, though, that besides the names and room assignments of all the guests who arrived before June 20, we would also like to see listed the names of the rooms that were *not* assigned during this period. Rows exist for these rooms in table ROOMS, but the rooms are not listed in the rows selected from GUEST_ROSTER because they were not assigned then. By using an outer join, we can cause these unassigned rooms to be listed too.

In the join condition, the plus sign goes in the column from the table where nulls may have to be added, namely GUEST_ROSTER. In the result, nulls are added to both columns that derive from GUEST_ROSTER.

```
SELECT GUEST_ROSTER.NAME, GUEST_ROSTER.ROOM, ROOMS.NAME
FROM GUEST_ROSTER, ROOMS
WHERE GUEST_ROSTER.ROOM(+) = ROOMS.ROOM
AND ARRIVAL < 20-JUN-1988;

GUEST_ROSTER.NAME          GUEST_ROSTER.ROOM  ROOMS.NAME
=========================  =================  ===============
BETTE MIDRIFF              1                  ANNATTO RM
                                              CARMINE RM
JEAN-PAUL ROTUNDO          3                  CERISE RM
MICHAEL JOHNSON            4                  CHERRY RM
                                              MAROON RM
                                              PEACH RM
                                              MARIGOLD SUITE
WARREN AMOROSO             9                  GOLD RM
MARLON SPANDEX             10                 AMBER RM
HETAERA                    10                 AMBER RM
                                              BEIGE RM
                                              SAND RM
                                              JADE SUITE
                                              MYRTLE SUITE
MEL GIMLET                 15                 TURQUOISE RM
```

```
JANE FYUNDAI              18         DAHLIA SUITE
DYAN HOWITZER             19         OLIVE SUITE
                                     PEARL SUITE
SEAN PENCIL               6          PUCE RM
DON JACKSON               16         MARINE RM
ROBERT DINERO             17         INDIGO RM

21 ROWS SELECTED
```

Next, notice the difference if we specify column ROOMS.ROOM rather than column GUEST_ROSTER.ROOM in the SELECT list. No nulls appear in the column now. This is because a row exists in ROOMS.ROOM for every room name, whereas in GUEST_ROSTER.ROOM only rows relating to guests who arrived before June 20 are listed.

```
SELECT GUEST_ROSTER.NAME, ROOMS.ROOM, ROOMS.NAME
FROM GUEST_ROSTER, ROOMS
WHERE GUEST_ROSTER.ROOM(+) = ROOMS.ROOM
AND ARRIVAL < 20-JUN-1988;

GUEST_ROSTER.NAME         ROOMS.ROOM ROOMS.NAME
========================  ========== ================
BETTE MIDRIFF             1          ANNATTO RM
                          2          CARMINE RM
JEAN-PAUL ROTUNDO         3          CERISE RM
MICHAEL JOHNSON           4          CHERRY RM
                          5          MAROON RM
                          7          PEACH RM
                          8          MARIGOLD SUITE
WARREN AMOROSO            9          GOLD RM
MARLON SPANDEX            10         AMBER RM
HETAERA                   10         AMBER RM
                          11         BEIGE RM
                          12         SAND RM
                          13         JADE SUITE
                          14         MYRTLE SUITE
MEL GIMLET                15         TURQUOISE RM
JANE FYUNDAI              18         DAHLIA SUITE
DYAN HOWITZER             19         OLIVE SUITE
                          20         PEARL SUITE
SEAN PENCIL               6          PUCE RM
DON JACKSON               16         MARINE RM
ROBERT DINERO             17         INDIGO RM

21 ROWS SELECTED
```

Self Joins

Sometimes you may want to join a table with itself. This is a way of treating one table as, in effect, two tables in order to make possible certain types of queries.

Suppose that we want to select all guests who receive the same discount as Joannie Rivulets. All the information we want is in table GUEST_ROSTER, which looks like this:

```
SELECT * FROM GUEST_ROSTER;

NAME                     ROOM  TRAINER   ARRIVAL      DEPARTURE    DISCOUNT
========================  ====  ========  ===========  ===========  ========
JEAN-PAUL ROTUNDO         3     JULIO     15-JUN-1988  17-JUN-1988       .2
MARCELLO HISTRIONI        2     TODD      26-JUN-1988                    .1
BETTE MIDRIFF             1     MICHAEL   14-JUN-1988  16-JUN-1988
MICHAEL JOHNSON           4     JULIO     15-JUN-1988  19-JUN-1988
CLINT WESTWOOD            5     MICHAEL   25-JUN-1988                   .15
SEAN PENCIL               6     TODD      15-JUN-1988  20-JUN-1988      .05
HETAERA                   7     SERENA    24-JUN-1988
JOANNIE RIVULETS          8     SERENA    25-JUN-1988                   .15
WARREN AMOROSO            9     TODD      16-JUN-1988  23-JUN-1988       .2
MARLON SPANDEX            10    JULIO     16-JUN-1988  23-JUN-1988      .05
OLYMPIA WELCH             11    MICHAEL   22-JUN-1988  27-JUN-1988       .1
HEATHER STARLETTE         12    SERENA    22-JUN-1988                   .05
DOLLY BRISKET             13    SERENA    22-JUN-1988
JOAN TONIC                14    MICHAEL   23-JUN-1988                   .05
SEAN PENCIL               9     TODD      23-JUN-1988                    .1
MEL GIMLET                15    YVETTE    17-JUN-1988  24-JUN-1988
DON JACKSON               16    TODD      17-JUN-1988  25-JUN-1988       .1
HETAERA                   10    SERENA    14-JUN-1988  20-JUN-1988       .2
ROBERT DINERO             17    YVETTE    18-JUN-1988  25-JUN-1988       .1
JANE FYUNDAI              18    MICHAEL   19-JUN-1988  26-JUN-1988       .1
DYAN HOWITZER             19    YVETTE    19-JUN-1988  26-JUN-1988
BIANCA JOGGER             20    TODD      20-JUN-1988  27-JUN-1988      .15

22 ROWS SELECTED
```

We could, of course, use one query to select DISCOUNT where NAME equals "JOANNIE RIVULETS" and then a second query to select NAME and DISCOUNT where DISCOUNT equals the result from our first query. But suppose we want to do things more elegantly, and with less trouble, using a single query.

Our task may look straightforward enough. We might begin to construct our query as follows:

```
SELECT NAME, DISCOUNT
FROM GUEST_ROSTER
WHERE DISCOUNT = ...?
```

Here, however, we come to an impasse. We want to say something like WHERE DISCOUNT = (Joannie Rivulets' discount), and there does not seem to be any way to say that.

Notice how easy the query would be, though, if instead of dealing with only one table we were dealing with two, so that we were able to get our information about Joannie Rivulets from one, and our information about everybody else from the other. Then, letting A and B differentiate the two otherwise identical tables, we could say

```
SELECT A.NAME, A.DISCOUNT
FROM GUEST_ROSTER A, GUEST_ROSTER B
WHERE A.DISCOUNT = B.DISCOUNT
AND B.NAME = 'JOANNIE RIVULETS';
```

Chapter 6: Queries That Draw on More than One Table: Joins

```
A.NAME                       A.DISCOUNT
==========================   ==========
CLINT WESTWOOD                      .15
JOANNIE RIVULETS                    .15
BIANCA JOGGER                       .15

3 ROWS SELECTED
```

As you can see from the result, this is in fact exactly the way to handle this sort of query, called a self join.

In a self join, temporary table names, called *correlation names*, or *labels*, are the key to letting you join a table to itself. The correlation names are assigned in the FROM list, in which you establish that the table in question is now to be known by these correlation names. Then elsewhere in the query you use the correlation names to prefix the column names you want to use.

By the way, you are not confined to using correlation names just in connection with self joins. You may use them with any join in which they will save you from typing complete table names as prefixes.

Here is another example. In this query we want to know if there are any guests who have been assigned the same room at the same time:

```
SELECT A.NAME, B.NAME
FROM GUEST_ROSTER A, GUEST_ROSTER B
WHERE A.NAME != B.NAME
AND A.ROOM = B.ROOM
AND B.ARRIVAL BETWEEN A.ARRIVAL AND A.DEPARTURE;

A.NAME                       B.NAME
==========================   ==========================
HETAERA                      MARLON SPANDEX
WARREN AMOROSO               SEAN PENCIL

2 ROWS SELECTED
```

Oops.

Here is a slightly different example. This time we want to know the name and discount of everyone receiving a *larger* discount than Joannie.

```
SELECT A.NAME, A.DISCOUNT
FROM GUEST_ROSTER A, GUEST_ROSTER B
WHERE A.DISCOUNT > B.DISCOUNT
AND B.NAME = 'JOANNIE RIVULETS';

A.NAME                       A.DISCOUNT
==========================   ==========
JEAN-PAUL ROTUNDO                    .2
WARREN AMOROSO                       .2
HETAERA                              .2

3 ROWS SELECTED
```

Later we see how to use a query containing another query inside it— a subquery—as an alternative way of dealing with this sort of situation.

Other Types of Joins

Notice that the last query was not an equijoin: that is, the join condition was not based on an equality but rather on the relation "is greater than" (>).

Sometimes joins like this that are not based on an equality are known by the euphonious name "non-equijoins." The term encompasses all joins built on any relational operator other than equality (=). Not all implementations of SQL allow you to perform joins of this kind.

In other respects, queries embodying such joins are structurally no different from the queries we have been discussing. In the next example, the query contains five join conditions, the last one using the relational predicate BETWEEN.

In this query, we select data from three tables to learn what guests, if any, have a recorded weight that falls in the range of acceptable weights for their sex, build, and height. To save typing, correlation names are used. (Now and in later queries, to help us relate columns to tables, we sometimes attach these prefixes even where technically we could get by without them. In the following query, for instance, we do not strictly need them with columns NAME, MIN_WT, MAX_WT, and GUEST.)

```
SELECT A.NAME, B.WEIGHT, C.MIN_WT, C.MAX_WT
FROM GUESTS A, GUEST_WT B, WEIGHT_CHART C
WHERE NAME = B.GUEST
AND A.SEX = C.SEX
AND A.BUILD = C.BUILD
AND A.HEIGHT = C.HEIGHT
AND B.WEIGHT BETWEEN MIN_WT AND MAX_WT;
```

A.NAME	B.WEIGHT	C.MIN_WT	C.MAX_WT
MICHAEL JOHNSON	183	159	183
MARLON SPANDEX	165	152	165
OLYMPIA WELCH	165	152	173
OLYMPIA WELCH	159	152	173
HEATHER STARLETTE	143	130	143
DON JACKSON	159	149	161
DYAN HOWITZER	128	126	139
BIANCA JOGGER	113	105	118
BIANCA JOGGER	109	105	118

9 ROWS SELECTED

Joins in Complex Queries

We close this chapter with an illustration of how joins, when used with arithmetic expressions, aggregate functions, and so forth, can let you perform highly complex manipulations of your data with a single query.

The next query, for instance, selects for female guests (only) the guest's name and the most by which that guest's weight exceeds the maximum allowable weight for a female of that guest's build and height.

In the SELECT list, the query draws data from three columns, each column from a different table. It features an arithmetic expression embedded in an aggregate function, a GROUP BY clause, and multiple search and join conditions:

```
SELECT A.NAME, MAX(B.WEIGHT - C.MAX_WT)
FROM GUESTS A, GUEST_WT B, WEIGHT_CHART C
WHERE NAME = B.GUEST
AND A.SEX = C.SEX
AND A.BUILD = C.BUILD
AND A.HEIGHT = C.HEIGHT
AND A.SEX = 'F'
AND WEIGHT > MAX_WT
GROUP BY NAME;

A.NAME                     MAX(B.WEIGHT - C.MAX_WT)
=========================  ========================
BETTE MIDRIFF                                     7
DOLLY BRISKET                                     7
HEATHER STARLETTE                                 4
HETAERA                                           6
JANE FYUNDAI                                      9
JOAN TONIC                                        4

6 ROWS SELECTED
```

In the line "A.SEX = 'F'", the correlation name is necessary even though we have already specified in a join condition that we are interested only in rows where the value of A.SEX is identical to the value of C.SEX. The database always requires unambiguous column references when it looks for data, even when it may happen that the values across ambiguous references are identical. If the database is not given an unambiguous reference, it looks no farther and an error is returned.

Summary

A single query can draw data from more than one table by using the WHERE clause to contain one or more search conditions whose terms are drawn from different tables. Such search conditions are called join conditions, and queries embodying join conditions are called joins. Joins make possible complex manipulations of data in a single query.

A join condition can be based on an identity of the rows in a column from one table with those in a column from another table, in which case the join condition is an equijoin; or the join condition can be based on some other relational operator.

Even apart from the type of join condition, there are different types of joins, for example, outer joins and self joins.

CHAPTER 7

Queries in Other Statements

In this chapter, we discuss three types of SQL statements that contain more than one SELECT. The first type uses the keyword UNION to merge result tables of two or more autonomous SELECT statements into a single result table. The second type is a SELECT statement that contains other SELECT statements in a WHERE or HAVING clause. The third type is an INSERT statement that uses a SELECT to fetch the data to be inserted.

A fourth type is discussed in the next chapter, in connection with CREATE VIEW statements.

Queries nested in another SELECT statement are called *subqueries*. When the statement immediately containing a query is not itself a query (that is, it is an INSERT statement or a CREATE VIEW statement), the nested SELECT statement is more properly called a *subselect*.

UNIONs of Queries

The keyword UNION merges the results of successive queries linked by the keyword. Duplicate rows are suppressed.

Queries that will be used with UNION must contain the same number of items in the SELECT list, and column for column the data types and lengths must match. That is, if the first column named in the SELECT list of the first query is a VARCHAR(25) column, for instance, then the first column named in the SELECT list of each subsequent query in the UNION statement must also be a VARCHAR(25) column. For instance, these columns cannot be VARCHAR(8) columns and they cannot be numeric or date or time columns. Finally, if any column is NOT NULL, then all columns to be merged with that column must similarly be NOT NULL.

The next example merges the names of the guests from table GUESTS with the names from GUEST_ROSTER. Because duplicate rows are eliminated, the result is the same in this instance as if we had issued just the first query by itself.

Both NAME columns are of type VARCHAR. The column heading in the result is taken from the column heading in the SELECT list of the first query. This is a convention of SQLBase; in DB2, for instance, no column heading would appear.

```
SELECT NAME FROM GUESTS
UNION
SELECT NAME FROM GUEST_ROSTER;

NAME
==========================
BETTE MIDRIFF
BIANCA JOGGER
CLINT WESTWOOD
DOLLY BRISKET
DON JACKSON
DYAN HOWITZER
ENGLEBERT HUMPTYDUMPTY
HEATHER STARLETTE
      .
      .
      .

24 ROWS SELECTED
```

The SELECT statements in a UNION can contain functions, WHERE clauses, and GROUP BY clauses, and an ORDER BY clause can be attached to the UNION as a whole.

There is no limit on the number of queries whose results can be merged in a UNION. The following example contains three. The UNION statement merges the names of all guests, past or present, who are of medium build or currently have Todd as their trainer or for whom a weight is recorded that falls between 130 and 155. An ORDER BY clause orders the single result column in descending order.

An ORDER BY in a UNION must use an integer to specify a result column. The integer refers to the column's position in the SELECT list.

Again, duplicate rows are suppressed.

```
SELECT NAME FROM GUESTS
WHERE BUILD = 'M'
UNION
SELECT NAME FROM GUEST_ROSTER
WHERE TRAINER = 'TODD'
UNION
SELECT GUEST FROM GUEST_WT
WHERE WEIGHT BETWEEN 130 AND 155
ORDER BY 1 DESC;
```

```
NAME
==========================
WARREN AMOROSO
STELLA SHIELDS
SHIRLEY O'SHADE
SEAN PENCIL
MEL GIMLET
MARLON SPANDEX
MARCELLO HISTRIONI
JOAN TONIC
HETAERA
HEATHER STARLETTE
DON JACKSON
CLINT WESTWOOD
BIANCA JOGGER
BETTE MIDRIFF

14 ROWS SELECTED
```

By the slightly tricky expedient of selecting constants (see Chapter 4, "Using Queries to Manipulate Data"), we can flag each name in the result with the criterion it satisfies to earn a place there.

The UNION statement in the next example is just like that in the preceding example except each component query now additionally selects a constant that summarizes the search condition for that query. These constants, like the respective columns selected in a UNION statement, must be identical with respect to data type and length. They satisfy the first requirement just by being string constants: all selected string constants are considered to be VARCHAR. To make the length of all three the same, the constant "tr. todd " includes two trailing spaces. Like the other column in the result, the column for these constants takes its name from the item selected in the top query.

There are duplicate values in the NAME column this time. These are names that appear in more than one of the columns merged. But because each name is associated with a different string constant depending on what table it is from, the result contains no duplicate rows:

```
SELECT NAME, 'med. build' FROM GUESTS
WHERE BUILD = 'M'
UNION
SELECT NAME, 'tr. todd  ' FROM GUEST_ROSTER
WHERE TRAINER = 'TODD'
UNION
SELECT GUEST, 'wt 130-155' FROM GUEST_WT
WHERE WEIGHT BETWEEN 130 AND 155
ORDER BY 1 DESC;

NAME                        'MED. BUILD'
==========================  ============
WARREN AMOROSO              med. build
WARREN AMOROSO              tr. todd
STELLA SHIELDS              med. build
```

```
SHIRLEY O'SHADE            med. build
SEAN PENCIL                tr. todd
SEAN PENCIL                wt 130-155
MEL GIMLET                 med. build
MARLON SPANDEX             med. build
MARCELLO HISTRIONI         med. build
MARCELLO HISTRIONI         tr. todd
JOAN TONIC                 med. build
JOAN TONIC                 wt 130-155
HETAERA                    wt 130-155
                             .
                             .
                             .
21 ROWS SELECTED
```

Simple Nested Queries

We remarked in connection with self joins that the same result could be obtained by using two separate queries—that is, by taking the result of one query and feeding it to the second—but that it was more economical doing the work in a single pass.

The same can be said of queries that embody another query, of which there are several varieties. They are a powerful device for doing the work of several queries in a single query.

A subquery is a SELECT statement nested in the WHERE or HAVING clause of another query. In any statement with subqueries, the subqueries are worked first and the results are used in working the outer statement.

Here again is our first example of a self join, in which we wanted to find the name and discount of everyone receiving the same discount as Joannie Rivulets:

```
SELECT A.NAME, A.DISCOUNT
FROM GUEST_ROSTER A, GUEST_ROSTER B
WHERE A.DISCOUNT = B.DISCOUNT
AND B.NAME = 'JOANNIE RIVULETS';
```

We can get the same information by using a subquery to select Joannie Rivulets' discount and then framing the main query to select everyone whose discount is equal to the result of the subquery. The subquery is enclosed in parentheses.

```
SELECT NAME, DISCOUNT
FROM GUEST_ROSTER
WHERE DISCOUNT =
      (SELECT DISCOUNT
       FROM GUEST_ROSTER
       WHERE NAME = 'JOANNIE RIVULETS');
```

```
NAME                        DISCOUNT
========================    ==========
CLINT WESTWOOD                   .15
JOANNIE RIVULETS                 .15
BIANCA JOGGER                    .15

3 ROWS SELECTED
```

You cannot use an ORDER BY clause in a subquery. Also, except when you are using the EXISTS predicate (discussed a few paragraphs further on), the SELECT list of a subquery can contain only a single column name or expression. In other respects, subqueries are just like any other query.

Besides the equal sign (=), you can use other relational operators, such as "<" and ">", in the WHERE clause, but only where the subquery yields a single value.

The query below uses the ">" operator in the WHERE clause. It selects the name and number of assigned guests of every trainer having more guests than Julio. This time the subquery is in the HAVING clause:

```
SELECT TRAINER, COUNT(NAME)
FROM GUEST_ROSTER
GROUP BY TRAINER
HAVING COUNT(NAME) >
       (SELECT COUNT(NAME)
        FROM GUEST_ROSTER
        WHERE TRAINER = 'JULIO');

TRAINER   COUNT(NAME)
========  ===========
MICHAEL        5
SERENA         5
TODD           6

3 ROWS SELECTED
```

If the subquery will yield more than one value, you must use IN in the WHERE clause.

The following query uses IN to find the name and trainer of everyone who has the same trainer as either Clint Westwood or Warren Amoroso. Because the subquery returns the names of two different trainers, we cannot use "=" in place of IN in the WHERE clause without making the clause incoherent.

```
SELECT NAME, TRAINER
FROM GUEST_ROSTER
WHERE TRAINER IN
       (SELECT TRAINER
        FROM GUEST_ROSTER
        WHERE NAME = 'CLINT WESTWOOD'
        OR NAME = 'WARREN AMOROSO');

NAME                        TRAINER
------------------------    --------
MARCELLO HISTRIONI          TODD
BETTE MIDRIFF               MICHAEL
```

```
CLINT WESTWOOD          MICHAEL
SEAN PENCIL             TODD
WARREN AMOROSO          TODD
OLYMPIA WELCH           MICHAEL
JOAN TONIC              MICHAEL
SEAN PENCIL             TODD
DON JACKSON             TODD
JANE FYUNDAI            MICHAEL
BIANCA JOGGER           TODD

11 ROWS SELECTED
```

Subqueries may also be attached by means of the EXISTS predicate. In fact, this predicate, unlike predicates BETWEEN, IN, NULL, and LIKE, can be used only with subqueries, which is why we have deferred discussing it until now.

For each row in GUEST_ROSTER, the following query selects NAME and DISCOUNT if there exist any rows in GUEST_ROSTER in which DISCOUNT > .15.

```
SELECT NAME, DISCOUNT
FROM GUEST_ROSTER
WHERE EXISTS
        (SELECT DISCOUNT
         FROM GUEST_ROSTER
         WHERE DISCOUNT > .15);

NAME                      DISCOUNT
==========================  ==========
JEAN-PAUL ROTUNDO               .2
MARCELLO HISTRIONI              .1
BETTE MIDRIFF
MICHAEL JOHNSON
CLINT WESTWOOD                  .15
SEAN PENCIL                     .05
HETAERA
JOANNIE RIVULETS                .15
               .
               .
               .

22 ROWS SELECTED
```

The preceding query is deliberately artificial to illustrate the special character of the EXISTS predicate, namely, that EXISTS returns only a TRUE/FALSE response: EXISTS cares only whether any rows in the result set of the subquery exist. If any do, the predicate returns a value of TRUE; otherwise it returns a FALSE.

The preceding query says, for each row, to select NAME and DISCOUNT if it is true that there exists *any row at all* in which DISCOUNT > .15. There do exist such rows—the result set of the subquery is not empty—so the outer query selects NAME and DISCOUNT for every row of GUEST_ROSTER. To select instead only those rows where DISCOUNT > .15, we would change the WHERE clause to read simply

```
WHERE DISCOUNT > .15
```

and drop the EXISTS operator and subquery.

Chapter 7: Queries in Other Statements **97**

Here is another example. In this query, we select just those names from GUESTS for which a row also exists in GUEST_ROSTER:

```
SELECT NAME
FROM GUESTS A
WHERE EXISTS
      (SELECT *
       FROM GUEST_ROSTER
       WHERE A.NAME = NAME);
```

```
NAME
==========================
DETTE MIDRIFF
MARCELLO HISTRIONI
JEAN-PAUL ROTUNDO
MICHAEL JOHNSON
CLINT WESTWOOD
JOANNIE RIVULETS
WARREN AMOROSO
            .
            .

20 ROWS SELECTED
```

This example is somewhat contrived too, actually, in the respect that we might more plausibly have gotten the information we want as follows, without using the EXISTS predicate:

```
SELECT NAME
FROM GUESTS A
WHERE A.NAME =
    (SELECT NAME
     FROM GUEST_ROSTER
     WHERE NAME = A.NAME);
```

Like the other predicates, EXISTS works with NOT, too. In the next and final example, we select just those names from GUESTS for which a row *does not* also exist in GUEST_ROSTER:

```
SELECT NAME
FROM GUESTS A
WHERE NOT EXISTS
      (SELECT *
       FROM GUEST_ROSTER
       WHERE A.NAME = NAME);
```

```
NAME
==========================
ENGLEBERT HUMPTYDUMPTY
SHIRLEY O'SHADE
SHARE
STELLA SHIELDS

4 ROWS SELECTED
```

You may have noticed a special feature of the last two examples that is not found in the other ones illustrating subqueries, namely, that the subquery contains a search condition—WHERE A.NAME = NAME—that refers to a column in the outer query. This is actually a significant difference. Queries embodying this feature are discussed in their own right in the section "Correlated Subqueries."

Compound Nested Queries

Queries containing more than a single subquery are called compound nested queries. The multiple subqueries can be on the same level—for instance, linked by AND—or they can be nested in other subqueries.

The example below selects the name, discount, and trainer of every guest with the same discount as Joannie Rivulets but having a different trainer. In this example, the two subqueries are on the same level. One returns Joannie Rivulets' discount and the other her trainer:

```
SELECT NAME, DISCOUNT, TRAINER
FROM GUEST_ROSTER
WHERE DISCOUNT =
        (SELECT DISCOUNT
         FROM GUEST_ROSTER
         WHERE NAME = 'JOANNIE RIVULETS')
AND TRAINER !=
        (SELECT TRAINER
         FROM GUEST_ROSTER
         WHERE NAME = 'JOANNIE RIVULETS');

NAME                        DISCOUNT TRAINER
========================== ========== =====
CLINT WESTWOOD                   .15 MICHAEL
BIANCA JOGGER                    .15 TODD

2 ROWS SELECTED
```

Here is an example of a subquery inside another subquery. We want to select all male guests of medium build whose maximum acceptable weight according to the weight chart is between 146 and 171, and we also want the trainers assigned to them.

```
SELECT TRAINER, NAME
FROM GUEST_ROSTER
WHERE NAME IN
        (SELECT NAME
         FROM GUESTS
         WHERE SEX = 'M'
         AND BUILD = 'M'
         AND HEIGHT IN
                (SELECT HEIGHT
                 FROM WEIGHT_CHART
                 WHERE SEX = 'M'
                 AND BUILD = 'M'
                 AND MAX_WT BETWEEN 146 AND 171));
```

```
TRAINER   NAME
========  =========================
TODD      MARCELLO HISTRIONI
TODD      WARREN AMOROSO
JULIO     MARLON SPANDEX
YVETTE    MEL GIMLET
TODD      DON JACKSON

5 ROWS SELECTED
```

You can create as many layers of subqueries as you want.

Correlated Subqueries

One type of nested query deserves special notice. This type embodies a *correlated subquery*. We have already seen some examples in connection with our discussion of the EXISTS predicate.

Ordinarily, an inner query is run once and for all and the same result applied for every row of the outer query. A correlated subquery, on the other hand, requires information from the rows of the outer query and so must be run once for each of these rows. In this respect, the subquery is correlated with the outer query and not independent of it.

Let's look again at a query we mentioned in connection with the EXISTS predicate:

```
SELECT NAME
FROM GUESTS A
WHERE A.NAME =
      (SELECT NAME
       FROM GUEST_ROSTER
       WHERE NAME = A.NAME);

NAME
==========================
BETTE MIDRIFF
MARCELLO HISTRIONI
JEAN-PAUL ROTUNDO
MICHAEL JOHNSON
CLINT WESTWOOD
JOANNIE RIVULETS
         .
         .
         .

20 ROWS SELECTED
```

The query as a whole selects every NAME value in GUESTS that also occurs in the NAME column of GUEST_ROSTER. The subquery runs once for each row of GUESTS.NAME, to see whether it can find a match. It cannot run once for all rows of the outer query because of the search condition in the subquery's WHERE clause. This search condition requires the subquery to compare with a row of

A.NAME in the outer query for each row of NAME that the subquery considers returning. In this respect, the subquery is *correlated* with the outer query: it cannot run autonomously.

In the next example, we want to select the name, trainer, and length of stay of each guest with a longer stay than average for guests assigned *to that guest's trainer*. Here the average length of stay required by the inner query must be computed afresh for each trainer in each row of the outer query:

```
SELECT NAME, TRAINER, DEPARTURE - ARRIVAL
FROM GUEST_ROSTER A
WHERE DEPARTURE - ARRIVAL >
      (SELECT AVG(DEPARTURE - ARRIVAL)
       FROM GUEST_ROSTER
       WHERE TRAINER = A.TRAINER);
```

```
NAME                      TRAINER   DEPARTURE - ARRIVAL
==========================  ========  ===================
WARREN AMOROSO            TODD                        7
MARLON SPANDEX            JULIO                       7
OLYMPIA WELCH             MICHAEL                     5
DON JACKSON               TODD                        8
JANE FYUNDAI              MICHAEL                     7
BIANCA JOGGER             TODD                        7

6 ROWS SELECTED
```

Again the search condition in the inner query requires the subquery to go to the outer query for the value of A.TRAINER. Thus, the subquery must run once for each row in the outer query. Because of this, incidentally, queries with correlated subqueries are apt to take longer to run.

The following example is built around a join. In this case we want to find each trainer's tallest guest, also listing the trainer and the guest's height. Labels A and B are assigned to avoid ambiguity, because both GUEST_ROSTER and GUESTS contain a NAME column. The correlation name X is assigned to ensure that the subquery looks at each row of the *outer query* for the value of TRAINER in GUEST_ROSTER. The subquery finds the maximum height among guests assigned to a particular trainer.

```
SELECT TRAINER, A.NAME, HEIGHT
FROM GUESTS A, GUEST_ROSTER X
WHERE A.NAME = X.NAME
AND HEIGHT =
        (SELECT MAX(HEIGHT)
         FROM GUESTS A, GUEST_ROSTER B
         WHERE A.NAME = B.NAME
         AND B.TRAINER = X.TRAINER)
ORDER BY TRAINER;
```

```
TRAINER   A.NAME                       HEIGHT
========  ==========================   ==========
JULIO     MICHAEL JOHNSON                    71
JULIO     MARLON SPANDEX                     71
```

```
MICHAEL   CLINT WESTWOOD                      73
SERENA    HEATHER STARLETTE                   66
TODD      WARREN AMOROSO                      70
TODD      DON JACKSON                         70
YVETTE    MEL GIMLET                          70

7 ROWS SELECTED
```

If we simply want to find the tallest guest (and his or her height and trainer) we still need a subquery, but it does not have to be correlated. In particular, we can delete from the subquery all reference to table GUEST_ROSTER and associated join conditions, and we need a correlation name or label for GUEST_ROSTER only to avoid ambiguity over the two NAME columns. No correlation takes place in the subquery, which in this form runs only once, without referring to the outer query:

```
SELECT TRAINER, A.NAME, HEIGHT
FROM GUESTS A, GUEST_ROSTER B
WHERE A.NAME = B.NAME
AND HEIGHT =
      (SELECT MAX(HEIGHT)
       FROM GUESTS);

TRAINER   A.NAME                          HEIGHT
========  ============================    ==========
MICHAEL   CLINT WESTWOOD                      73

1 ROW SELECTED
```

Using Queries To Insert Data

One last use for subselects must be mentioned. Besides being used to select data for an outer query, they may be used to insert data where the outer statement is an INSERT.

Suppose that we want to create a table MALE_GUESTS to be just like table GUESTS except, instead of listing sex, build, and height for all previous and current guests, MALE_GUESTS will contain data for male guests only (and so will not list sex). The following statement creates the table:

```
CREATE TABLE MALE_GUESTS (NAME VARCHAR(25), BUILD CHAR(1),
HEIGHT INTEGER);

TABLE CREATED
```

Now we need to insert data. The data we want is already in table GUESTS and can be extracted and inserted using an INSERT statement containing a query:

```
INSERT INTO MALE_GUESTS
SELECT NAME, BUILD, HEIGHT
FROM GUESTS
WHERE SEX = 'M';

11 ROWS INSERTED
```

The only restrictions on inserting data by this method are these:

The number of columns in the SELECT must match the number of columns listed in the insert statement or, as in our example, contained in the table itself, if the columns are not listed.

The data type and data length of the selected data must be compatible with specifications of the columns in the destination table. For instance, numbers can be inserted in a character-type column, but character data cannot be inserted in a column of numeric data type.

Summary

This chapter covered three types of SQL statements that contain a SELECT statement as a component: UNION statements, queries with subqueries, and INSERT statements.

UNION statements merge the results of successive queries linked by the keyword UNION.

SELECT and INSERT statements containing SELECT statements use the interior queries to supply data that is then used to work the outer statement.

CHAPTER 8

Virtual Tables: Views

A view is a named result table of a query. After you have created a view (that is, named the result table of a certain query), you can query it just as you would query an actual table.

Views have a variety of uses. A principal one is that they let you replace long, complex queries with simpler ones that accomplish the same thing. They also in effect provide a way to use aggregate functions in search conditions.

Another important feature is that they give you added flexibility in maintaining the security of your system. With views, you can grant other users access just to selected data in a table; users do not even have to know that additional data exists.

Finally, you can create views to have a CHECK option that helps you maintain the integrity of your data by ensuring that updates and insertions of data meet certain conditions you can specify.

Each of these uses is discussed below.

Replacing Complex Queries with Simpler Ones

Long, complicated queries are time-consuming to type, and they can be a particular nuisance when you have to enter different versions of the same long, complicated query frequently.

Views can often help. Whenever you find yourself repeatedly having to put the same kinds of complicated queries to tables, you should consider creating a view.

You can then address simpler queries to the view rather than more complicated ones to the tables.

For instance, to find Bette Midriff's acceptable weight range directly from the tables, given her sex, build and height, we need a query like the following one. This query joins table GUESTS, containing Bette's statistics, with table WEIGHT__CHART to display the row appropriate to Bette from the columns MIN__WT and MAX__WT, which list her acceptable weight range:

```
SELECT NAME, A.SEX, A.BUILD, A.HEIGHT, MIN_WT, MAX_WT
FROM GUESTS A, WEIGHT_CHART B
WHERE A.SEX = B.SEX
AND A.BUILD = B.BUILD
AND A.HEIGHT = B.HEIGHT
AND NAME = 'BETTE MIDRIFF';
```

NAME	A.SEX	A.BUILD	A.HEIGHT	MIN_WT	MAX_WT
BETTE MIDRIFF	F	M	66	130	143

1 ROW SELECTED

It would be aggravating to have to type all this very often. If we frequently have occasion to issue this sort of query, we might do well to create a view listing all guests' acceptable weight ranges. We can then address simpler versions of this query to the view.

The following CREATE VIEW statement creates a view listing every guest's name, sex, build, height, and acceptable weight range. This statement is similar to the statement CREATE TABLE, with the difference that CREATE VIEW contains a query (which may in turn contain subqueries, in fact).

In this instance, the query the CREATE VIEW statement contains is the identical query in the preceding query, minus the last line that restricts the result just to the row for Bette Midriff. The result table of this query in the CREATE VIEW statement becomes the view.

Notice that although we do have to supply what we want to be column names for the view, we do not need to supply information about data type and data length. This information is automatically taken from the original columns selected in the query.

Notice, too, that the query used to construct the view is a join and thus draws on more than one table. Views can be constructed from queries that address any number of tables. Views cannot, however, be created from a SELECT statement that contains an ORDER BY clause or from multiple SELECT statements whose results are merged with the UNION keyword.

As a reminder that the view is a view and not a table proper, we build ''VIEW'' into its name:

```
CREATE VIEW PROPER_WT_VIEW (NAME, SEX, BUILD, HEIGHT,
MIN_WT, MAX_WT) AS
SELECT NAME, A.SEX, A.BUILD, A.HEIGHT,
MIN_WT, MAX_WT
FROM GUESTS A, WEIGHT_CHART B
WHERE A.SEX = B.SEX
AND A.BUILD = B.BUILD
AND A.HEIGHT = B.HEIGHT;

VIEW CREATED
```

The view looks like this:

```
SELECT * FROM PROPER_WT_VIEW;
```

NAME	SEX	BUILD	HEIGHT	MIN_WT	MAX_WT
BETTE MIDRIFF	F	M	66	130	143
MARCELLO HISTRIONI	M	M	66	137	149
JEAN-PAUL ROTUNDO	M	L	70	156	179
MICHAEL JOHNSON	M	L	71	159	183
CLINT WESTWOOD	M	M	73	159	173
JOANNIE RIVULETS	F	S	65	117	130
WARREN AMOROSO	M	M	70	149	161
MARLON SPANDEX	M	M	71	152	165
OLYMPIA WELCH	F	L	70	152	173
HEATHER STARLETTE	F	M	66	130	143
DOLLY BRISKET	F	S	61	105	118
JOAN TONIC	F	M	62	118	132
MEL GIMLET	M	M	70	149	161
DON JACKSON	M	M	70	149	161
ROBERT DINERO	M	L	69	163	175
JANE FYUNDAI	F	L	65	137	156
DYAN HOWITZER	F	S	68	126	139
BIANCA JOGGER	F	S	61	105	118
ENGLEBERT HUMPTYDUMPTY	M	L	72	163	187
SHIRLEY O'SHADE	F	M	64	124	138
SHARE	F	S	71	135	148
STELLA SHIELDS	F	M	65	127	141
SEAN PENCIL	M	S	65	131	137
HETAERA	F	S	63	111	124

```
24 ROWS SELECTED
```

Now if we are interested in Bette Midriff's acceptable weight range, we have only to issue the following query:

```
SELECT NAME, MIN_WT, MAX_WT
FROM PROPER_WT_VIEW
WHERE NAME = 'BETTE MIDRIFF';
```

NAME	MIN_WT	MAX_WT
BETTE MIDRIFF	130	143

```
1 ROW SELECTED
```

Queries Requiring a View

Sometimes a view provides the only way to issue a certain query.

Suppose that, referring to the records of periodic weighings in the GUEST_WT table, we want to list the guests whose average weight falls in a certain range. We might begin to frame our query as follows:

```
SELECT GUEST, AVG(WEIGHT)
FROM GUEST_WT
```

But then what? If we continue as follows, we run into the prohibition stated in Chapter 4, "Using Queries to Manipulate Data," against including an aggregate function in the WHERE clause:

```
SELECT GUEST, AVG(WEIGHT)
FROM GUEST_WT
WHERE AVG(WEIGHT) BETWEEN 140 AND 170
GROUP BY 1
```

The information we want seems straightforward enough, but we cannot get it by any of the methods explored so far.

The solution is to construct a view that contains a column listing every guest's average weight. Then we can frame our query to refer in the WHERE clause *to this column* where we want to use the aggregate function.

We can create such a view with the following statement:

```
CREATE VIEW AVG_WEIGHT_VIEW (GUEST, AVG_WEIGHT) AS
SELECT GUEST, AVG(WEIGHT)
FROM GUEST_WT
GROUP BY GUEST;

VIEW CREATED
```

Here is what the view looks like:

```
SELECT *
FROM AVG_WEIGHT_VIEW;
```

GUEST	AVG_WEIGHT
BETTE MIDRIFF	149.25
BIANCA JOGGER	111
CLINT WESTWOOD	179.25
DOLLY BRISKET	123.5
DON JACKSON	162
DYAN HOWITZER	126.5
HEATHER STARLETTE	145
.	
.	
.	

20 ROWS SELECTED

Now we can get around our difficulty. If you recall, the problem was that, because AVG(WEIGHT) is an aggregate function, it cannot go in the WHERE clause. But now column AVG__WEIGHT of the view contains the identical information. This means that, by addressing the view rather than the table, we can retrieve this information without using an aggregate function: we simply refer to column AVG__WEIGHT in the WHERE clause where we wanted to use the aggregate function AVG(WEIGHT):

```
SELECT GUEST, AVG_WEIGHT
FROM AVG_WEIGHT_VIEW
WHERE AVG_WEIGHT BETWEEN 140 AND 170;

GUEST                        AVG_WEIGHT
===========================  ==========
BETTE MIDRIFF                    149.25
DON JACKSON                         162
HEATHER STARLETTE                   145
JANE FYUNDAI                      162.5
MARCELLO HISTRIONI               157.75
MARLON SPANDEX                      168
MEL GIMLET                        164.5
OLYMPIA WELCH                       162
SEAN PENCIL                      149.75
WARREN AMOROSO                   165.25

10 ROWS SELECTED
```

Joins on Views

We can do joins on views, too. The next query joins the two views we have created and tells us by how much each guest's average weight exceeds his or her maximum acceptable weight.

The query below is simple enough on the surface, but actually requires some fairly involved operations. Consequently, this query takes longer to run than its length might suggest:

```
SELECT NAME, AVG_WEIGHT - MAX_WT
FROM PROPER_WT_VIEW, AVG_WEIGHT_VIEW
WHERE NAME = GUEST;

NAME                         AVG_WEIGHT - MAX_WT
===========================  ===================
BETTE MIDRIFF                               6.25
MARCELLO HISTRIONI                          8.75
JEAN-PAUL ROTUNDO                           10.5
MICHAEL JOHNSON                              1.5
CLINT WESTWOOD                              6.25
JOANNIE RIVULETS                           -14.5
```

```
WARREN AMOROSO                          4.25
MARLON SPANDEX                          3
                         .
                         .
                         .
20 ROWS SELECTED
```

Views can be used anywhere you can use a table, and in the same way. Next, we join a view and a table to select Robert Dinero's name and acceptable weight range (from PROPER_WT_VIEW) and his trainer (from table GUEST_ROSTER):

```
SELECT A.NAME, MIN_WT, MAX_WT, TRAINER
FROM PROPER_WT_VIEW A, GUEST_ROSTER B
WHERE A.NAME = B.NAME
AND A.NAME LIKE 'ROBERT%';

A.NAME                       MIN_WT     MAX_WT TRAINER
==========================  ==========  ========== =======
ROBERT DINERO                   163        175 YVETTE

1 ROW SELECTED
```

Security and Dropping a View

We talk more about security in Chapter 11, "The System Catalog and Sharing a Database," in which we discuss granting privileges and authority levels. But the topic comes up in connection with views, too, because views provide a way of giving users access to data in a table selectively, without giving them access to all data in the table.

A view is sometimes spoken of as a "window" on a table—hence the name "view." This language is apt because a view, like a window, can be trained on selected portions of a table.

For example, we can create a view that represents a table in its entirety, or we can create a view that contains only a couple of columns. We can put restrictions on the rows we want included, too.

The following statement creates a view GUEST_LIST that is identical to table GUEST_ROSTER:

```
CREATE VIEW GUEST_LIST (NAME, ROOM, TRAINER, ARRIVAL,
DEPARTURE, DISCOUNT) AS
SELECT * FROM GUEST_ROSTER;

VIEW CREATED
```

Suppose that we do not want the clerk at the reception desk to know the discounts the various guests receive. An easy way to keep this information confidential is to create a view that omits column DISCOUNT and then have the clerk work exclusively from this view rather than from the table from which the view derives.

We can use a DROP statement to discard the view we have just created. This statement can also be used to drop tables, as we will see in Chapter 9, "Changing Tables and Data."

The following DROP VIEW statement erases view GUEST_LIST from the database:

```
DROP VIEW GUEST_LIST;

VIEW DROPPED
```

The following CREATE VIEW statement creates a revised version of the original GUEST_LIST, for use at the reception desk. This time the view does not contain DISCOUNT:

```
CREATE VIEW GUEST_LIST (NAME, ROOM, TRAINER, ARRIVAL, DEPARTURE) AS
SELECT NAME, ROOM, TRAINER, ARRIVAL, DEPARTURE
FROM GUEST_ROSTER;

VIEW CREATED
```

The view looks like this:

```
SELECT * FROM GUEST_LIST;
```

NAME	ROOM	TRAINER	ARRIVAL	DEPARTURE
JEAN-PAUL ROTUNDO	3	JULIO	15-JUN-1988	17-JUN-1988
MARCELLO HISTRIONI	2	TODD	26-JUN-1988	
BETTE MIDRIFF	1	MICHAEL	14-JUN-1988	16-JUN-1988
MICHAEL JOHNSON	4	JULIO	15-JUN-1988	19-JUN-1988
CLINT WESTWOOD	5	MICHAEL	25-JUN-1988	
SEAN PENCIL	6	TODD	15-JUN-1988	20-JUN-1988

.
.
.

22 ROWS SELECTED

If the clerk works from this view rather than from table GUEST_ROSTER, information about guests' discounts can be kept confidential.

Inserting Data into a View

If the clerk is to work successfully with the view in place of the table, he needs to be able to add new rows to the view and change old ones.

There are three structural requirements of any view that is to be updateable:

1. The view must not be created from a join—that is, only one table name can appear in the FROM list of the CREATE VIEW statement.

2. No columns of the view may be derived from aggregate functions.

3. The view must not be created from a SELECT statement that uses the DISTINCT keyword to suppress duplicate rows or contains a GROUP BY or HAVING clause. Nor does standard SQL allow the SELECT statement to contain subqueries, although DB2 and SQLBase permit them.

Also, for a user to be able to update old rows or insert new ones even in a view meeting these three conditions, there is a fourth requirement:

4. The user must possess appropriate privileges (SELECT, INSERT, UPDATE, DELETE: see Chapter 11, "The System Catalog and Sharing a Database") on the corresponding columns of the underlying table.

Any view that does not satisfy the first three conditions is a read-only view and cannot be changed or added to.

Besides fully updateable views, there can also be partially updateable views. Any view containing a column derived from an arithmetic expression or non-aggregate function is only partially updateable: only the columns not derived from an arithmetic expression or function can be updated. An attempt to update the derived columns generates an error. Partially updateable views must also satisfy the original four conditions just listed.

View GUEST_LIST satisfies the first three requirements, and we will posit that we satisfy the fourth, so GUEST_LIST is for us a fully updateable view.

How to change data in a table or view is discussed in the next chapter. Here we use GUEST_LIST only to show how to insert new rows. Our discussion is brief because new rows are inserted into a view in exactly the same way they are inserted into a table: with the INSERT statement.

In fact, any rows inserted in a view actually are inserted in the underlying table. This holds for other modifications of a view as well: besides modifying the view, they also modify the underlying table, through the view.

Suppose that former guest Stella Shields shows up at 10 a.m., June 23, wanting to stay for two days in the Cherry Room, which turns out to be available, and to have Michael as her trainer. The following statement inserts into GUEST_LIST a row with this information:

```
INSERT INTO GUEST_LIST
VALUES ('STELLA SHIELDS','4','MICHAEL',23-JUN-1988,
25-JUN-1988);

1 ROW INSERTED
```

As when inserting into a table, string data must be in single quotation marks.

Now let's confirm that the row was inserted:

```
SELECT *
FROM GUEST_LIST
WHERE NAME = 'STELLA SHIELDS';
```

```
NAME                          ROOM  TRAINER    ARRIVAL     DEPARTURE
==========================    ====  ========   ==========  ==========
STELLA SHIELDS                4     MICHAEL    23-JUN-1988 25-JUN-1988

1 ROW SELECTED
```

The following query confirms that the row was also inserted in table GUEST_ROSTER:

```
SELECT *
FROM GUEST_ROSTER
WHERE NAME = 'STELLA SHIELDS';
```

```
NAME                          ROOM  TRAINER    ARRIVAL     DEPARTURE   DISCOUNT
==========================    ====  ========   ==========  ==========  ==========
STELLA SHIELDS                4     MICHAEL    23-JUN-1988 25-JUN-1988

1 ROW SELECTED
```

No discount was inserted, so DISCOUNT is null.

Ensuring Data Integrity: The CHECK Option

Views have one more beneficial feature, the CHECK option, that can in many cases make it advantageous to work with a view in preference to a table.

The CHECK option ensures that inserts or updates of a view do not violate the defining characteristic of the view, as stated in the WHERE clause of the subquery in the CREATE VIEW statement.

For example, suppose that all guests receiving a discount of at least 15 percent and whose names have previously been entered in table GUESTS are eligible for other special perquisites, and suppose that we want a view of the guest roster that lists only these guests. We create the view as follows, with the CHECK option:

```
CREATE VIEW PREFERRED_GUESTS AS
SELECT NAME, DISCOUNT
FROM GUEST_ROSTER
WHERE DISCOUNT !< .15
AND NAME IN
        (SELECT NAME
         FROM GUESTS)
WITH CHECK OPTION;

VIEW CREATED
```

Now suppose that we try to add Stella Shields to this list, giving her a discount of only 5 percent. The CHECK option prevents us because Stella's discount is not at least 15 percent:

```
INSERT INTO PREFERRED_GUESTS
VALUES ('STELLA SHIELDS',.05);
INSERT INTO PREFERRED_GUESTS
VALUES ('STELLA SHIELDS',.05)
              ^
Error: not enough non-null values
```

Without the CHECK option, we would be allowed to insert Stella because no checking would be done to ensure that the new row did not violate a condition of the view.

Standard SQL requires that, to use the CHECK option, the defining conditions to be checked must (a) contain no subqueries and (b) refer only to columns in the table on which the view is based. In other words, in assessing whether a new row is consistent with a condition of a view, it must be possible to check the row by considering just the row itself, without having to look at any other row.

Thus the CHECK option can enforce the condition WHERE DISCOUNT !< .15 just by checking a new row to see that DISCOUNT is not less than .15. However, in standard SQL, it *cannot* enforce the other condition, containing the subquery: there is no way to tell whether STELLA SHIELDS is in GUESTS.NAME without actually looking at rows in GUESTS.

SQLBase has extended standard SQL here and dropped this restriction. In SQLBase, the CHECK option can enforce even a condition containing a subquery and referring to a column in another table—a condition like that in the AND clause of the SELECT used to create the view.

For example, suppose that trainer Todd attempts to add himself to the list of preferred guests:

```
INSERT INTO PREFERRED_GUESTS
VALUES ('TODD',.2);
INSERT INTO PREFERRED_GUESTS
VALUES ('TODD',.2)
          ^
Error: not enough non-null values
```

SQLBase's implementation of the CHECK option disallows the new row even in this case, because Todd is not listed in GUESTS.NAME.

In the same way that the CHECK option checks inserts, it also prevents our *changing* data already in the view in such a way that it violates the view definition. For example, we would again receive an error message if we tried to use the UPDATE statement, discussed in the next chapter, to update the view by reducing Warren Amoroso's 20 percent discount to 5 percent.

Summary

A view is a named result table of a query. A view can be used anywhere a table can be, and in the same way. In fact, there are often advantages to using them rather than tables.

Views can be used to replace long, complex queries with simpler ones that accomplish the same thing. They are also useful where we would like to use an aggregate function in a WHERE clause—something we are unable to do: we can instead create a view with a column containing the same information that would be returned by the aggregate function and then refer in the query to that column rather than to the aggregate function itself.

Views also make it possible to grant other users access just to selected data in a table.

Finally, views can be created to have a CHECK option that helps maintain the integrity of data by ensuring that updates and insertions meet certain conditions you can specify when you create the view.

Like tables, views can be updated, but there are some restrictions.

CHAPTER 9

Changing Tables and Data

So far we have dealt mostly with queries—the SELECT statements that allow us to get data in one form or another from a table. In this chapter, we discuss examples of two other types of SQL statements: *data-manipulation statements*, used to change the data in a database; and *data-definition statements*, used to make structural changes to the database itself.

In the first half of this chapter, we look at data-manipulation statements that let us update and delete rows of data. In the remainder of the chapter, we discuss two kinds of data-definition statements that let us change or drop tables or views themselves.

Throughout this chapter, we make a number of changes to the tables we have created. To be able to undo just these changes without undoing everything done so far, readers who have used the information in Appendix D to set up a SPA database of their own and are issuing the sample SQL statements as they work through the book should issue the following statement before proceeding:

```
COMMIT;
```

This statement lets us undo the changes we are about to make without dropping the tables we have created. The statement is discussed later in this chapter.

Changing the Data

A data-manipulation statement we have already encountered is the INSERT statement, which adds new rows.

Besides INSERT, there are two other types of data-manipulation statements: UPDATE statements and DELETE statements. Like the INSERT statement, both types let you change the data in a database. UPDATE lets you alter existing rows and DELETE lets you remove them.

Both UPDATE and DELETE can be used with either tables or views. The only restrictions on using these statements with views are the same that apply to using INSERT with views, namely, that the view must be updateable, and that the user must have the appropriate privileges. See Chapter 8, "Virtual Tables: Views," for the requirements of being able to update a view.

Updating Data in a Row

Suppose that one day Hetaera informs us that she has decided to change her name to Virginia and would like her name to appear that way henceforth in our records. We can use the following UPDATE statement to make the change in table GUEST_ROSTER:

```
UPDATE GUEST_ROSTER
SET NAME = 'VIRGINIA'
WHERE NAME = 'HETAERA';

2 ROWS UPDATED
```

The name of the table or view to be updated is specified in the first line of the example. In the second line appears the name of the column to be updated and the nature of the change. In the third line appears a search condition. As with queries, if there is no search condition, the operation ranges over all rows.

Suppose that Virginia also wants her room changed from 10, which she has been forced to share with Marlon Spandex, to 11, which she hopes to have to herself; and that she persuades us that she ought to receive an additional 2 percent discount on top of her original 20 percent.

We can use the UPDATE statement to put through both these changes at once. The second search condition specifying the arrival date is necessary because there are two rows for Virginia in GUEST_ROSTER, and we do not want to change the room number for Virginia's other stay.

```
UPDATE GUEST_ROSTER
SET ROOM = '11', DISCOUNT = DISCOUNT + .02
WHERE NAME = 'VIRGINIA'
AND ARRIVAL = 14-JUN-1988;

1 ROW UPDATED
```

As the example shows, you can update more than one column at once, and you can use arithmetic expressions to specify the new, replacement value.

You cannot, however, update more than one table or view at a time. Thus a separate UPDATE statement must be issued for each table listing Virginia by her former name. And you cannot update columns derived from a function or arithmetic expression. This last statement just follows from the requirements (listed in Chapter 8, "Virtual Tables: Views") of a view's being updateable.

Nor can you use aggregate functions to specify the replacement value. Thus the following variation on our example is illegal:

```
UPDATE GUEST_ROSTER
SET ROOM = '11', DISCOUNT = MAX(DISCOUNT)
WHERE NAME = 'VIRGINIA';
```

The next example contains a subquery in the search condition. Here we raise the discounts of all female guests by 5 percent.

```
UPDATE GUEST_ROSTER
SET DISCOUNT = DISCOUNT + .05
WHERE NAME IN
      (SELECT NAME FROM GUESTS
       WHERE SEX = 'F');
10 ROWS UPDATED
```

Deleting Rows

We can remove rows from a table or updateable view by using the DELETE statement. As with the UPDATE statement, any row acted on by the statement in a view is similarly affected in the table underlying the view.

Even rows from partially updateable views can be deleted with the DELETE statement. These, you recall, are views that contain columns derived from an arithmetic expression or nonaggregate function. Such columns cannot be updated with INSERT or UPDATE, but rows from tables containing these columns can be removed with DELETE.

The following statement deletes from GUEST_ROSTER all rows for guests who have given departure dates:

```
DELETE FROM GUEST_ROSTER
WHERE DEPARTURE IS NOT NULL;
15 ROWS DELETED
```

To delete all rows from a table or view, do not append a search condition.

The following statement deletes all rows from the view PREFERRED_GUESTS (and hence those same rows from underlying table GUEST_ROSTER):

```
DELETE FROM PREFERRED_GUESTS;
2 ROWS DELETED
```

Undoing and Saving Changes

In the previous two sections, we made numerous changes to the database. We can undo these changes by issuing the following statement:

```
ROLLBACK;
TRANSACTION ROLLED BACK
```

Issuing this statement, we have restored all rows we deleted, and we have replaced the original data whenever we did any updates. Had we earlier dropped any tables or views entirely, using the DROP statement (discussed later in this chapter), those would have been restored too.

ROLLBACK undoes all changes to the database since the last COMMIT or, if none has been issued, since the user connected to the database.

Analogously, COMMIT saves, or *commits*, all changes to the database since the last COMMIT was issued or, if none has been issued, since the user connected to the database. Changes committed to a database can no longer be undone in a wholesale fashion.

Now you can see why we advised issuing a COMMIT at the beginning of this chapter. A COMMIT placed there lets us roll back changes made in this chapter without rolling back changes made in earlier chapters. The effect of the ROLLBACK stops at the last COMMIT.

As you have seen, the COMMIT statement is issued like this:

```
COMMIT;
TRANSACTION COMMITTED
```

The SQL (or other) statements issued by a user between COMMIT statements or between a COMMIT and a ROLLBACK are called collectively a *transaction*.

A new transaction begins with any SQL statement issued after a COMMIT (or with your initially connecting to the database). A transaction can terminate either successfully or unsuccessfully. It is considered to terminate successfully in the case of a subsequent COMMIT being issued, and unsuccessfully in the case of a ROLLBACK.

Changing a Table

Besides allowing us to change a table's data, SQL also includes a statement, ALTER TABLE, for changing the structure of the table itself. Another SQL statement, DROP, discussed at the end of this chapter, lets us drop an entire table or view.

Exactly how many features of a table we can change depends on how ALTER TABLE is implemented. ALTER TABLE offers a selection of different clauses or continuations, corresponding to the operations you can use the statement to perform, and the number of these varies with the particular implementation of SQL. Standard SQL and most implementations limit the options to two, the ADD and MODIFY continuations on the following list. SQLBase supplements this standard set with three additional possible continuations.

Suppose, for instance, that we have begun an ALTER TABLE statement as follows:

```
ALTER TABLE GUEST_ROSTER
```

In SQLBase, we have a choice of five clauses or continuations with which to proceed, depending on which of the following five operations we want to perform:

ADD	a new column
MODIFY	an existing column's data length and whether the column is to accept nulls
DROP	an existing column
RENAME	an existing column
RENAME TABLE	

We begin with the first option, dropping a column.

Dropping a Column

Suppose that we decide we no longer want to give discounts. We can drop the column DISCOUNT from GUEST_ROSTER as follows:

```
ALTER TABLE GUEST_ROSTER
DROP DISCOUNT;

COLUMN(S) DROPPED
```

Had we wanted to, we could have dropped other columns from GUEST_ROSTER in the same statement, separating the column names with commas, as in a SELECT list. For example:

```
ALTER TABLE GUEST_ROSTER
DROP ROOM, DEPARTURE;

COLUMN(S) DROPPED
```

Table GUEST_ROSTER now looks like

```
SELECT * FROM GUEST_ROSTER;

NAME                     TRAINER   ARRIVAL
========================  ========  ===========
JEAN-PAUL ROTUNDO        JULIO     15-JUN-1988
MARCELLO HISTRIONI       TODD      26-JUN-1988
BETTE MIDRIFF            MICHAEL   14-JUN-1988
MICHAEL JOHNSON          JULIO     15-JUN-1988
CLINT WESTWOOD           MICHAEL   25-JUN-1988
```

```
SEAN PENCIL              TODD      15-JUN-1988
HETAERA                  SERENA    24-JUN-1988
JOANNIE RIVULETS         SERENA    25-JUN-1988
                          .
                          .
                          .
23 ROWS SELECTED
```

We cannot use ALTER TABLE to act on more than one table at a time, however.

Any views that refer to dropped columns are themselves automatically dropped. Thus in dropping column DISCOUNT we have also dropped the view PREFERRED__GUESTS, which uses that column.

A column having an index on it cannot be dropped unless the index is dropped first. Indexes are discussed in Chapter 10, "Using Indexes to Maximize Performance."

Adding a Column

We use the ADD clause of ALTER TABLE to add a column.

Adding a column is slightly more involved than dropping one because we must specify data type, data length where appropriate, and also whether the column is to accept nulls, just as we do when we create columns in a table in the first place.

The following statement adds a new column DISCOUNT like the one we dropped:

```
ALTER TABLE GUEST_ROSTER
ADD DISCOUNT DECIMAL(2,2);

COLUMN(S) ADDED
```

We specified the DECIMAL data type and a data length of (2,2). We wanted the column to accept nulls, so we did not specify NOT NULL, although we could have. Here is what GUEST__ROSTER looks like now:

```
SELECT * FROM GUEST_ROSTER;
NAME                      TRAINER    ARRIVAL       DISCOUNT
========================  ========   ===========   ==========
JEAN-PAUL ROTUNDO         JULIO      15-JUN-1988
MARCELLO HISTRIONI        TODD       26-JUN-1988
BETTE MIDRIFF             MICHAEL    14-JUN-1988
MICHAEL JOHNSON           JULIO      15-JUN-1988
CLINT WESTWOOD            MICHAEL    25-JUN-1988
SEAN PENCIL               TODD       15-JUN-1988
HETAERA                   SERENA     24-JUN-1988
JOANNIE RIVULETS          SERENA     25-JUN-1988
                            .
                            .
                            .
23 ROWS SELECTED
```

The new column DISCOUNT is empty, that is, contains only nulls, because as yet no data has been inserted into it. The column would contain these initial nulls even if we specified NOT NULL. NOT NULL only ensures that no new nulls will be accepted in any update.

As when we drop a column, we could have specified more than one column at a time to add.

The following statement adds new columns DEPARTURE and WAITER:

```
ALTER TABLE GUEST_ROSTER
ADD DEPARTURE DATE, WAITER VARCHAR(10);

COLUMN(S) ADDED
```

Views using a table to which a column has been added are unaffected.

Modifying a Column

The MODIFY clause of ALTER TABLE lets you increase the data length of columns with a variable-length data type. You cannot *decrease* the data length, however, and you cannot change the data type itself.

For instance, you can change a VARCHAR(5) to a VARCHAR(10), but you cannot change a VARCHAR column to an INTEGER type.

You can also modify a column that does not accept nulls to accept them, and you can modify a column that does accept nulls not to accept them any longer, provided that the column presently contains none.

For instance, it happens that there are no nulls in the TRAINER column of GUEST_ROSTER, so we can, if we want, change TRAINER to be NOT NULL. But we cannot do the same with column DISCOUNT, because DISCOUNT contains nulls.

The statement below changes TRAINER from a data length of 8 to 25 and defines the column as NOT NULL:

```
ALTER TABLE GUEST_ROSTER
MODIFY TRAINER VARCHAR(25) NOT NULL;

COLUMN(S) MODIFIED
```

We can modify more than one column at a time in the same way that we add or drop more than one column at a time, namely, by listing the columns in the MODIFY clause, separated by commas:

```
ALTER TABLE GUEST_ROSTER
MODIFY TRAINER VARCHAR(30) NULL, NAME NULL;

COLUMN(S) MODIFIED
```

Renaming a Table or Column

The final two options of the ALTER TABLE statement are RENAME, for renaming columns, and RENAME TABLE, for renaming tables.

The following example renames column WAITER in GUEST_ROSTER to SERVER:

```
ALTER TABLE GUEST_ROSTER
RENAME WAITER SERVER;
COLUMN(S) RENAMED
```

There is no need to give data type or column length because these are not affected by the change.

RENAME TABLE functions similarly except that, because the present name is already specified in the ALTER TABLE clause, we need to specify only the new name of the table in the RENAME TABLE clause.

The following statement changes the name of GUEST_ROSTER to ROSTER:

```
ALTER TABLE GUEST_ROSTER
RENAME TABLE ROSTER;
TABLE RENAMED
```

Renaming a column or table on which a view is based has the effect of dropping the view. Indexes are unaffected.

Dropping a Table

To drop an entire table, you must use the DROP statement.

DROP is like ALTER TABLE in being really several statements in one. Depending on how you complete the statement, DROP can be used to drop a table, a view, an index, or a synonym. Here we describe only how to drop tables and views. Indexes and synonyms are discussed in later chapters.

The following statement drops table ROOMS:

```
DROP TABLE ROOMS;
TABLE DROPPED
```

When a table is dropped from the database, all views based on the table, all synonyms and indexes defined for the table, and all privileges granted on the table are dropped with it.

If we try to query ROOMS now, we receive a message that the table has not been created.

```
SELECT * FROM ROOMS;
SELECT * FROM ROOMS
                  ^
Error: table has not been created
```

Dropping a table removes the table and its data from the database—that is, changes the database. Thus a COMMIT must be issued for the operation finally to go through, and until a COMMIT is issued, the effects of dropping the table can be undone by issuing a ROLLBACK. As explained earlier in this chapter, a ROLLBACK undoes all changes to the database effected in the current transaction.

The next SQL statement drops the view AVG_WEIGHT_VIEW:

```
DROP VIEW AVG_WEIGHT_VIEW;
VIEW DROPPED
```

When a view is dropped, any other views whose definitions depend on the view are also dropped, and all privileges on the dropped view (or views) are removed.

Now we issue a ROLLBACK to undo all changes since the last COMMIT:

```
ROLLBACK;
```

Summary

This chapter discussed examples of two types of SQL statements that are not queries: data-manipulation statements, used to change the data in a database; and data-definition statements, used to make structural changes to the database itself.

There are three kinds of data-manipulation statements: INSERT, UPDATE, and DELETE. INSERT statements add new rows to a table; UPDATE statements change data in existing rows; and DELETE statements drop specified rows.

The concept of a transaction was introduced. A new transaction begins when a user logs on or issues a SQL statement after a COMMIT. A COMMIT statement saves to the database changes made by issuing, for instance, data-manipulation or data-definition statements. Until a COMMIT is issued, all changes effected in the course of a current transaction can be undone wholesale by issuing a ROLLBACK statement.

The two statements ALTER TABLE and DROP were discussed. The SQLBase ALTER TABLE statement allows you to add or drop columns, to change a column's length and whether it accepts nulls, and also to rename a column or table. The DROP statement is used to drop tables, views, indexes, and synonyms. Dropping tables and views was explained.

CHAPTER 10

Using Indexes To Maximize Performance

Notice that the rows in table GUEST_ROSTER are not displayed in any particular order. That is, in none of the columns do the entries appear in any coherent alphabetical or numerical sequence. Rather, they generally appear in the order in which they were entered.

```
SELECT * FROM GUEST_ROSTER;
NAME                      ROOM TRAINER  ARRIVAL     DEPARTURE   DISCOUNT
========================= ==== ======== =========== =========== ==========
JEAN-PAUL ROTUNDO            3 JULIO    15-JUN-1988 17-JUN 1988        .2
MARCELLO HISTRIONI           2 TODD     26-JUN-1988                    .1
BETTE MIDRIFF                1 MICHAEL  14-JUN-1988 16-JUN-1988
MICHAEL JOHNSON              4 JULIO    15-JUN-1988 19-JUN-1988
CLINT WESTWOOD               5 MICHAEL  25-JUN-1988                   .15
SEAN PENCIL                  6 TODD     15-JUN-1988 20-JUN-1988       .05
HETAERA                      7 SERENA   24-JUN-1988
JOANNIE RIVULETS             8 SERENA   25-JUN-1988                   .15
WARREN AMOROSO               9 TODD     16-JUN-1988 23-JUN-1988        .2
                             .
                             .
                             .
23 ROWS SELECTED
```

If we are searching for a particular name, we might have to scan the entire NAME column before we find it. And the database engine is no better off than we are: in any search of its own, it too has to scan all the data in the column until it finds the name it is looking for.

Indexes provide a way to speed the search. When you create an index on a column, the column is sorted in such a way that, whenever that column is referred to in a query, the database engine can use the index to go directly to the data it wants instead of having to scan the entire column. Indexes are thus particularly useful in connection with queries that refer to single rows. Generally speaking, they are useful on any column that is referred to often.

An index is a database object like a table or view. In other words, it is not an ephemeral thing like a query, that has no lasting effect on the database. You create an index with the CREATE INDEX statement, and the index is automatically updated as its associated column or columns are changed.

An index remains in existence until you use the DROP INDEX statement to erase it or drop the table the index is on.

You can create an index on one column or on several jointly. The latter sort of index is called a *concatenated* or *composite* index.

The less duplication of data in a column, the more useful an index on that column alone will be. If a column contains so much duplication that by itself it is virtually useless for picking out a particular row, then a concatenated index on that column plus another or others is in order.

For example, the SEX column in table WEIGHT_CHART contains only two values, M and F. To pick out a particular row in WEIGHT_CHART, we need to specify values not only for SEX but for HEIGHT and BUILD as well. So we might consider creating a concatenated index on HEIGHT, SEX, and BUILD.

There is no limit on the number of indexes you can create, but they do take up considerable disk space and you will want to avoid creating so many that the database optimizer gets bogged down in choosing among them. The optimizer is the subsystem of the database engine that chooses access paths and decides how best to extract the data required by a query. It is the optimizer that decides which available indexes to use, if any; you do not need to be concerned with when to use one.

Indexes can considerably speed performance. In fact, the improvement is greater the more rows an index contains. In the examples in the next few sections, we list the reduction in run-time that results from using indexes on some of the comparatively small tables in the SPA database. If these tables had thousands of rows rather than 20 or 90 rows, the degree of improvement would be much more pronounced.

An index called a *unique index* can also help safeguard the integrity of your data. A unique index, created by adding the keyword UNIQUE in the CREATE INDEX statement, ensures that in the column or columns indexed all rows are unique, that is, that none are duplicates. With a unique index, any attempt to insert, update, or delete that results in duplicate rows in the indexed columns generates an error.

To create or drop an index, a user needs the INDEX privilege on the particular table. An index is dropped with the DROP INDEX statement.

Using an Index

The following query draws on two tables to give the name, trainer, and height of every guest.

```
SELECT A.NAME, TRAINER, HEIGHT
FROM GUEST_ROSTER A, GUESTS B
WHERE A.NAME = B.NAME;
```

A.NAME	TRAINER	HEIGHT
JEAN-PAUL ROTUNDO	JULIO	70
MARCELLO HISTRIONI	TODD	66
BETTE MIDRIFF	MICHAEL	66
MICHAEL JOHNSON	JULIO	71
CLINT WESTWOOD	MICHAEL	73
SEAN PENCIL	TODD	65
HETAERA	SERENA	63
JOANNIE RIVULETS	SERENA	65
.		
.		
.		

23 ROWS SELECTED

Column NAME of GUEST_ROSTER contains only two duplicate rows, so it is a good candidate for an index. We use the CREATE INDEX statement to create one, specifying first the table, GUEST_ROSTER, and then, in parentheses, the column or columns to be indexed. We can also include keyword ASC or DESC with the column name to specify that the column be indexed in ascending or descending order. Ascending order is the default.

```
CREATE INDEX NAME_IDX
ON GUEST_ROSTER (NAME);
```

INDEX CREATED WITH 23 ROWS

The index speeds execution of the previous query by about 13 percent on a PC/AT.

Using a Unique Index

The query we have used involves a join on two tables. We can create an index on the second table as well.

We did not specify NAME_IDX to be a unique index because column GUEST_ROSTER.NAME contains duplicate names: both Hetaera and Sean Pencil appear on the roster twice, having made two visits to the spa. A unique index cannot be created on a column or group of columns that contains duplicate rows.

Table GUESTS, however, represents our archival table of all guests past and present, and as such contains each guest's name only once. Moreover, we want to enforce that the NAME column of GUESTS contains each guest's name only once, so it is appropriate for us to make our index on this table unique.

The following statement creates a unique index on column NAME of table GUESTS:

```
CREATE UNIQUE INDEX NAME1_IDX
ON GUESTS (NAME);

INDEX CREATED WITH 24 ROWS
```

We call this index NAME1_IDX because we already have an index NAME_IDX, and indexes must all have unique names even when they are on columns of different tables.

We can demonstrate the uniqueness feature of this index by trying to insert an additional row for Jean-Paul Rotundo, whose name already appears in the indexed column:

```
INSERT INTO GUESTS
VALUES ('JEAN-PAUL ROTUNDO','M','L',70);
INSERT INTO GUESTS
                ^
Error: non-unique data
```

Because of the index, the duplicate value was not accepted.

Now, with two indexes to draw on, the query with which we began this section runs about 20 percent faster on a PC/AT.

Using a Concatenated Index

Whenever we want to look up someone's acceptable weight range in the WEIGHT_CHART table, we need to specify values for the three columns HEIGHT, SEX, and BUILD.

Chapter 10: Using Indexes To Maximize Performance

The following query is a case in point. It selects the name, trainer, and acceptable weight range for all guests. NAME and TRAINER come from GUEST_ROSTER; each guest's height, sex, and build are gotten from GUESTS and are used to look up each guest's acceptable weight range in WEIGHT_CHART:

```
SELECT A.NAME, TRAINER, MIN_WT, MAX_WT
FROM GUEST_ROSTER A, GUESTS B, WEIGHT_CHART C
WHERE A.NAME = B.NAME
AND B.SEX = C.SEX
AND B.HEIGHT = C.HEIGHT
AND B.BUILD = C.BUILD;
```

A.NAME	TRAINER	MIN_WT	MAX_WT
BETTE MIDRIFF	MICHAEL	130	143
BIANCA JOGGER	TODD	105	118
CLINT WESTWOOD	MICHAEL	159	173
DOLLY BRISKET	SERENA	105	118
.			
.			
.			

```
23 ROWS SELECTED
```

We can significantly reduce the time it takes to run this query by creating a concatenated index on HEIGHT, SEX, and BUILD:

```
CREATE INDEX WEIGHT_IDX
ON WEIGHT_CHART (HEIGHT, SEX, BUILD);

INDEX CREATED WITH 90 ROWS
```

The concatenated index improves the run time of the query by about 38 percent on a PC/AT.

Dropping an Index

Any index on a table is dropped automatically when the table is dropped. To drop an index manually, we use the DROP statement. This is the same statement we used to drop tables and views, only in this case we complete the statement so as to specify an index.

The following statement drops the index WEIGHT_IDX that we created on table WEIGHT_CHART:

```
DROP INDEX WEIGHT_IDX;

INDEX DROPPED
```

The underlying table or view is not affected when an index is dropped.

Summary

An index on a column or group of columns enables the database to find rows faster in much the same way that an index in a book helps a reader find a reference: by looking it up.

An index can be created on a single column or on several columns jointly. Indexes are most useful when the columns they are created on contain few or no duplicate rows. A unique index can be created to prevent operations that would create duplicate rows in the column or group of columns indexed. This feature helps preserve the integrity of the data.

CHAPTER 11

The System Catalog and Sharing a Database

Information about the database is kept track of in a set of permanent tables maintained by the database and variously called *system tables*, the *system catalog*, or the *data dictionary*. Here you can find out such information as the number of tables in the database, the name, length and data type of each column, which columns have indexes on them, and information about users' database authority levels and privileges. These tables are updated by the database itself. They are always current and can be queried like any other tables.

The exact number and makeup of the tables in the system catalog varies with the proprietary implementation of SQL. SQLBase presently maintains the ten tables listed below.

Table Name	Contains Information About
SYSTABLES	All tables and views in the database
SYSCOLUMNS	All columns in the database
SYSVIEWS	All views
SYSINDEXES	All indexes
SYSKEYS	All columns in any index
SYSCOMMANDS	All precompiled statements
SYSSYNONYMS	All synonyms of any table or view
SYSUSERAUTH	All users' passwords and authority levels
SYSTABAUTH	All users' table privileges
SYSCOLAUTH	All users' column update privileges

132 Part I: Using SQL Interactively

In this chapter, we begin by looking at the first five of these tables. The tables in this group contain summary information about tables, views, and indexes.

The next table on the list, SYSCOMMANDS, is used with a command that precompiles and stores in the database selected statements for later execution. The command in question is a special feature of Gupta Technologies command interfaces and not part of the body of commonly implemented SQL functions proper, so we do not discuss it.

The last four tables lead us into the topic of sharing a database with other users. We examine these tables in the context of a wider discussion of database authority levels and privileges.

Tables, Views, and Indexes

In this section, we examine the five system catalog tables SYSTABLES, SYSCOLUMNS, SYSVIEWS, SYSINDEXES, SYSKEYS.

We begin with SYSTABLES.

SYSTABLES

SYSTABLES, also known as SYSCATALOG in some implementations, contains a row for each table and view, including rows for the various system tables themselves. In the following query, we select only certain columns because the combined length of the table's seven columns is too great to fit in the display.

In fact, we have to cheat a bit even to fit these five in. To get REMARKS to show, we have to preface the query with a SQLTalk command to narrow the width of that column to 20 characters. Readers working the examples in SQLTalk can issue this command as follows:

```
COLUMN 5 WIDTH 20;
```

Now here is the query:

```
SELECT CREATOR, NAME, COLCOUNT, TYPE, REMARKS
FROM SYSTABLES;

CREATOR   NAME                COLCOUNT TYPE REMARKS
========  ==================  ======== ==== ====================
SYSADM    SYSTABLES                  7 T
SYSADM    SYSCOLUMNS                11 T
SYSADM    SYSINDEXES                 6 T
SYSADM    SYSKEYS                    6 T
SYSADM    SYSCOLAUTH                 4 T
SYSADM    SYSTABAUTH                10 T
SYSADM    SYSUSERAUTH                4 T
SYSADM    SYSSYNONYMS                4 T
```

```
SYSADM      SYSVIEWS              5  T
SYSADM      SYSCOMMANDS           3  T
SYSSQL      SYSTABLES             5  V
SYSSQL      SYSCOLUMNS           10  V
SYSSQL      SYSINDEXES            6  V
SYSSQL      SYSKEYS               6  V
SYSSQL      SYSSYNONYMS           4  V
SYSADM      GUESTS                4  T
SYSADM      GUEST_ROSTER          6  T
SYSADM      GUEST_WT              3  T
SYSADM      ROOMS                 4  T
SYSADM      WEIGHT_CHART          5  T
SYSADM      MALE_GUESTS           3  T
SYSADM      PROPER_WT_VIEW        6  V
SYSADM      AVG_WEIGHT_VIEW       2  V
SYSADM      GUEST_LIST            5  V
SYSADM      PREFERRED_GUESTS      2  V

25 ROWS SELECTED
```

Column CREATOR lists the owner of the table, who is ordinarily the creator too. You own any table or view you create, and your ownership gives you privileges on the table that are discussed later in this chapter.

Column NAME contains the name of every table or view in the database.

In the example, there are two distinct names in the CREATOR column, SYSADM and SYSSQL. These two names are authorization IDs, or users, that are created by the system. In SQLBase, "SYSADM" is the authorization ID of the system administrator of the database; this user owns all the system tables. Consequently, SYSADM is listed as CREATOR even though the system tables are actually created by the system.

SYSSQL is listed as CREATOR in five rows. These rows contain listings in NAME that duplicate other listings in which SYSADM appears as CREATOR. These duplicate listings are views, as can be seen by referring to column TYPE. In this column a *T* appears if the item in NAME is a table, a *V* if it is a view. These views, like the system tables themselves, are created by the system and are substantially the same as the similarly named tables on which they are based. They are included for technical reasons having to do with making SQLBase fully compatible with DB2.

Column COLCOUNT gives the number of columns in each table or view listed in the NAME column. For example, reading the row for SYSTABLES, we can see that SYSTABLES contains seven columns, or two columns in addition to those shown. These two columns relate to features of SQLTalk, the command interface extension of SQLBase, that fall outside our scope here. One of the columns, SNUM, contains serial numbers used with the SQLTalk UNLOAD command for unloading data from tables to a file. The other column, LABEL, has to do with a report-writing feature.

Notice the REMARKS column at the right. You can use a statement we have not yet discussed, COMMENT ON, to insert remarks of up to 254 characters here about any table or view listed in SYSTABLES. COMMENT ON can also be used with another system table, SYSCOLUMNS, to insert remarks about any *column* of any table or view.

Next we use COMMENT ON to add the note "Temporary table" in the REMARKS column of the row for table MALE_GUESTS:

```
COMMENT ON TABLE MALE_GUESTS
IS 'Temporary table';

COMMENT UPDATED

SELECT CREATOR, NAME, COLCOUNT, TYPE, REMARKS
FROM SYSTABLES
WHERE NAME = 'MALE_GUESTS';

CREATOR   NAME                COLCOUNT  TYPE REMARKS
========  ==================  ========  ==== ====================
SYSADM    MALE_GUESTS                3  T    Temporary table

1 ROW SELECTED
```

At this point, readers working the examples in SQLTalk should issue the following SQLTalk command to remove the width setting of 20 characters that enabled us to display the REMARKS column:

```
COLUMN 5 WIDTH OFF;
```

SYSCOLUMNS

The following query selects 6 of the 11 columns in SYSCOLUMNS. This table has a row for every column in a table or view:

```
SELECT NAME, TBNAME, TBCREATOR, COLNO, COLTYPE, LENGTH
FROM SYSCOLUMNS;

NAME                TBNAME              TBCREATOR   COLNO COLTYPE      LENGTH
==================  ==================  =========  ====== ========  ==========
CREATOR             SYSTABLES           SYSADM          1 CHAR               8
NAME                SYSTABLES           SYSADM          2 VARCHAR           18
COLCOUNT            SYSTABLES           SYSADM          3 SMALLINT           2
REMARKS             SYSTABLES           SYSADM          4 CHAR             254
TYPE                SYSTABLES           SYSADM          5 CHAR               1
SNUM                SYSTABLES           SYSADM          6 INTEGER            4
LABEL               SYSTABLES           SYSADM          7 CHAR              30
NAME                SYSCOLUMNS          SYSADM          1 VARCHAR           18
TBNAME              SYSCOLUMNS          SYSADM          2 VARCHAR           18
TBCREATOR           SYSCOLUMNS          SYSADM          3 CHAR               8
                           .
                           .
                           .
TRAINER             GUEST_LIST          SYSADM          3 VARCHAR            8
ARRIVAL             GUEST_LIST          SYSADM          4 DATE              10
```

```
DEPARTURE         GUEST_LIST          SYSADM        5 DATE            10
NAME              PREFERRED_GUESTS    SYSADM        1 VARCHAR         25
DISCOUNT          PREFERRED_GUESTS    SYSADM        2 DECIMAL          2
133 ROWS SELECTED
```

The NAME column lists every column in every table or view in the database. For each entry in NAME, the other columns display the table or view containing the column (TBNAME), its creator (CREATOR), the position of the column in the table (COLNO), its data type (COLTYPE), and its length (LENGTH). SYSCOLUMNS also has columns, not addressed by the preceding query, that list the scale of a decimal data-type column (SCALE), whether the column accepts nulls (NULLS), whether the column can be updated—not all columns in views can be, you recall— (UPDATES), and any remarks that have been inserted with the COMMENT ON COLUMN version of the COMMENT ON statement (REMARKS).

The following query shows some of these columns of SYSCOLUMNS that would not fit in our first display.

```
SELECT NAME, TBNAME, SCALE, NULLS, UPDATES
FROM SYSCOLUMNS;

NAME                TBNAME                SCALE NULLS UPDATES
================    ==================    ===== ===== =======
CREATOR             SYSTABLES                 0 Y     Y
NAME                SYSTABLES                 0 Y     Y
COLCOUNT            SYSTABLES                 0 Y     Y
                        .
                        .
                        .
NAME                GUEST_ROSTER              0 N     Y
ROOM                GUEST_ROSTER              0 Y     Y
TRAINER             GUEST_ROSTER              0 Y     Y
ARRIVAL             GUEST_ROSTER              U N     Y
DEPARTURE           GUEST_ROSTER              0 Y     Y
DISCOUNT            GUEST_ROSTER              2 Y     Y
GUEST               GUEST_WT                  0 N     Y
                        .
                        .
                        .
133 ROWS SELECTED
```

In columns NULLS and UPDATES, a *Y* indicates that the column named accepts nulls or updates. An *N* indicates that it does not.

SYSVIEWS

Table SYSVIEWS contains one or more rows for every view:

```
SELECT NAME, CREATOR, SEQNO, CHECKFLAG
FROM SYSVIEWS;
```

Part I: Using SQL Interactively

```
NAME               CREATOR    SEQNO  CHECKFLAG
================== ========   ====== =========
SYSTABLES          SYSSQL         1  N
SYSTABLES          SYSSQL         2  N
                        .
                        .
                        .
PROPER_WT_VIEW     SYSADM         5  N
PROPER_WT_VIEW     SYSADM         6  N
AVG_WEIGHT_VIEW    SYSADM         1  N
AVG_WEIGHT_VIEW    SYSADM         2  N
AVG_WEIGHT_VIEW    SYSADM         3  N
GUEST_LIST         SYSADM         1  N
GUEST_LIST         SYSADM         2  N
PREFERRED_GUESTS   SYSADM         1  Y
PREFERRED_GUESTS   SYSADM         2  Y
PREFERRED_GUESTS   SYSADM         3  Y
PREFERRED_GUESTS   SYSADM         4  Y
PREFERRED_GUESTS   SYSADM         5  Y
PREFERRED_GUESTS   SYSADM         6  Y

46 ROWS SELECTED
```

An *N* in CHECKFLAG signifies that the view was not created with the CHECK option (see Chapter 8, "Virtual Tables: Views,"), a *Y* that it was.

Notice that SYSVIEWS devotes 16 rows to view SYSSQL.SYSTABLES. These rows are numbered in column SEQNO (the sole purpose of this column). The reason that several of the views have multiple rows like this in SYSVIEWS has to do with the column TEXT of SYSVIEWS, shown in the following example. This column displays the text of the SELECT statement used in the CREATE VIEW statement that created the view. In the case of SYSSQL.SYSTABLES, this text runs to 16 lines and so requires 16 rows in the table.

The following query shows the SELECT statement used in creating view SYSSQL.SYSTABLES. Again, for the information of SQLTalk users working the examples, to get the result to display as shown, we must first issue a SQLTalk command to adjust the column width of the display. We give the SQLTalk command first, followed by the query:

```
COLUMN 1 WIDTH 79;

SELECT TEXT
FROM SYSVIEWS
WHERE NAME = 'SYSTABLES';

TEXT
===================================================================
SELECT CREATOR, NAME, COLCOUNT, TYPE, REMARKS
       FROM    SYSADM.SYSTABLES
       WHERE   (USER = CREATOR)      OR
               (USER = 'SYSADM')     OR
               EXISTS (SELECT SYSADM.SYSTABAUTH.GRANTEE,SYSADM.SYSTABAUTH.TCR
```

```
        M.SYSTABAUTH.SELECTAUTH,SYSADM.SYSTABAUTH.UPDATEAUTH FROM SYSADM.SYSTA
                   WHERE ((GRANTEE = USER) OR (GRANTEE = 'PUBLIC')) AND
                         (TCREATOR = CREATOR) AND (TTNAME = NAME)  AND
                         ((ALTERAUTH  = 'Y') OR
                          (DELETEAUTH = 'Y') OR
                          (INDEXAUTH  = 'Y') OR
                          (INSERTAUTH = 'Y') OR
                          (SELECTAUTH = 'Y') OR
                          (UPDATEAUTH = 'Y')
                         )
                   )
16 ROWS SELECTED
```

Here is the entry in TEXT for the view GUEST_LIST:

```
SELECT TEXT
FROM SYSVIEWS
WHERE NAME = 'GUEST_LIST';

TEXT
========================================================================
SELECT NAME, ROOM, TRAINER, ARRIVAL, DEPARTURE
FROM GUEST_ROSTER

2 ROWS SELECTED
```

SQLTalk users should now issue the following command to turn off the special column width setting:

```
COLUMN 1 WIDTH OFF;
```

SYSINDEXES

Table SYSINDEXES contains a row for every index, as follows:

```
SELECT * FROM SYSINDEXES;

NAME                 CREATOR   TBNAME              TBCREATOR UNIQUERULE  COLCOUNT
================== ======== ================== ========= ========== ==========
SYS$INDEXA           SYSADM    SYSTABLES           SYSADM    D                  2
SYS$INDEXB           SYSADM    SYSCOLUMNS          SYSADM    D                  3
                       .
                       .
                       .
SYS$INDEXM           SYSADM    SYSROWIDLISTS       SYSADM    D                  2
SYS$INDEXN           SYSADM    SYSCOMMANDS         SYSADM    D                  2
NAME_IDX             SYSADM    GUEST_ROSTER        SYSADM    D                  1
NAME1_IDX            SYSADM    GUESTS              SYSADM    U                  1

16 ROWS SELECTED
```

Indexes with names like "SYS$INDEXA" are created by the system.

A *D* in column UNIQUERULE signifies that the index accepts duplicates; a *U* signifies that the index is a unique index and does not allow duplicate rows.

The number in COLCOUNT shows how many columns each index is on.

SYSKEYS

We can find which columns are indexed by referring to table SYSKEYS, which has a row for every column in an index. The column or columns in an index are called the *index key*.

```
SELECT * FROM SYSKEYS;
```

IXNAME	IXCREATOR	COLNAME	COLNO	COLSEQ	ORDERING
SYS$INDEXA	SYSADM	CREATOR	1	1	A
SYS$INDEXA	SYSADM	NAME	2	2	A
SYS$INDEXB	SYSADM	TBCREATOR	3	1	A
.					
.					
SYS$INDEXM	SYSADM	NAME	1	1	A
SYS$INDEXM	SYSADM	CREATOR	2	2	A
SYS$INDEXN	SYSADM	NAME	2	1	A
SYS$INDEXN	SYSADM	CREATOR	1	2	A
NAME_IDX	SYSADM	NAME	1	1	A
NAME1_IDX	SYSADM	NAME	1	1	A

34 ROWS SELECTED

Column COLNO gives the numerical position of the column in its home table.

Column COLSEQ gives the numerical position of a column in the key.

Column ORDERING gives the order of the column in the key: An *A* signifies ascending order; a *D*, descending.

Authority Levels and Privileges

The four catalog tables we have yet to consider—SYSSYNONYMS, SYSUSERAUTH, SYSTABAUTH, and SYSCOLAUTH—keep track of the access levels and database objects (that is, tables, views, and so forth) of multiple users. Before looking at these tables, we have to talk a bit about database authority levels and privileges.

Up to now, for the most part we have assumed that the database has only a single user, or authorization ID, namely, the system administrator—SYSADM, in our case. Because SYSADM owns all system tables and any other tables he creates, the topic of access to tables in the database has not come up.

However, SYSADM can create other users and grant them various levels of access to the database.

The type of access a user has is defined by the user's *authority level* and *privileges*. These are conferred by SYSADM using various types of GRANT statement. How many types of GRANT statement are available varies with the particular SQL implementation, as does the exact number and nature of the authority levels and privileges themselves. In SQLBase, there are just two GRANT statements: GRANT (Database Authority) and GRANT (Table Privileges). The authority levels and privileges conferred with these statements are similar to those used in the IBM SQL/DS relational database product.

No matter what authority and privileges SYSADM grants, SYSADM always retains the highest authority and full privileges on all tables, whether created by SYSADM or by other users.

Authority Levels

SYSADM can grant three levels of authority with GRANT (Database Authority). These levels are listed below in ascending order from least to greatest. They are not exclusive: a user may have more than one.

CONNECT allows the user to log on to the database and exercise any of the privileges assigned him for specific tables and views, but does not allow him to create tables or views of his own or to grant any privileges. This authority level creates the user, in the sense that a user may have other levels of authority in addition to this but must have this authority to log on.

RESOURCE allows the user to create tables and views of his own, drop any tables or views he creates, and to grant (and revoke) privileges on those tables and views to other users. The user has full privileges on any tables or views he creates.

DBA confers full privileges on all tables and views in the database and also the right to grant (and revoke) privileges on any of them. This authority level differs from that of SYSADM only in that a user with DBA authority cannot create new users or change the passwords or authority levels of existing ones.

The GRANT (Database Authority) statement permits three variations, corresponding to the three authority levels the statement can be used to grant. These variations are shown below in somewhat simplified form:

```
GRANT RESOURCE TO authorization_ID
GRANT DBA TO authorization_ID
GRANT CONNECT TO authorization_ID IDENTIFIED BY password
```

The statement REVOKE (Database Authority) is used to revoke authority. We show how to use these GRANT and REVOKE statements after we talk about privileges in the next section.

Privileges

A user is said to *own* any table or view that he himself creates. Users have all of the following privileges on any tables or views they own:

Privilege	*Confers ability to*
SELECT	Select data from a table or view
INSERT	Insert record into a table or view
DELETE	Delete records from a table or view
UPDATE	Update a table or view: may be granted on the entire table or view or only on selected columns
INDEX	Create or drop indexes for a table
ALTER	Alter a table or view

With the GRANT (Table Privileges) statement, any user can grant other users any or all of these privileges on the grantor's own tables or views. If the phrase WITH GRANT OPTION is added to the statement, then the user being granted the privilege can in turn grant that privilege to other users.

The syntax of the GRANT (Table Privileges) statement is as follows:

GRANT *privilege(s)* ON *table* or *view* TO *authorization ID* WITH GRANT OPTION

A user who has only CONNECT authority can be granted any number of privileges on tables or views by other users, but he can grant none himself because he has no tables or views of his own.

The statement REVOKE (Table Privileges) is used to revoke privileges that have been granted.

Granting Authority and Privileges

The following statement grants CONNECT authority to a user whose authorization ID is USER1 and whose password is PWD1:

```
GRANT CONNECT
TO USER1
IDENTIFIED BY PWD1;

CONNECT AUTHORITY GRANTED
```

We can create several users with the same statement:

```
GRANT CONNECT
TO USER2, USER3, USER4
IDENTIFIED BY PWD2, PWD3, PWD4;

CONNECT AUTHORITY GRANTED
```

We have now created four users. But they have no tables of their own and have not been granted any privileges on existing tables, so they are still unable to use any tables in the database. Nor are any of these users presently logged on to the system.

SQL does not itself provide a specific statement to be used for logging on to a database: the mechanics of logging on are left up to particular implementations. All methods, however, establish a connection to a database by opening a transaction for a specified user name, or authorization ID.

Suppose that we have connected to the database as USER1 (who still has no privileges). If as USER1 we try to query a table GUEST_ROSTER, we get an error:

```
SELECT *
FROM GUEST_ROSTER;
SELECT *
FROM GUEST_ROSTER
     ^
Error: table has not been created
```

The system first looks for a table GUEST_ROSTER that USER1 owns. It does not find one, and USER1 has no privileges on SYSADM's table GUEST_ROSTER, so the system returns the message that no table GUEST_ROSTER owned by USER1 exists.

The following GRANT (Table Privileges) statement (issued by SYSADM) grants USER1 the privilege to query SYSADM's table GUEST_ROSTER:

```
GRANT SELECT
ON GUEST_ROSTER
TO USER1;

PRIVILEGE(S) GRANTED ON TABLE OR VIEW
```

SYSADM can use the following GRANT (Table Privileges) statement to grant SELECT, INSERT, and DELETE privileges to both USER1 and USER2. Granting USER1 privileges he already has has no effect, so he can be included in the same statement that grants SELECT privileges to USER2.

```
GRANT SELECT, INSERT, DELETE
ON GUEST_ROSTER
TO USER1, USER2;

PRIVILEGE(S) GRANTED ON TABLE OR VIEW
```

The next example grants UPDATE privileges. UPDATE privileges can be granted on an entire table or view or just on selected columns. The following statement grants USER1 and USER2 UPDATE privileges on just the two columns NAME and ARRIVAL of GUEST_ROSTER:

```
GRANT UPDATE (NAME, ARRIVAL)
ON GUEST_ROSTER
TO USER1, USER2;

PRIVILEGE(S) GRANTED ON TABLE OR VIEW
```

142 Part I: Using SQL Interactively

If we want to grant all privileges to some user or users, we do not have to list the privileges. We can instead specify ALL in the statement. Similarly, if we want to include all users among the recipients, we can use the keyword PUBLIC instead of listing everyone.

The following statement grants all privileges to all users on table GUEST_WT:

```
GRANT ALL
ON GUEST_WT
TO PUBLIC;

PRIVILEGE(S) GRANTED ON TABLE OR VIEW
```

We turn now to granting authority levels.

Suppose that we want to let USER3 create his own tables. For this he needs a higher authority level than CONNECT. We give him RESOURCE authority. To do this we use the GRANT (Database Authority) statement, the same statement we used to grant the CONNECT authority:

```
GRANT RESOURCE
TO USER3;

RESOURCE AUTHORITY GRANTED
```

The statement below gives USER4 the highest authority level next to SYSADM, namely, DBA. Again, we use a GRANT (Database Authority) statement:

```
GRANT DBA
TO USER4;

DBA AUTHORITY GRANTED
```

Now we are in a position to examine the three system tables SYSUSERAUTH, SYSTABAUTH, and SYSCOLAUTH. These record the authority level and privileges assigned to any user. We examine each table in turn.

SYSUSERAUTH

System table SYSUSERAUTH lists each user's password and authority level:

```
SELECT * FROM SYSUSERAUTH;

NAME      RESOURCEAUTH  DBAAUTH  PASSWORD
========  ============  =======  ========
SYSADM    G             G        SYSADM
SYSSQL                           SYSSQL
USER1                            PWD1
USER2                            PWD2
USER3     Y                      PWD3
USER4     Y             Y        PWD4

6 ROWS SELECTED
```

The first three columns correspond to the three possible authority levels: NAME lists all users having CONNECT authority—that is, all users; RESOURCEAUTH and DBAAUTH show whether a user also has RESOURCE or DBA authority. A *Y* in either of these columns signifies that the user has been granted that authority. A *G* in either column signifies that the user not only has the authority but can grant it to others. The PASSWORD column lists passwords. Only SYSADM can read this column.

Now let's look at SYSTABAUTH.

SYSTABAUTH

System table SYSTABAUTH contains ten columns and lists each user's privileges.

We have granted privileges on GUEST_ROSTER and GUEST_WT, so we'll select the first seven columns (all that fit in the display) from SYSTABAUTH for those two tables. TTNAME in the search condition is the column listing the table or view on which privileges are held. The initial *T* in the name stands for "target":

```
SELECT GRANTEE, TCREATOR, TTNAME, UPDATECOLS, ALTERAUTH, DELETEAUTH,
INDEXAUTH
FROM SYSTABAUTH
WHERE TTNAME IN ('GUEST_ROSTER', 'GUEST_WT');

GRANTEE   TCREATOR  TTNAME             UPDATECOLS  ALTERAUTH  DELETEAUTH  INDEXAUTH
========  ========  =================  ==========  =========  ==========  =========
USER1     SYSADM    GUEST_ROSTER           *                      Y
USER2     SYSADM    GUEST_ROSTER           *                      Y
PUBLIC    SYSADM    GUEST_WT                           Y          Y           Y

3 ROWS SELECTED
```

The columns contain the following information:

GRANTEE lists the user who has received the privileges.

TCREATOR lists the user who created the table or view on which privileges are held.

TTNAME gives the name of the target table or view on which privileges are held.

UPDATECOLS contains a blank if no updates are allowed for this user on the target table or if updates are allowed on the entire table. Contains an asterisk (*) if the user has UPDATE privileges on only certain columns of the target table. The particular columns are listed in SYSCOLAUTH.

ALTERAUTH contains a *Y* if the user is allowed to alter the target table.

DELETEAUTH contains a *Y* if the user is allowed to delete rows from the target table or view.

INDEXAUTH contains a *Y* if the user is allowed to create or drop indexes on the target table.

The following query selects GRANTEE and TTNAME plus three columns of SYSTABAUTH that would not fit in our initial display:

```
SELECT GRANTEE, TTNAME, INSERTAUTH, SELECTAUTH, UPDATEAUTH
FROM SYSTABAUTH
WHERE TTNAME IN ('GUEST_ROSTER', 'GUEST_WT');

GRANTEE   TTNAME              INSERTAUTH SELECTAUTH UPDATEAUTH
========  ==================  ========== ========== ==========
USER1     GUEST_ROSTER        Y          Y          Y
USER2     GUEST_ROSTER        Y          Y          Y
PUBLIC    GUEST_WT            Y          Y          Y

3 ROWS SELECTED
```

The three new columns are described below:

INSERTAUTH contains a *Y* if the user is allowed to insert rows into the target table or view.

SELECTAUTH contains a *Y* if the user is allowed to read rows from the target table or view.

UPDATEAUTH contains a *Y* if the user is allowed to update rows in the target table or view.

Again, a *Y* means that a user, or grantee, has the particular privilege.

We look now at system table SYSCOLAUTH to find on what specific columns of GUEST_ROSTER USER1 and USER2 have UPDATE privileges.

SYSCOLAUTH

Table SYSCOLAUTH lists the individual columns of a table or view on which users have the UPDATE privilege in cases in which the privilege does not extend to all columns of a table.

```
SELECT *
FROM SYSCOLAUTH;

GRANTEE   CREATOR   TNAME               COLNAME
========  ========  ==================  ==================
USER1     SYSADM    GUEST_ROSTER        ARRIVAL
USER1     SYSADM    GUEST_ROSTER        NAME
USER2     SYSADM    GUEST_ROSTER        ARRIVAL
USER2     SYSADM    GUEST_ROSTER        NAME

4 ROWS SELECTED
```

TNAME lists the table and COLNAME the column on which GRANTEE holds UPDATE privileges.

Synonyms

It might seem that because USER1 has been granted SELECT privileges on table GUEST_ROSTER he ought to be able to select from it. And so he can, with one proviso concerning how he frames his query. For having more than one user of the database makes a certain difference in how we refer to tables.

Although so far we have had no occasion to make a note of it, formally the full name of a table consists of the identifier its owner gave it—for example, "GUEST_ROSTER"—plus another component. This second component is the owner's name, as a prefix. Thus, formally, the full name of GUEST_ROSTER is actually "SYSADM.GUEST_ROSTER", even though till now we have been able to refer to it informally and omit the prefix.

As long as we deal only with our own tables, we can refer to them informally this way, without the qualifying prefix. When we omit the prefix, the table name is implicitly qualified by our own user name and the database understands that we are referring to one of our own tables.

If GUEST_ROSTER is not our own table, though, and we omit the prefix, the database looks for a table *of ours* by that name. If it fails to find one, it returns an error to the effect that the table has not been created, as in the case a few examples earlier where USER1 attempted to query GUEST_ROSTER.

USER1 can avoid this error by referring to the table by its full, qualified name, "SYSADM.GUEST_ROSTER". For example:

```
SELECT *
FROM SYSADM.GUEST_ROSTER;
```

It would be inconvenient to have to supply a prefix every time we want to exercise our access privileges on another user's table, and fortunately SQL provides a way to avoid having to. We can create our own *synonym* name for the table and use that rather than the full, qualified name. A synonym is not another version of the table or a view; it is simply another name for a table or view.

Synonyms are created with the CREATE SYNONYM statement. The following statement, which is issued by USER1, creates the synonym ROSTER for SYSADM.GUEST_ROSTER:

```
CREATE SYNONYM ROSTER
FOR SYSADM.GUEST_ROSTER;

SYNONYM CREATED
```

Now USER1 can use the synonym to put his query:

```
SELECT *
FROM ROSTER;
```

```
NAME                        ROOM  TRAINER   ARRIVAL      DEPARTURE    DISCOUNT
==========================  ====  ========  ===========  ===========  ==========
JEAN-PAUL ROTUNDO              3  JULIO     15-JUN-1988  17-JUN-1988         .2
MARCELLO HISTRIONI             2  TODD      26-JUN-1988                      .1
BETTE MIDRIFF                  1  MICHAEL   14-JUN-1988  16-JUN-1988
MICHAEL JOHNSON                4  JULIO     15-JUN-1988  19-JUN-1988
                               .
                               .
                               .

23 ROWS SELECTED
```

To create a synonym name for a table or view, a user must have at least one privilege on the table or view.

Synonyms, like table names themselves, are implicitly qualified by a user's own authorization ID, so only the user who creates a synonym can use it. Other users must create their own. However, the prefix individuates different users' synonyms, so the rest of the name can be the same: for example, every user who wants to can create a synonym "ROSTER" for GUEST_ROSTER.

If many users will be granted privileges on a certain table, SYSADM or the table's owner or a DBA can use CREATE SYNONYM with the keyword PUBLIC to create a public synonym that all users with privileges on the table can use. This saves everyone from having to create their own.

The following statements, issued by SYSADM, create a public synonym "G_WEIGHT" for table GUEST_WT:

```
CREATE PUBLIC SYNONYM G_WEIGHT FOR GUEST_WT;

SYNONYM CREATED
```

Synonyms, like privileges and authority levels, are kept track of in the system tables. We can look up a list of current synonyms in the SYSSYNONYMS table:

```
SELECT *
FROM SYSSYNONYMS;

NAME                  CREATOR   TBNAME              TBCREATOR
====================  ========  ==================  =========
ROSTER                USER1     GUEST_ROSTER        SYSADM
G_WEIGHT              PUBLIC    GUEST_WT            SYSADM

2 ROWS SELECTED
```

In the table, NAME lists the synonyms and column CREATOR gives the users to whom they belong (ordinarily, the actual creator). Because synonym G_WEIGHT can be used by everyone, PUBLIC is listed as its creator even though SYSADM actually created it.

The two other columns, TBNAME and TBCREATOR, give the table and the creator of the table to which a synonym applies.

To drop a synonym, we use the DROP SYNONYM statement. The following statement drops USER1's synonym ROSTER. Because we are currently connected as SYSADM, we must refer to the synonym by its qualified name "USER1.ROSTER" to prevent the database from looking for a synonym "SYSADM.ROSTER" and returning an error:

```
DROP SYNONYM USER1.ROSTER;
SYNONYM DROPPED
```

Granting Access to the System Catalog

As we have said, all of the system tables are owned by SYSADM. SYSADM can perform on these tables the actions in the following list:

SELECT rows from a system table
CREATE a VIEW on a system table
CREATE a SYNONYM on a system table
CREATE an INDEX on any column of a system table
(ALTER TABLE) ADD user-defined columns to a system table
(ALTER TABLE) DROP user-defined columns
UPDATE the user-defined columns of a system table

Only user-defined columns previously added by a user to a system table can be dropped from a system table; none of the original columns can be dropped. Nor can any user, including SYSADM, use INSERT or DELETE to add or remove rows from any tables in the system catalog.

Because all the system tables are owned by SYSADM, SYSADM can, if desired, restrict access to these tables by other users. For example, instead of granting SELECT privileges on these tables to PUBLIC (that is, all users), as SQLBase does automatically, it may be preferable to create selective views of the tables and grant access only to the views. This option allows SYSADM to make available to other users information on tables, and so on, of their own without giving them free range of other information in the system tables.

SQLBase has a special keyword, USER, that makes this easy to do. The keyword takes as its value the authorization ID of the current user and can be used in a SELECT list or WHERE clause in place of a particular user name. By using this keyword in a CREATE VIEW statement, SYSADM can create a single view of, say, SYSTABLES that all users can use but which lists for each user only rows for tables that a given user owns (that is, tables for which that user is listed as CREATOR in SYSTABLES).

For example, SYSADM might create such a view, MYTABLES, as follows, using the keyword USER in the search condition:

```
CREATE VIEW MYTABLES AS
SELECT * FROM SYSTABLES
WHERE CREATOR = USER;

VIEW CREATED
```

Now suppose that USER3, who has RESOURCE authority, has created a table FEMALE_GUESTS for himself and wants to look up in SYSTABLES all the information there about the tables he owns. Suppose, too, that SYSADM has denied all users access to the system tables themselves but has granted access to MYTABLES to PUBLIC. USER3 can get the information he wants by querying SYSADM's view MYTABLES:

```
SELECT CREATOR, NAME, COLCOUNT, TYPE
FROM SYSADM.MYTABLES;

CREATOR   NAME                 COLCOUNT  TYPE
========  ===================  ========  ====
USER3     FEMALE_GUESTS               3  T

1 ROW SELECTED
```

USER3 can also create a synonym for this view to save typing the qualifier.

If SYSADM queries the same view, as follows, just those rows in SYSTABLES where SYSADM is creator are shown:

```
SELECT CREATOR, NAME, COLCOUNT, TYPE
FROM MYTABLES;

CREATOR   NAME                 COLCOUNT  TYPE
========  ===================  ========  ====
SYSADM    AVG_WEIGHT_VIEW             2  V
SYSADM    GUESTS                      4  T
            .
            .
            .
SYSADM    SYSTABAUTH                 10  T
SYSADM    SYSTABLES                   7  T
SYSADM    SYSUSERAUTH                 4  T
SYSADM    SYSVIEWS                    5  T
SYSADM    WEIGHT_CHART                5  T

22 ROWS SELECTED
```

And similarly for all other users.

Revoking Authority and Privileges

Privileges and authority levels that have been granted can also be revoked.

Just as there are separate statements for granting authority and privileges, there are separate statements for revoking authority and privileges: REVOKE (Database Authority) and REVOKE (Table Privileges).

A user requires RESOURCE authority to grant any privileges, and he can revoke any privileges he has granted. A DBA user can revoke not only privileges he has granted, but also privileges granted by any RESOURCE user, though he cannot change authority levels. And SYSADM can revoke any privileges and authority whatsoever.

To show how the REVOKE statements work, we revoke, as SYSADM, all the privileges and authority levels we have just granted. We begin by using REVOKE (Table Privileges) to revoke privileges, as follows:

```
REVOKE UPDATE
ON GUEST_ROSTER
FROM USER1;

PRIVILEGE(S) REVOKED ON TABLE

REVOKE UPDATE, SELECT, INSERT, DELETE
ON GUEST_ROSTER
FROM USER1, USER2;

PRIVILEGE(S) REVOKED ON TABLE

REVOKE ALL
ON GUEST_WT
FROM PUBLIC;

PRIVILEGE(S) REVOKED ON TABLE
```

Now we use REVOKE (Database Authority) to revoke authority:

```
REVOKE RESOURCE
FROM USER3;

RESOURCE AUTHORITY REVOKED

REVOKE DBA
FROM USER4;

DBA AUTHORITY REVOKED

REVOKE CONNECT
FROM USER2, USER3, USER4;
REVOKE CONNECT
FROM USER2, USER3, USER4
                    ^
Error: table(30) exist for specified user
```

Notice that the REVOKE CONNECT statement failed. USER3 still owns table FEMALE_GUESTS, and we are not allowed to revoke connect authority from a user who still has tables.

This constraint is a safety measure. Revoking connect authority removes a user just as granting connect authority creates one. In revoking connect authority from a user who has tables, the system would also have to remove the tables, to prevent their being left without an owner. We may have forgotten about these when we set about removing the user, and they may contain data we would not want to lose. So, to save us from ourselves, the system refuses to remove a user until we have first disposed of his tables.

The following statement removes FEMALE_GUESTS. We are then able to put through the statement revoking connect authority from the three users:

```
DROP TABLE USER3.FEMALE_GUESTS;

TABLE DROPPED

REVOKE CONNECT
FROM USER2, USER3, USER4;

CONNECT AUTHORITY REVOKED
```

Changing a Password

There are two ways to change a password in SQLBase, depending on whether the password you want to change is your own or someone else's. SYSADM can change anyone's password with the GRANT (Database Authority) statement, and users can change their own password with the ALTER PASSWORD statement.

SYSADM can change any user's password, including his own, with a GRANT CONNECT statement. Recall that a GRANT CONNECT is used to create a user and establish his password in the first place. To change a password, the same statement is issued again, with the new password replacing the old one.

The following statement, issued by SYSADM, changes USER1's password from PWD1 to SECRET:

```
GRANT CONNECT
TO USER1
IDENTIFIED BY SECRET;

CONNECT AUTHORITY GRANTED
```

In SQLBase, if not in all other implementations of SQL, a user can change his own password, too, using the ALTER PASSWORD statement. Below, SYSADM changes his own password from SYSADM to TIGER:

```
ALTER PASSWORD SYSADM
TO TIGER;

PASSWORD ALTERED
```

Summary

Information about the database is kept track of in a set of permanent tables maintained by the database and variously called system tables, the system catalog, or the data dictionary. These tables list and contain information about all tables, columns, indexes, views, users, and so forth in the system.

Initially, there is only one user, the special system administrator user, created by the system. In SQLBase, this user is called SYSADM. However, SYSADM can create other users and grant them various levels of access to the database.

Access to the database is controlled through a system of privileges and authority levels. There are three authority levels and a variety of privileges that can be granted. These, too, are kept track of in the system tables.

A user is said to own any table or view that he himself creates. Users have, and can grant, privileges on any table or view they own.

Authority levels and privileges can be revoked as well as granted.

CHAPTER 12

Database Utilities and Recovery

The SQL language has many virtues as a tool for managing data in a relational database, but there are certain other important functions that it has not been equipped to perform. For example, no provision is made in standard SQL for loading more than a row at a time of data into a database in the first place or for bulk unloading or transferring of data out, whether to a different application, to another database, or to an external backup file.

The various implementations of SQL remedy these and other shortcomings by supplementing a more or less shared core of SQL statements with other commands. Certain of these are worth discussing here, even though they are extensions of SQL, because similar utilities can be found in virtually every SQL implementation; these utilities thus represent a de facto consensus on how a particular lack in SQL will be supplied.

In this chapter, we discuss SQLTalk versions of four such utilities. Two, the SQLTalk LOAD and UNLOAD commands, transfer quantities of data in and out of a database; another command, REORGANIZE, consolidates a fragmented database file to improve performance; and the fourth utility, journaling (actually a complex of commands), enables data to be recovered when a media failure has destroyed some or all of a database.

SQL itself has provisions for automatic recovery from certain types of catastrophe other than a media failure. We conclude the chapter with a look at these.

The LOAD Command

The SQLTalk LOAD command is used to load data from an external file into the current database. The command accepts data in three formats—SQL, ASCII, and DIF—and can be used to bulk load data from spreadsheet programs, other databases, backup files created with the SQLTalk UNLOAD command, or files created by a user.

SQL Format

For each table to receive data, files in SQL format contain a SQL INSERT statement incorporating program variables, followed by rows of data in program variable format (see Part II). SQL format files may also contain CREATE TABLE statements to create the tables and CREATE INDEX statements to create certain indexes on the tables.

Most often, files in SQL format are created with the SQLTalk UNLOAD command and are intended for backup purposes.

The following command loads the SQL-format file STAFF.SQL:

```
LOAD SQL STAFF.SQL;
```

ASCII Format

Files in ASCII format contain only data, with individual items appearing separated by commas and character data delimited by, that is, enclosed in, double quotation marks (" ").

Because these files contain only data, the destination table must be specified when the file is loaded. If the table does not exist, the data cannot be loaded.

ASCII-format files are particularly useful for transferring data from another database. The following example loads data from ASCII-format file STAFF.ASC into table STAFF:

```
LOAD ASCII STAFF.ASC STAFF;
```

DIF Format

The DIF (Data Interchange Format) file format is popular for use with microcomputer spreadsheet and database products. A file in this format contains data for a single table; it can also, optionally, contain the names of the table and columns. In the latter case, if the table does not already exist, SQLTalk will create it on loading the file.

How a DIF file is loaded depends on whether it contains the name of the destination table. If it contains only data and no name, then the destination table must exist to receive the data in order for the load to succeed. On the other hand, if the file contains the table name, then the table must *not* already exist or the load will fail when SQLTalk tries to create the table.

The following example shows using the LOAD command to load the data-only DIF file STAFF.DIF into table STAFF. Because the file is data-only, the command specifies the destination table:

```
LOAD DIF STAFF.DIF STAFF;
```

The UNLOAD Command

The SQLTalk UNLOAD command has two purposes. It is used both to create external files for transferring data to other databases or applications, and it is also used to make backup files of the contents of a database.

To ensure that the database is not changed while data is being unloaded, all users must be disconnected before the UNLOAD command is used. However, some systems (including SQLBase) also offer other utilities that permit the database to be unloaded without first being "quiesced" in this fashion.

The UNLOAD command can be used to create files in any of the three formats discussed in connection with the LOAD command. For doing backups, the SQL format is particularly apt. Not only can files in this format contain, in addition to data, SQL statements to recreate tables, indexes, and so forth, but the format lends itself to use with multiple tables.

Somewhat simplified, the syntax of the UNLOAD command is

```
UNLOAD format  file_name  table_name, table_name, ...;
```

Except in permitting the listing of multiple table names, the basic syntax of UNLOAD is similar to that of the LOAD command. UNLOAD, however, presents more options.

For instance, an optional keyword DATA can be included before specifying the format. In the case of SQL-format files, this omits the CREATE TABLE and CREATE INDEX statements that would otherwise be included in the file. Instead, the file is made to contain only INSERT statements and data. Thus, when the file is loaded, it does not rebuild the tables whose data it contains or any indexes existing on the tables when they were unloaded, as the file would otherwise do. This option is useful where you are more likely to want to reinstate data in existing tables than to rebuild the tables in a new database.

The DATA keyword has a similar effect with DIF files: the keyword causes these files to consist just of data; they do not also receive the names of the table and its columns where the data originates. As a result, SQLTalk does not try to create the table if the file is subsequently used with the LOAD command.

The following command unloads only the data, in DIF format, from table GUEST_ROSTER to file GUEST_ROSTER.DIF:

```
UNLOAD DATA DIF GUEST_ROSTER.DIF GUEST_ROSTER;
```

Another important optional keyword is ALL, which can be used to unload all tables in the database to a SQL-format file. For example, the following command uses this keyword in place of a table name to unload all tables in database SPA to SQL-format file SPA.SQL:

```
UNLOAD SQL SPA.SQL ALL;
```

To prevent users from gaining access to tables that they do not have privileges on, only the SYSADM user can use the ALL keyword with the UNLOAD SQL format.

There are two variations on the UNLOAD command, UNLOAD ALL (not to be confused with ALL used with UNLOAD SQL) and UNLOAD DATABASE.

UNLOAD ALL can be used by any user to unload all of his own tables and indexes in a SQL-format file.

UNLOAD DATABASE can be used only by SYSADM. This command unloads the entire database in SQL format, including tables, views, indexes and synonyms, such that a complete duplicate of the database can be created from the file. The following command unloads the SPA database to a file SPA.SQL:

```
UNLOAD DATABASE SPA.SQL;
```

The UNLOAD DATABASE version of the UNLOAD command is specially suited to doing backups.

The REORGANIZE Command

A database is a file, and it can become fragmented from repeated changes and dropping of tables and so forth just like any other file repeatedly saved to disk. In time, this fragmentation can adversely affect the speed of database response.

To address this situation, many systems have a utility such as the REORGANIZE command that optimally reorganizes the database to which you are currently connected. The command has the same effect as unloading and then reloading the entire database: it consolidates the database.

The following command reorganizes the SPA database:

```
REORGANIZE SPA;
```

Journaling

If a database is physically damaged or destroyed, as by a media failure, a backup file like those discussed in connection with the UNLOAD command can be used to restore the database on a new drive. However, by itself a backup file enables recovery only up to the point when the backup file was made. We are still at risk of losing subsequent changes to the database.

We can ensure recovery of changes made subsequent to the last backup by turning on a utility called *journaling*. The command to do this in SQLTalk is

    SET JOURNAL ON;

or

    SET JOURNAL file_name;

Setting journaling on creates a *roll-forward journal* file that logs any changes committed to the database. Thus the file records any data-manipulation, data-definition, or data-control statements when the transactions in which these statements are issued are committed.

To avoid missing any changes, the journal should be turned on immediately after the backup is made, with no users logged on to the system. Also, because the point of using journaling is to protect against the consequences of a media failure on the drive containing the database, the journal file should be located on a different drive—ideally, on a different device—from the database itself.

With a backup of the entire database, plus a journal file logging all changes committed since the backup was made, the entire database can be rebuilt up through the last COMMIT.

The procedure to restore a database from a backup and a journal has two steps: First the backup file is loaded into a newly initialized database. This restores the database up through when the backup was made. Then a command is issued to *apply* the journal file to the database, thus executing all the changes recorded in the journal and bringing the database up to date. In SQLTalk, the command to do this is APPLY JOURNAL. The following command applies journal file SPA.JOR:

    APPLY JOURNAL SPA.JOR;

The following command turns journaling off:

    SET JOURNAL OFF;

Automatic Recovery

Backups and journaling are necessary only to protect against media failure, that is, a failure that physically destroys data committed to the database. SQL recovers automatically from power failures and the like; these are different from a media failure in that changes that have been committed are written to disk and so are not affected. But still, what of changes made in the course of a current transaction that is aborted by, say, a power failure? How does the database maintain consistency of data when several transactions are aborted before COMMIT statements have been issued?

The short answer is that all these transactions are rolled back. Thus the net effect is the same as with a media failure in which a backup and up-to-date journal file exist: the database is restored up through the last COMMIT, and only uncommitted changes are lost. With the type of failure we are discussing now, though, the recovery is handled automatically by the system. The key to how this is done is the before image log.

Whenever during a transaction you issue a statement such as an UPDATE or DELETE that changes data in the database, a backup image of the original records, the way they were before being changed, is stored in a file called the *before image log*. This file is maintained by the system. In the file, the records are flagged with a *transaction ID* identifying the transaction in which they were changed.

The before image log is what makes it possible to roll back changes to the database. If changes you make are subsequently committed, the images associated with these changes in the before image log are erased; but if your transaction is aborted and the changes are not committed, the images associated with your transaction in the before image log are used to return any records you changed to the way they were before you changed them.

In Chapter 9, "Changing Tables and Data," we described how to perform a rollback by issuing a ROLLBACK command. Such rollbacks, initiated by the user, are called *explicit* rollbacks. But a rollback, in this case called an *implicit* rollback, can also be initiated by the system. An implicit rollback is issued in any case where a transaction is unsuccessfully terminated and a ROLLBACK command was not issued explicitly by the user. These cases fall into two classes: those where a particular user's transaction is unsuccessfully terminated but the system itself is unaffected, as would happen if, for instance, the user's node lost power or the user rebooted without exiting first; and those where the system itself crashes.

In the first case, the system automatically and immediately rolls back all changes made in the course of the user's current transaction.

In the second case, where the system itself goes down, everybody's transactions are rolled back. In this case, the rollback takes place as soon as the system is started up again, at which time the system always checks the before image log and automatically rolls back any uncommitted changes.

Thus in the case of power failures and the like, the system itself provides for consistent recovery of data and limits loss of data just to changes that were not committed.

Chapter 12: Database Utilities and Recovery 159

Summary

There are certain important functions that standard SQL has not been equipped to perform. For instance, there is no way in standard SQL to load more than a row at a time of data into a database or to do bulk unloading or transferring of data out.

The chapter discusses SQLTalk versions of four utilities representative of the ways that some of standard SQL's deficiencies are commonly remedied. Two of the utilities, the SQLTalk LOAD and UNLOAD commands, transfer bulk quantities of data in and out of a database in a variety of formats; another command, REORGANIZE, consolidates a fragmented database file to improve performance; and the fourth utility, journaling, enables data to be recovered when a media failure has destroyed some or all of a database.

The chapter concludes with a discussion of provisions standard SQL does have for recovery from power failures and the like.

Part II

Programming with SQL

CHAPTER 13

SQL Programming Concepts

In Part I, "Using SQL Interactively," we showed how to use SQL interactively—that is, how to execute SQL statements directly, by typing them at the keyboard. Now, in Part II, "Programming with SQL," we take up the topic of *programming* with SQL—that is, of *embedding* SQL statements in programs written in another language, such as C or COBOL.

In this chapter, we give an overview of the dialogue that takes place between the database engine and a program when you use embedded SQL, and we describe the phases in the processing of embedded SQL statements. Collectively, these phases are sometimes called the *database access cycle*. In the chapters that follow in Part II, we show how these phases are provided for in actual programs.

Why Embedded SQL

As we mentioned in the Introduction, SQL is not a programming language, or even an interactive language. You cannot write programs in SQL, and, practically speaking, you cannot execute SQL statements directly. You need to execute them *through* a program that makes various arrangements for you with the database engine and handles things that SQL was not designed to handle.

We did not emphasize the fact, but even the SQL statements used in Part I, "Using the SQL Language," were executed through a program—the SQLTalk interactive-SQL command interface. SQLTalk not only supplements, or extends, SQL with additional commands and functions; SQLTalk also performs various services behind the scenes and handles communications with the database engine even when you issue ordinary SQL statements. And SQLTalk is written in C.

163

But what, then, is the difference between interactive and embedded SQL? The answer is that interactive SQL is just SQL embedded in a program to let you issue SQL statements interactively. This may sound circular, but it isn't really. You can write programs to do many things with SQL, and executing SQL statements from the keyboard is just one of these things. In the next three sections, we discuss some of the things SQL does not do that make it either necessary or desirable to embed SQL in a program.

Row-at-a-Time Processing

SQL is a special-purpose language. It is designed specifically to perform certain tasks—namely, those having to do with database management, described in Part I.

Because SQL is a special-purpose language, you do not have to spell out in detail *how* to do the things you want to use SQL to do. You just have to say *what* you want to do—select all rows from GUEST_ROSTER where the trainer is Todd, for instance. Because SQL was built to let you do this kind of operation, the SQL implementation takes matters from there, and the database engine executes the statement.

This feature makes SQL very straightforward to use in some ways. For contrast, consider what would be involved if you wanted to do a query using a general-purpose *procedural* language such as C, which knows nothing about databases. You would have to make explicit every step, or procedure, that needed to be taken to select the rows, and you would have to use numerous conditionals, with looping and branching, as you specify what to do in different situations. You would have to write a program that said, "Open the GUEST_ROSTER table. Take a look at the first record. Does TRAINER = 'TODD'? If it doesn't, go to the next record. If it does, get me that record." And so on.

SQL is not a procedural language and does not need if-then statements for its ordinary business of processing queries and so forth. But we miss if-then statements when it comes to dealing with the *results* of these queries.

For instance, suppose that you want to pull out the rows for Todd's female trainees from the result of the query just mentioned. Suppose that you want to highlight these rows somehow or simply discard all the other rows. SQL provides no way to do this. If you have not set up your query itself to select only Todd's female trainees, there is no way to pick out just these rows from the result.

And even if you could pick them out, you cannot do anything with them in SQL. You cannot flag certain rows with a check mark, say, or prefix a value representing a sum of money with a dollar sign, or round decimals after two places. SQL does not provide a way to do anything with the result at all. To format it, print it, or display it, you need a program. SQL delivers just the set of rows.

This raises another point: what if the set is too large for you to handle? SQL is *set-oriented* in that it operates on the *set* of all rows that meet the criteria of the SQL statement. There are mechanisms in the database engine to examine each candidate row separately to see whether it qualifies, but there is no way to say in a SQL statement "Hold off after the first five rows." The entire set specified in the SQL statement is operated on. If 20 rows qualify, then SQL selects all 20 in a body. If a million rows qualify, then SQL delivers a million.

To process the rows SQL returns from a query, you need a program—such as SQLTalk—that looks at each row individually and decides what to do with it. Then you can use the procedural features of the language in which the program is written to sort, format, print, or display the rows.

The operation that takes rows from a query result one at a time is called *fetching*, and the phase of executing or processing a query in which this operation takes place is called the *fetch phase*. Later in this chapter, we describe this and the other two principal phases in the execution of a SQL statement.

Substituting for Variables

In Part I, we did not demonstrate inserting more than one row at a time because the SQL INSERT statement can handle only one row. Except when you use a subselect, it is impossible to insert multiple rows with a single INSERT statement unless SQL is embedded in a program. You would have to issue a separate SQL statement for each row. If you wanted to insert a hundred rows, you would have to issue a hundred INSERT statements.

If you embed SQL in a program, however, you can use the INSERT statement with variables defined in the enveloping programming language. By substituting successive rows of data for the variables, you can insert multiple rows with a single INSERT statement.

The following example uses variables in an INSERT statement entered interactively through SQLTalk. The statement inserts multiple rows into table GUEST_ROSTER.

The variables are called *program variables*. They are the numbers preceded by colons—:1, :2, :3, :4, :5, and :6—in the VALUES clause of the INSERT statement, where data ordinarily goes. The program feeds the database engine a row of data, the data is substituted for the variables, and the statement is executed. If there are more rows to insert, the program gives the engine the next row, this row in turn is substituted for the variables, and the statement is executed again. The process continues in a loop until there are no more rows to insert:

```
INSERT INTO GUEST_ROSTER
VALUES(:1, :2, :3, :4, :5, :6)
\
```

```
BETTE MIDRIFF,1,MICHAEL,14-JUN-1988,16-JUN-1988,,
MICHAEL JOHNSON,4,JULIO,15-JUN-1988,19-JUN-1988,,
CLINT WESTWOOD,5,MICHAEL,25-JUN-1988,,.15
SEAN PENCIL,6,TODD,15-JUN-1988,20-JUN-1988,.05
HETAERA,7,SERENA,24-JUN-1988,,,
JOANNIE RIVULETS,8,SERENA,25-JUN-1988,,.15
        .
        .
        .
JANE FYUNDAI,18,MICHAEL,19-JUN-1988,26-JUN-1988,.1
DYAN HOWITZER,19,YVETTE,19-JUN-1988,26-JUN-1988,,
BIANCA JOGGER,20,TODD,20-JUN-1988,27-JUN-1988,.15
/
```

The program variables represent the relative position of the data for each variable in the rows of data being inserted. A program variable can also be the name of a variable previously declared in a program—for instance (if these were previously declared variables), :name, or :arg1.

A backslash (\) appears after the INSERT statement to signify that the statement is complete and that data follows. Next are the rows of data, with values separated by commas. A slash (/) terminates the statement. This use of the slash and backslash is a convention of SQLTalk; it is followed only when entering multiple rows interactively. In an application program, the data would be assigned to variables elsewhere in the program and the delimiting slash and backslash would not be used.

When the statement is executed, variable :1 is substituted for the first value, :2 for the second, :3 for the third, and so on. These values are substituted in the SQL statement in place of the respective variables and inserted into table GUEST_ROSTER. The process is repeated in a loop until there are no more values.

Program variables, in addition to their use in the VALUES clause of an INSERT statement, can be used in the WHERE clause of any SQL statement and in the SET clause of an UPDATE statement. For example:

```
UPDATE TABLE GUEST_ROSTER
SET DISCOUNT = :2
WHERE NAME = :1
```

Variable :1 takes the first value to appear in the rows of data; variable :2 takes the second.

Error Handling

Another job a program does is to handle errors returned by the system. The system's work is done when the error is returned. To *process* the result or the message in a useful way requires a program.

Recall some of the error messages in Part I, "Using the SQL Language," such as "`Table does not exist`" and "`Set function not allowed here`". With each error message, the SQL statement in question was displayed, and a caret (^) pointed to the place in the statement where the error was generated.

Both these jobs were performed by the enveloping program, SQLTalk. SQLTalk processed the error message to show the offending SQL statement and the caret. But errors do not have to be treated this way. The program could have been written to append to a list each error message as it is generated. This less helpful approach to error handling would be like retrieving all the rows from a query in one block, without providing row-at-a-time fetching.

SQL itself does not do anything with error messages. You need a program, an implementation like SQLTalk, for instance, to intercept the errors and provide useful information about them. This information can then help the person or program using SQL decide what to do.

Phases of Processing SQL Statements

Both fetching and substitution of variables are easier to understand when viewed in the larger context of the phases of processing and executing SQL statements.

The three major phases in the processing of SQL statements are the *compile* phase, the *execute* phase, and the *fetch* phase (see fig. 13.1). All SQL statements go through the first two phases, but only SELECT statements—queries—go through all three. The third phase, the fetch phase, is entirely concerned with processing query results. Because only queries return results, only queries need a fetch phase.

***Fig. 13.1.** The phases of processing SQL statements.*

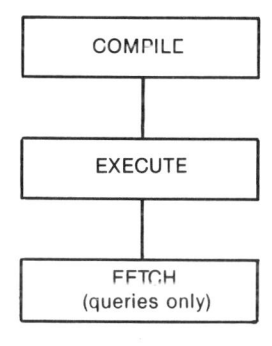

```
┌─────────────┐
│   COMPILE   │
└──────┬──────┘
       │
┌──────┴──────┐
│   EXECUTE   │
└──────┬──────┘
       │
┌──────┴──────┐
│    FETCH    │
│(queries only)│
└─────────────┘
```

The Compile Phase

Four actions take place in the compile phase: the statement is *parsed*, a *security check* is performed on it, an *access path* is constructed for the statement's execution, and the SQL statement is translated into a series of executable procedures (see fig. 13.2).

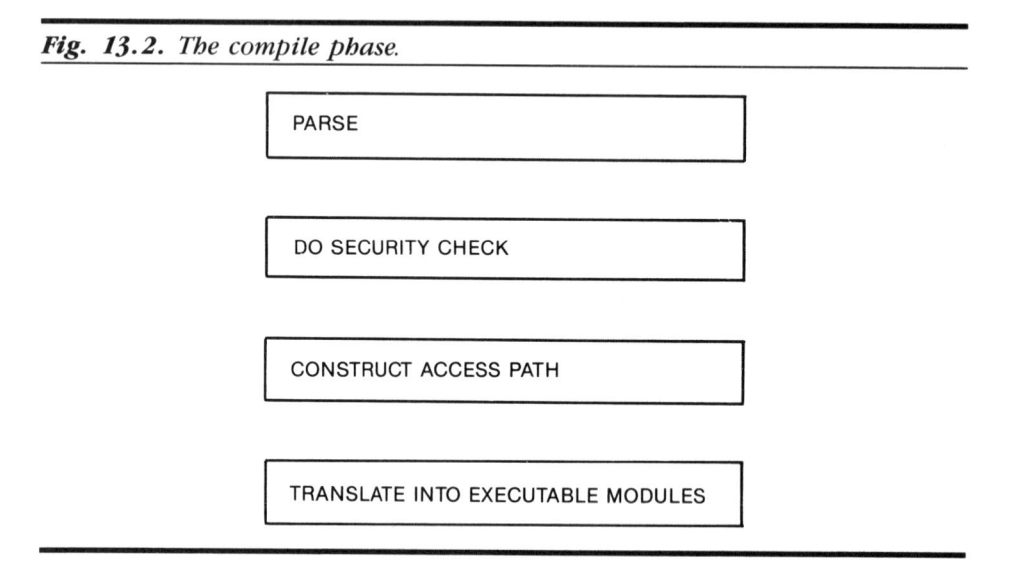

Fig. 13.2. The compile phase.

```
┌─────────────────────────────────┐
│            PARSE                │
└─────────────────────────────────┘

┌─────────────────────────────────┐
│       DO SECURITY CHECK         │
└─────────────────────────────────┘

┌─────────────────────────────────┐
│      CONSTRUCT ACCESS PATH      │
└─────────────────────────────────┘

┌─────────────────────────────────┐
│  TRANSLATE INTO EXECUTABLE MODULES │
└─────────────────────────────────┘
```

Parsing a statement involves checking the statement for validity. The engine reviews the syntax of the statement and checks that all columns, tables, users, and so on referred to in the statement exist. If the statement fails any of these checks, the engine returns an error and the statement is not processed any further.

When a statement containing program variables is parsed, the variables serve as placeholders for data. Actual values are not known until data is substituted for the variables in the execution phase. But the statement still can be checked for validity in other respects without these values. This is part of the advantage of using variables: you do not need a separate SQL statement for each row of data, and the one SQL statement you do need is compiled only once, no matter how many substitutions you want to make.

After the statement is parsed, the engine performs a security check, confirming that the user issuing the statement has the authority and privileges to direct the engine to do what the statement says. For instance, if you have issued a syntactically and semantically valid statement to update a table that you do not have update privileges on, the engine halts processing of the statement and returns an error.

After the security check, the database engine determines which indexes to apply, if any, and the best access path to the data. Then the engine converts the statement from English to a series of procedures, little pseudo-programs or executable modules, that are run later to execute the statement. The engine stores these in its memory until the execution phase.

In some implementations, such as SQLBase, you can store the compiled version of the statement in the database and execute it when you choose. Being able to store queries or other statements in the database is useful with complex statements that need a long time to compile. By compiling such statements in advance (*precompiling*), compile time can be saved from the time it takes to run the statements.

The Execute Phase

The execute phase follows the compile phase. Essentially two things take place in this phase: buffers are established by the program, as necessary, and the compiled statement—whether just compiled or compiled some time ago—is run, or executed.

Buffers are reserved areas of memory established, or *declared*, by the program. Two kinds of buffers are involved in the execute phase: input buffers and output buffers.

Input buffers contain the program data that is substituted for program variables in a SQL statement. Each variable in a SQL statement must be provided with buffer space for its own data. These are *input* buffers in the sense that their data is used as input from the program to the engine. Data is placed in the appropriate buffers either by the programmer or through execution of a prior SQL statement that retrieves that data.

Output buffers are a place to put data returned by the engine in the fetch phase of a query. These are *output* buffers in the sense that they hold data that is output from the engine. Output buffers are also called SELECT buffers because their data originates as the result of a query, or SELECT statement.

In addition to establishing the buffers in the first place, the program must also tell the database which buffers to use. With input buffers, this step is called *binding* the data. For each bind variable in a SQL statement, the program must *bind* that variable to a particular buffer area so that the engine knows where to look for the data to use for that variable.

A similar step is necessary with output buffers; the program must tell the engine where to put the data for each field in a row retrieved by a fetch. This step involves *setting* the output buffers for the particular fields.

Figure 13.3 shows the various operations in the execute phase. As you can see, the details of what happens in this phase for any particular SQL statement vary depending on whether the statement contains program variables and whether the statement is a query.

***Fig. 13.3.** The execute phase.*

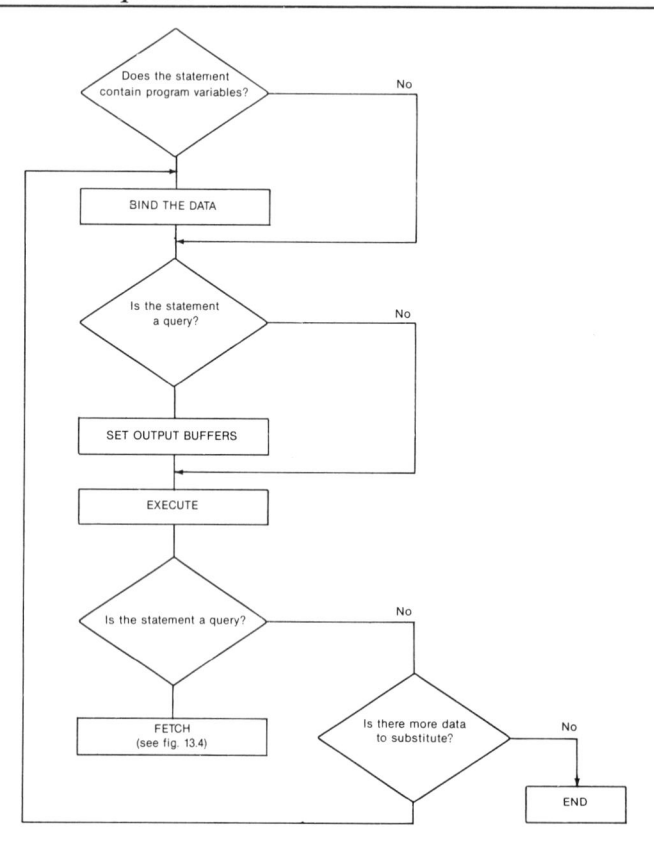

[Flowchart: Does the statement contain program variables? → If yes: BIND THE DATA. Is the statement a query? → If yes: SET OUTPUT BUFFERS → EXECUTE → Is the statement a query? → If yes: FETCH (see fig. 13.4); If no: Is there more data to substitute? → If yes: loop back; If no: END.]

After any variables in a statement are bound to data in the appropriate buffers, a set of data is substituted for the variables and the statement is run, or executed. Then, if more data remains, the engine performs another substitution and the statement is executed again with the new values. This process is repeated until all data in the input buffers has been substituted into the statement.

If the statement is a query, the process of performing successive substitutions is essentially the same as we have just described, but the process is extended into the fetch phase.

The Fetch Phase

Queries are the only type of SQL statement that require a fetch phase. With every other type of SQL statement, after the statement is executed, the engine is finished with the statement and is free to do another. With a query, though, executing the statement merely positions the engine to deliver the first row of the result set. If you want to see the row, you have to do a fetch. In fact, you must do a fetch for *each* row that you want to see in the result set.

As we said earlier, the point of fetching is to move the result of a query one row at a time into work areas, or buffers, where you can do things with the rows that you cannot do in SQL. Any operations on the rows you fetch— any formatting, printing, or displaying—must be provided for in your program; the engine is not involved. Often, 90 percent or more of an application deals with examining and processing rows fetched into the output buffer by the engine.

Figure 13.4 diagrams what takes place in the fetch phase.

Fig. 13.4. The fetch phase.

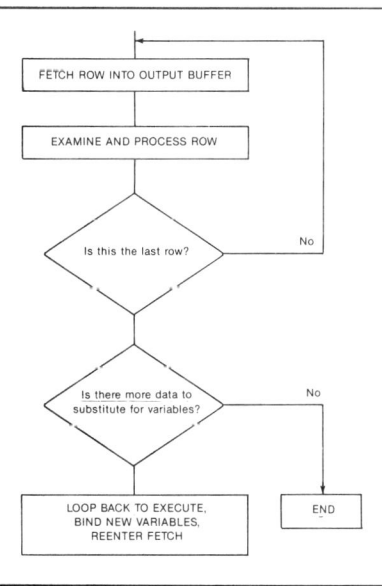

```
         ┌──────────────────────────────┐
         │  FETCH ROW INTO OUTPUT BUFFER │
         └──────────────────────────────┘
                        │
         ┌──────────────────────────────┐
         │   EXAMINE AND PROCESS ROW    │
         └──────────────────────────────┘
                        │
                     ◇ Is this the last row? ◇ ── No ──┐
                        │                              │
                        │                              │
                     ◇ Is there more data to           │
                       substitute for variables? ◇ ── No ──┐
                        │                                  │
         ┌──────────────────────────────┐           ┌─────┐
         │  LOOP BACK TO EXECUTE,       │           │ END │
         │  BIND NEW VARIABLES,         │           └─────┘
         │  REENTER FETCH               │
         └──────────────────────────────┘
```

The program continues to instruct the engine to fetch rows until there are no more rows to fetch. Then the processing of the statement ends, or, if the query contains program variables and there is more data to substitute for these, the process loops back to the execute phase. At the execute phase, the engine performs a new substitution for the variables and positions itself at the first row of the new result set, ready to reenter the fetch phase.

Cursors

The preceding section described the engine positioning itself at a particular row of a result set. The mechanism for doing this is a *cursor*.

If result rows are fetched one at a time, the engine needs a way to locate itself in the result set: it cannot fetch the next row if it does not know which row the next row is. To enable the engine to keep track of its position in a result set, embedded SQL provides *cursors*. A cursor in SQL picks out a row position in the result set; it represents where the engine is in the set.

Counting the FETCH statement itself, four statements are provided in embedded SQL for working with cursors.

First, a program must issue a DECLARE statement, which defines a cursor for a query. This associates the cursor with the query. Then, to execute the query, the program issues a command to OPEN the cursor. This causes the engine to position the cursor at the first row of the result set. When the program issues a FETCH statement, the engine returns the row.

With each FETCH statement, the cursor advances through the result set a row at a time until it reaches the end of the set. Then the program issues a command to CLOSE the cursor. If the query contains variables, new values can be substituted at this point. The query can be run again with the new values by issuing another OPEN statement.

Connecting and Disconnecting

The steps in the processing of an embedded SQL statement have been arranged into three main phases—compile, execute, and fetch. But before a program can issue a SQL statement for processing, the program—like a user of interactive SQL—first has to log on to the system.

In a general way, the process is similar to the process for connecting with interactive SQL (covered in Part I). First, you get a connection ID, called a *handle*, that identifies the connection to the engine. In some implementations, you give this a name; in some, the system names it for you.

Second, you give your user name and password. This establishes your authority in the database. Also, you may have to specify the *database name* if you can connect to more than one database, as in SQLBase.

A handle is like a service number in a shop: whatever you order is associated with the service number. This lets you identify your order to the shop and enables the shop to come back to the right customer when the order is filled.

The order itself, on this analogy, is the SQL statement that the engine is processing. You give the statement a name that the engine associates with your handle or you use the handle itself as a name, depending on the implementation.

Not all implementations support handles, incidentally. A handle is necessary only in an implementation, such as SQLBase, that can make multiple simultaneous connections to one or more databases. Because the system needs a way to tell the different connections apart, it assigns handles. In implementations that do not support multiple simultaneous connections, there is no concept of handles.

Chapter 15, "Advanced Programming with a Function Call Interface," discusses using multiple connections.

When the program has issued all the statements it wants processed, it is ready to *disconnect* from the database and finish operations.

Disconnecting from the system essentially consists in disconnecting all handles, or closing all cursors. In some implementations, such as SQLBase, the engine automatically commits any changes made during the program's transaction if the program has not already done so; in other implementations, uncommitted changes are automatically rolled back.

Programming Options

The following chapters in Part II examine three ways of using SQL in programs. One way is to embed SQL in programs written for a function call interface to a SQL implementation. The second way is to embed SQL in programs written for a precompiler (also called a preprocessor) interface. A third, newly available alternative is to use SQL with a dBASE-language interface.

With a function call interface, the programmer controls when the program interacts with the database. The interface provides a set of statements, called *function calls*, that the program uses to tell the database engine to do specific things—for example, to connect to a database, compile a statement, store a compiled statement, bind data, execute a particular statement, or fetch rows.

With a precompiler interface, however, the programmer does not have to manage operations on so fine a scale. In fact, using SQL in a program written for a precompiler is somewhat like using SQL interactively. The programmer does not need to tell the engine when to compile, when to execute, and so forth. The precompiler, almost like SQLTalk, translates SQL statements into appropriate function calls automatically.

The new dBASE-language interfaces are similar to a precompiler interface in that the programmer does not need to use function calls: SQL statements embedded in dBASE code are automatically translated into function calls to access a SQL database engine.

Most implementations of SQL provide function call interfaces and precompiler interfaces for one or more programming languages. These interfaces work similarly, but because different implementations define different function calls, no two interfaces are exactly alike. We will use SQLBase interfaces for the examples and sample programs in Part II. These interfaces are representative of the kinds of interfaces offered by other implementations.

The function call interface we will use is the SQLBase API (Application Programming Interface) for C. The C language is the most common language for programming with a function call interface. In Chapter 14, "Using a Function Call Interface," we look at code from a sample program using function calls for each major phase of the typical database access cycle. In Chapter 15, we discuss some advanced programming topics relating to function calls.

In Chapter 16, "Using a Precompiler Interface," and Chapter 17, "Using a COBOL SQL Precompiler," we use the SQLBase SQL/Preprocessor for COBOL to demonstrate programming with a precompiler, or preprocessor, interface. COBOL is the most popular language for use with SQL precompilers.

We discuss dBASE-language interfaces in Chapter 18, "Using a dBASE Interface." These are offered by Ashton-Tate Corporation (dBASE IV) and third-party vendors such as WordTech (dBXL and Quicksilver).

These next chapters are more technical than previous chapters and assume some familiarity with C, COBOL, and dBASE.

Summary

SQL by itself is neither an interactive language nor a programming language. To be used at all, SQL must be embedded in a program written in a procedural language. This lets you provide important features such as error handling, substitution of variables, and sorting and formatting of results.

The three main phases in the processing of SQL statements are the compile phase, the execute phase, and, for queries, the fetch phase.

Two additional operations also must be provided in any program containing embedded SQL: connecting and disconnecting to the database, analogous to logging on and logging off.

CHAPTER 14

Using a Function Call Interface

In this chapter, we look at excerpts from a sample application program written in the C language for a function call interface. The program creates a table, inserts rows of data into the table, and queries the table. The excerpts of code show how the program handles the various phases in the processing of SQL statements, described in Chapter 13, "SQL Programming Concepts."

The function call interface the program uses is the SQLBase API (Application Programming Interface) for the C programming language.

A complete annotated sample program appears in Appendix A, "Sample C Program." A list of the function calls available for the SQLBase API is given in Appendix B, "SQLBase API Function Calls."

Before We Begin

Some background matters must be explained before you look at the excerpts of code. We need to say a few words about practices we have followed in the code; special files, included with the API, that must be available for the code to access; provisions in the API for getting information about SQL statements being processed; and error handling.

Notes About the Sample Code

For simplicity, constants are used in some places where you might ordinarily expect variables (for example, for user name and password).

Second, when a function expects the length of a character buffer as an argument and the buffer contains a null-terminated string, we customarily pass a 0 and let SQLBase calculate the length.

Finally, an error message prints the error value returned by the API call, but the sample code does not provide additional error processing. In practice, a rollback, disconnect, and program exit ordinarily would be issued.

Special Files

Three files in the SQLBase API are referred to in the sample code:

sql.h   The `sql.h` file must be included with any .c files that make SQLBase calls. The `sql.h` file contains (among other things) definitions for SQLBase data types and other definitions used in API programming, codes for each type of SQL command, and system defaults. For instance, SQLTCUR, used in the sample code to declare a handle, is defined in this file.

error.sql   The `error.sql` file contains error codes and the associated text for each code.

errsql.h   The `errsql.h` file is an include file containing definitions for all SQLBase error codes.

Getting Information

Information about a SQL statement being processed through a particular handle can be requested by the application program. As we explained in Chapter 13, "SQL Programming Concepts," a handle is returned when an application program connects to a database. The handle is used in API calls to identify the SQL statement currently being processed for the connection associated with that handle.

SQLBase returns the information into a variable declared in the application. Information is requested with a function call of the following form:

```
sqlxxx (cur, &infobuffer1, &infobuffer2, and so on)
```

`sqlxxx` represents the function call appropriate to the information you want. Most of the API functions require that the database handle (`cur`) be passed so that the function is performed on a particular connection to the database. Other parameters may also be required. If a parameter will receive a value from the function, then a pointer to a buffer (variable) must be passed. The desired value is returned into this variable.

The ampersand symbol (&) means that the address of the variable is passed, not the value. This address of a variable is a pointer. When the function returns, the variable contains the new value. Each variable must be declared with the type appropriate for the value returned.

An application program can request the following kinds of information. Each item of information can be retrieved with a function call.

Return code: The return code is always returned by the function. If the operation was successful, a 0 is returned. In all other cases, a number representing an error or some other condition is returned.

Number of rows: You can get the number of rows affected by UPDATE, DELETE, INSERT, or FETCH as well as the number of rows in a table.

Error position: If a syntax error is returned from an API call, the location of the error in the SQL statement is represented as an offset from the beginning of the statement. The first character is position 0.

The error offset is most meaningful after a compile or an execute operation because it points to the precise position in a SQL statement where the error was detected.

Number of select items: The number of items in the select list is set after a SELECT statement is compiled.

Number of program variables: After a SQL statement is compiled, the number of program variables associated with the statement is set.

For example, the call sqlnbv (cur, &curnbv) returns a 2 in the unsigned char curnbv after compiling the following SQL statement:

```
UPDATE TABLE1 SET COL1 = :1
WHERE COL3 = :2
```

Rollback flag: The rollback flag is set to 1 when a transaction is rolled back by SQLBase, as a result of a deadlock or system failure. Ordinarily, the flag is set to 0, which means that no rollback has occurred.

Result command type: The command type is set after a compile operation and indicates the type of SQL statement that was compiled. A code is defined in the sql.h file for every type of SQL operation, such as SELECT, INSERT, UPDATE, ROLLBACK, and so on.

Errors

Each API function returns a code indicating success or an error condition. An API program should always check these return codes and proceed accordingly. When an error on the current statement affects previous statements in the transaction, you may want to roll back the entire transaction with the `sqlrbk` function and then disconnect and exit. In other cases, you may have anticipated the error condition and set the course of subsequent processing accordingly.

Text for error codes is commonly stored in a separate file—the `error.sql` file, in SQLBase. The SQLBase function `sqlerr` retrieves error text from this file into an application program.

The API Database Access Cycle

In this section, we look at sample code for the various stages of the database access cycle. The discussion is keyed to figure 14.1, an overview of the cycle.

Fig. 14.1. The database access cycle.

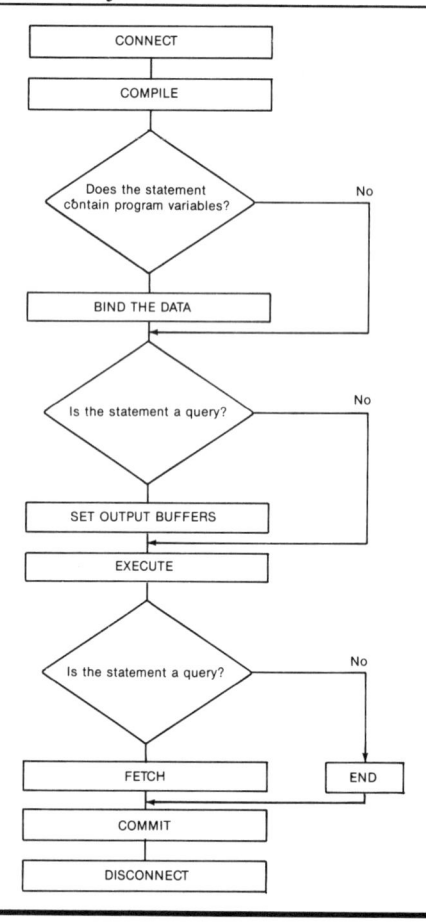

```
                    CONNECT
                       |
                    COMPILE
                       |
           Does the statement        No
           contain program variables? ----+
                       |                   |
                     Yes                   |
                       |                   |
                  BIND THE DATA            |
                       |<------------------+
                       |
           Is the statement a query?   No
                       |              ----+
                     Yes                   |
                       |                   |
               SET OUTPUT BUFFERS          |
                       |<------------------+
                       |
                    EXECUTE
                       |
           Is the statement a query?   No
                       |              ----+
                     Yes                   |
                       |                   |
                    FETCH                 END
                       |
                    COMMIT
                       |
                  DISCONNECT
```

Figure 14.1 is a slightly abridged compilation of the figures in Chapter 13, "SQL Programming Concepts." The sections of the figure correspond with passages in this section. Each passage gives an excerpt of sample code, with commentary, dealing with the indicated stage in the cycle.

The code in the excerpts uses SQL statements addressing the ITEM table, which follows:

Columns:	ITEM_NO	DESCRIPTION	PRICE	NOTES
Data Type:	number	char	decimal	long varchar
	=====	=======	=====	====
	3	BASIL	.89	{text}
	1	CINNAMON	.45	{text}
	2	SAGE	.95	{text}

The three SQL statements used in the sample code are

```
CREATE TABLE ITEM
(ITEM_NO NUMBER NOT NULL,
DESCRIPTION CHAR (25),
PRICE DECIMAL (5,2),
NOTES LONG VARCHAR)

INSERT INTO ITEM VALUES (:1,:2,:3,:4)

SELECT * FROM ITEM WHERE PRICE > :price
```

The INSERT and SELECT statements contain program variables.

CONNECT

You must include in the program the file containing definitions for data types, SQL commands, and system defaults. (In SQLBase, the file is sql.h.).

```
#include <sql.h>
```

Then you declare the SQL statements used in the code as static strings:

```
static char critem[] =
"CREATE TABLE ITEM (ITEM_NO NUMBER NOT NULL, DESCRIPTION\
   CHAR (25), PRICE DECIMAL (5,2), NOTES LONG VARCHAR)";

static char insitem [] =
"INSERT INTO ITEM VALUES (:1,:2,:3,:4)";

static char selitem [] =
"SELECT * FROM ITEM WHERE PRICE > :price";
```

To program with the API, you must connect to a database with a valid user authorization and password. To connect to a database and establish a handle, you use the sqlcnc call. We use the same handle, cur in this case, for each SQL statement.

The following lines of code establish a connection between the INVENTORY database and the program, returning the handle to be used in the variable cur.

```
#include "sql.h"
SQLTCUR cur;           /* Handle                */
char errmsg[80];       /* Buffer for error text */
short ret;

if (ret = sqlcnc (&cur, "inventory/tj/x",0))
{
   sqlerr(ret, errmsg);
   printf ("Failure on CONNECT: %s\n", errmsg);
}
```

The first argument to sqlcnc is a pointer to the variable that will contain the handle. The next argument is the database name, user name, and password, separated by slashes. The third argument is the data length of the second argument: 0 indicates a null-terminated string.

COMPILE

As we said in Chapter 13, "SQL Programming Concepts," a SQL statement must be compiled before it can be executed. SQL statements are compiled with the sqlcom function. The excerpt below compiles the INSERT statement for the sample program:

```
char errmsg[80];       /* Buffer for error text */
SQLTCUR cur;
short ret;
short errpos;

if (ret = sqlcom (cur, insitem, 0))
{
   sqlerr (ret, errmsg);
   sqlepo (cur, &errpos);
   printf ("COMPILE error:%s at %d \n", errmsg, errpos);
}
```

The first argument of sqlcom is a handle; this is followed by a pointer to the INSERT statement and then by the length of the buffer containing the SQL statement. The zero argument in this last case indicates a null-terminated string.

Data-definition statements, data-control statements, and queries that do not contain program variables can be compiled and executed in a single pass. Because these statements are executed only once, there is no advantage to having the program take back control after the compile stage, as there would be if the statement were going to be run again with different values. For these statements, we use SQLCEX to compile and execute the statement in a single function call.

The CREATE TABLE statement is a (data-definition) statement that is run only once. In the code that follows, we use the sqlcex call to compile and execute this statement, creating the ITEM table.

When the CREATE TABLE statement is executed, you are done with the database access cycle for this statement. If no other database accesses were required to complete the transaction, the program ordinarily would commit, either by issuing the API `sqlcmt` call or by compiling and executing a SQL COMMIT statement.

```
if (ret = sqlcex (cur, crtitem, 0))
{
   sqlerr (ret, errmsg);
   printf ("CEX error: %s\n", errmsg);
}
```

BIND DATA

The INSERT and SELECT statements we are using contain program variables. Data from the program will replace, or be bound to, these variables each time the statement executes.

The `sqlbnn` command is used to bind the program data for columns that are not LONG VARCHAR. The command associates a program variable in a SQL statement with a data buffer in the program where the data will be found.

Columns of type LONG bind their data using a different call, `sqlblo`, discussed in Chapter 15, "Advanced Programming with a Function Call Interface." In general, the way LONG columns are processed depends on the implementation.

The compiled INSERT statement is executed each time a row of data is inserted into the input buffer. Similarly, the SELECT statement (`selitem`) is executed each time new data is bound to the variable :price. Because of the new data in the statement, each execution generates a new result set of rows.

The INSERT statement (`insitem`) has four program variables; the last one refers to a LONG data column. Each variable must be associated with the location of the data in the program.

Suppose that the description and price are typed in at the terminal and are in the variables indicated in the example. The item number is a system-generated integer that increments the highest existing number by 1. Assume that you have derived the highest existing number by processing this statement:

```
SELECT MAX(ITEM_NO) FROM ITEM
```

Items and prices are entered as character strings and stored in the program as an array of null-terminated strings. The item number is an integer. The text for NOTES is read into the `notebuf` input buffer, as shown:

```
int item;              /* Item number                    */
int maxitem;           /* Highest item number            */
int len;               /* Length of bound data           */
int cols;              /* Program variable number        */
char itemdata[2][26];  /* Array of pointers to item data */
...
```

First, you bind `maxitem` to the ITEM column, represented by the program variable :1 in the INSERT statement:

```
/* Bind maxitem                              */
if (ret = sqlbnn(cur, 1, &maxitem, sizeof(int), 0, SQLPUIN))
{
/* Code to process error appears here */
}
```

The arguments are cursor, program variable number, pointer to data, length of data, scale, and data type of the program variable (in this case, an unsigned integer symbolized by the constant SQLPUIN).

The following code is a loop that binds the second and third columns (program variables :2 and :3, representing DESCRIPTION and PRICE) to the `itemdata` array. The number of program variables is set after a compile using the `sqlnbv` function to extract the number of program variables in the compiled statement.

```
unsigned char nbv;         /* Number of program variables        */
sqlnbv (cur, &nbv);
for (i=0,cols=2; cols < nbv; i++, cols++)
{
   len = strlen(itemdata[i]);
   if (ret = sqlbnn(cur,cols,itemdata[i],len, 0, SQLPSTR))
   {
                   /* Code to process error appears here */
   }
}
```

The loop begins with `cols` = 2 because 2 corresponds to the first variable we are binding (namely, :2). Program variable :4 refers to a LONG column. We therefore end the loop prior to 4 by using < rather than <= as the operator in the loop statement. LONG columns are bound using a different function, `sqlbln` ("bind LONG data by number").

```
if (ret = sqlbln (cur, 4))
{
/* Code to process error appears here */
}
```

The first argument is the current cursor; the second argument is the number indicating the program variable, in this case :4.

An alternate bind function, `sqlbnd`, is used for variables that are names rather than of numbers. This call has an additional argument (the length of the SQL program variable name).

The following example uses the `sqlbnd` call for the sample SELECT statement (SELECT * FROM ITEM WHERE PRICE > :price):

```
char pricebuf[25];
if (ret = sqlbnd (cur,"price", 0, pricebuf, 0,0,SQLTSTR))
{
/* Code to process error appears here */
}
```

SET OUTPUT BUFFERS

For a SQL statement that is a query (a SELECT statement), an output buffer must be set up to receive the column data fetched from the query.

The `sqlssb` function sets up an output buffer for each item in the select list of a SQL SELECT statement. The number of these is set following a compile operation using the function `sqlnsi`. In the example, SELECT * FROM ITEM WHERE PRICE > :price, the result contains four columns. The last column is a LONG and is processed separately; it uses a different function call, `sqlrlo` ("read LONG"), which identifies the buffer.

In the following example, the output buffers are declared to be a specific length.

```
char selbuf[3][26];       /* Buffers for fetched data */
int col, i;
unsigned char nsi;        /* Number of select items    */

/* Get the number of select items    */
sqlnsi (cur, &nsi);

/* Set buffers for the character columns. Ignore final
   column, which is a LONG */
for (col=1, i=0; col < nsi; i++, col++)
{
   if (ret = sqlssb (cur, col, SQLPSTR,selbuf[i], 0,
      0, SQLNPTR,SQLNPTR))
   {
      sqlerr (ret, errmsg);
      sqlepo (cur, &errpos);
      printf ("SSB error: %s at %d col %d\n", errmsg, errpos, col);
   }
}
```

Each item in the select list must be associated with an output buffer to receive the data. Thus, the `sqlssb` call is issued once for each item in the select list. The call's first argument is the current cursor handle. The second argument, `col`, is the column number in the select list, followed by the data type of the variable receiving the column data. The next argument, `selbuf[i]`, is a pointer to the data to be fetched. This is followed by a data length of 0, which indicates that the data should be converted to a null-terminated string. The next argument is for the scale of packed decimal data.

The last two arguments are optional. The sample code passes null pointers indicating that the information is not necessary to the application. When the arguments are used, they serve as a pointer to the length of the data most recently fetched and as a pointer to the fetch status code of the fetch operation. Following the `sqlssb` call, data is bound to the program variable "price" to complete the data component of the SQL statement.

Sometimes, you may not know the attributes of a column (such as column name or data length) you are selecting or binding data to. For example, if you are writing a general-purpose query processor, you might want to wait until run time to get certain key column information. The `sqldes` ("describe") function, does this for you. It returns the database data type, maximum column size, column name, precision, and scale for a specified column.

EXECUTE

After program variables are bound and output buffers are established for a query, the SQL statement can be executed.

```
short ret;
char errmsg [SQLMERR];
/* First write the long data for the NOTES column. */
if (sqlexe (cur))
{
   sqlrcd (cur &ret);      /* Get return code */
   sqlerr (ret, errmsg);   /* Get error text  */
   printf ("EXE error: %s\n", errmsg);
}
```

If the SQL statement is not a SELECT statement, database access is complete. The application can loop back, bind new data, and reexecute. In this case, another compile operation is not needed. If the database is no longer needed by the application, the user ordinarily commits (`sqlcmt`) and disconnects.

For our INSERT example (`insitem`), program variable :4 refers to a column of type LONG VARCHAR. Additional function calls are required before executing an INSERT or an UPDATE when any program variable refers to a LONG. In every implementation, LONG columns require special handling in various ways that tend to be specific to the implementation. Chapter 15, "Advanced Programming with a Function Call Interface," explains how LONG columns are handled in SQLBase.

FETCH

If the SQL statement is a query, rows of data must be fetched one at a time after the execute operation. The `sqlfet` function retrieves one row of data into the output buffer. A loop in the application program repeats the fetch operation until all the rows are fetched. A 0 return code means that the operation was successful and the row was fetched. An end-of-fetch (that is, a fetch attempt after the last successful fetch) returns a 1.

```
char line [80];
short ret; /* Return code */
for (; ;)
{
```

```
      if (ret = sqlfet(cur)) break;
      sprintf (line, "%s   %s   %s\n", selbuf[0],selbuf[1],
         selbuf[2]);
}
if (ret != 1)
{
   sqlerr (ret, errmsg);
   printf ("FETCH error: %s\n", errmsg);
}
```

For the sample query, SELECT * FROM ITEM, the first three columns are fetched into the selbuf array. The last column is a LONG and is read separately.

COMMIT

After you have completed all the statements in the transaction, you must permanently commit any changes made to the database. This also releases any locks you may have acquired (see Chapter 15, "Advanced Programming with a Function Call Interface").

There are two ways to commit changes through the SQLBase API. You can use the sqlcmt function, or you can compile and execute the SQL COMMIT command. The following example uses the sqlcmt function:

```
if (ret = sqlcmt(cur))
{
/* Code to process error appears here */
}
```

The next example commits by compiling and executing the SQL COMMIT command:

```
if (ret = sqlcex(cur, 'COMMIT'))
{
/* Code to process error appears here */
}
```

Alternatively, if you want to undo the changes you have made rather than commit them to make them permanent, you can issue the sqlrbk command to roll all the changes back, as follows:

```
if (ret = sqlrbk(cur))
{
/* Code to process error appears here */
}
```

DISCONNECT

A disconnect (sqldis) terminates access to a database through the handle named in the disconnect call. Disconnecting from a handle implies disconnecting from the database, assuming that no other handles are connected. You should disconnect from all active handles before exiting a program. In SQLBase, when you disconnect from the last handle in a transaction, the engine issues a commit if you have not already issued one.

```
if (ret = sqldis (cur))
/* Code to process error appears here */
```

Summary

This chapter showed excerpts of sample C code for operations in the database access cycle discussed more generally in Chapter 13, "SQL Programming Concepts."

Code was provided for the following operations: connecting to a database, compiling a SQL statement, binding data to variables, setting output buffers, executing the compiled statement, fetching individual rows, committing the transaction, and disconnecting the handle.

CHAPTER 15

Advanced Programming with a Function Call Interface

Chapter 14, "Using a Function Call Interface," covered the basic operations that must be provided for when you program for the function call API interface. In this chapter, we cover some advanced programming operations that can be done with the API. Here we discuss operations on LONG VARCHAR data columns, using result sets, and using multiple handles. We also take up the topic of database consistency and locking.

Manipulating LONG VARCHAR Columns

The LONG VARCHAR data type lets us store data that is longer than 254 characters. Data of any length can be stored in a column of type LONG VARCHAR.

SELECT, INSERT, and UPDATE statements can be used with LONG columns in the same way that they are used with columns of other data types, but there is an important difference in how LONG data is handled. Because the length of LONG data is essentially unlimited, program loops must be set up to read or write the data in installments of a specified length. Special function calls are thus provided for dealing with LONG data. For instance, the SQLBase function sqlrlo reads LONG columns *n* bytes at a time from a database, and the sqlwlo function writes LONG columns *n* bytes at a time. Another function, sqllsk, sets a position in the LONG data and reads from that position. The function sqlelo ("end long operation") terminates operations on LONG data.

The following sections explain the use of these functions.

Querying LONG Data

The function `sqlrlo` ("read long operation") is used when data of type LONG VARCHAR is requested by a SELECT statement. The function is used after the SELECT statement is compiled and executed and the row is fetched. In the example in this section, a loop is established to read the data from the NOTES column of the ITEM table into a 500-byte buffer.

The statement "SELECT ITEM__NO, DESCRIPTION, PRICE, NOTES FROM ITEM WHERE ITEM__NO = :1" sets the number of select items to 4; the fourth column contains the LONG data.

The function `sqlssb` ("set select buffer") does not have to be issued for the LONG column, but it must be issued for the other columns. The `sqlrlo` call replaces the `sqlssb` function.

The following code illustrates fetching a set of rows that includes a column of LONG data. The non-LONG data is fetched, and then a loop retrieves the LONG data. When all the LONG data is retrieved, the LONG operation is ended and the next row is fetched. Data retrieved by both methods is output as the application specifies. This operation is not shown in the code.

```
/* READ LONG: Do this for each fetch (sqlfet) */
int col = 4;                 /* Column number of NOTES  */
char notebuf[500];           /* Buffer for LONG data    */
int len = 0;                 /* Number of bytes read    */
char errmsg[SQLMERR];        /* Buffer for error text   */
for (; ;)
{
  /*Fetch non-long data */
  if (ret = sqlfet(cur))
    break;
  /* Output the data from the fetch as desired */
  for (; ;)
  /* Read LONG data for this row until no more data */
{
    if(ret =
       sqlrlo(cur,col,notebuf,sizeof(notebuf),&len))
    {
sqlerr (ret, errmsg);             /* Get error text */
       printf ("ERROR ON READ LONG - %s\n", errmsg)
       break;
    }
    if(len == 0)                  /* No more data for row    */
    {
      if (ret = sqlelo(cur))   /* End LONG operation */
      {
        break;
      }
      else
        /* Output the data from sqlrlo as desired */
```

Chapter 15: Advanced Programming with a Function Call Interface 189

```
      }
    }
    if (ret)                  /* API error occurred */
      {
        sqlerr (ret, errmsg)
        printf("failure on READ LONG:%s\n", errmsg);
        exit (1);
      }
  }
  if (ret != 1)               /* End of fetch */
  {
     sqlerr (ret, errmsg);
     printf("ERROR:%s\n", errmsg);
  }
```

In the sqlrlo call, col is the column number on which the operation will be performed, and notebuf is a pointer to the buffer that will contain the LONG data. The next argument contains the number of bytes to be read from the LONG field; in this case, the number of bytes equals the size of the notebuf buffer and is computed with the sizeof function. The last argument is a pointer to the number of bytes to be read (&len) by the function. A 0 in len indicates that the end of the LONG field was reached in the previous read. The sqlelo operation terminates the LONG operation and signals the resumption of regular operations.

Writing LONG Data

In SQLBase, the sqlwlo function inserts or updates rows with LONG columns. The following code segment illustrates an INSERT of a row that contains a LONG column or an UPDATE of a LONG column. This operation takes place after the compile (sqlcom) and bind operations but before the execute (sqlexe) operation. It is executed for each LONG column specified in the statement. The data is read from a file called LONGTEXT.

```
FILE *fp, *fopen();
int count;
unsigned char col = 4;
char notebuf[500];

if ((fp = fopen ("longtext", "r")) == NULL)
   ... process file open error and exit

/* Read until end of file (count == 0) */
while (count = fread (notebuf, 1,sizeof(notebuf), fp))
{
   if (sqlwlo(cur, notebuf, count))  /* Write LONG */
      {
          /* Code to process error appears here */
      exit (1);
```

```
            }
    }
    if (sqlelo(cur))           /* End long operation */
    {
            /* Code to process error appears here */
        exit (1);
    }
    /* Execute the INSERT or UPDATE */
    if (sqlexe(cur))
        . . .
```

Using Multiple Handles

Only one SQL statement at a time can be processed for a given connection. This lets one handle, or connection ID, identify the SQL statement being processed during a connection: statements are processed serially, not simultaneously.

In SQLBase and a few other implementations, you can process more than one SQL statement at a time by allowing the program to make simultaneous connections using multiple handles. Only by opening multiple handles can a program manipulate more than one SQL statement at a time.

A common reason for wanting to do this is to make it possible to use an UPDATE or DELETE statement to make changes on the fly while processing the result of a query. For instance, by processing an UPDATE and a SELECT statement together, you can update each successive row of the query result *as it is fetched*. The update is performed faster and more economically than it would be if done as a separate operation.

The different handles are necessary so that the program can distinguish the operations to be performed on the different SQL statements as they are processed. One handle in the transaction is associated with the query and one with the UPDATE statement. As each row is fetched through the query handle, the UPDATE statement is executed using the second handle.

The following example shows a multihandle transaction. It uses two handles, one for the SELECT and one for the UPDATE. In the example, prices of items are changed depending on the supplier. As each item is fetched, a decision about price is made. If the price will be changed, an UPDATE is executed based on the current cursor position in the result set of the query. This is the most recently fetched row. A special phrase, CURRENT OF *cursor*, is used to specify this position.

The following SQL statements are used in this transaction:

```
SELECT ITEM, DESCRIPTION, PRICE FROM ITEM
WHERE SUPPLIER = :1

UPDATE ITEM SET PRICE = :1 WHERE CURRENT OF NEWPRICE
```

First you connect to the database using two handles:

```
sqlcnc (&cur1, "inventory/tj/x", 0) /* Connect to handle 1 */
sqlcnc (&cur2, "inventory/tj/x", 0) /* Connect to handle 2 */
```

Handle 1 must be associated with a statement name to use a CURRENT OF *cursor* phrase:

```
sqlscn (cur1, "NEWPRICE" ...) /* Name handle 1 */
```

Handle 1 manages the SELECT statement.

```
sqlcom (cur1, insitem, 0)                               /* Compile handle 1 */
sqlbnn (cur1, 1, &maxitem, sizeof(int),0,SQLPIITN) /* Bind data           */
sqlssb (cur1, 1, SQLPUIN, &itemno, sizeof(itemno), 0 SQLNPTR, SQLNPTR)
                                                        /* Set fetch buffers */
```

Handle 2 is used for the UPDATE statement.

```
sqlcom (cur2, updprice, 0) /* Compile handle 2 */
sqlexe (cur1)              /* Execute SELECT   */
```

Next, the loop of fetch and update begins. The following two statements are executed repeatedly until there are no more rows in the transaction:

```
sqlfet (cur1)              /* Fetch a row */
/* Display data and enter new price */
sqlexe (cur2)              /* Update price */
```

The fetch and update loop ends.

```
sqlcmt (cur1)              /* Commit transaction */
```

Suppose that after changing the prices for one supplier, you want to proceed to the price changes for another supplier. The previous statements could be stored (with the `sqlsto` function), and then retrieved (with the `sqlret` function) for each new supplier. This eliminates the need to compile the statements again, though the new data must be bound and the select buffers reset.

Result Set Operations

ANSI has recently added to the SQL standard a feature called *scroll cursors* that lets you use the result set of one query as the basis for subsequent queries from the same table or tables. The feature works by internally storing the row identifiers of the rows in a result table and using these as an additional constraint in subsequent queries. In effect, the WHERE clause of the current query is appended to the WHERE clause of the previous query such that each subsequent query inherits the search conditions of its predecessors.

Using result sets this way is useful for browsing: you can continue to narrow the focus of your queries without reiterating the previous search conditions.

Although using result sets this way is recognized by the ANSI standards, the feature is not widely implemented. We give an example anyway, using function calls from the SQLBase API, because the feature is a handy one and seems likely to be more widely implemented in the future. In SQLBase the feature is presently called result set mode and can be used both to query and to perform updates. In standard SQL, scroll cursors cannot be used to update. The standard SQL treatment of scroll cursors is discussed in Chapter 19, "Promising Developments and Extensions."

Using Result Sets

In the following example of the SQLBase result set mode feature, a user creates a result set in order to change the prices of items. First, all items are selected where the number sold is less than 1000. Then the query is changed to fetch only rows from a certain supplier. These rows are fetched and displayed on the screen. The price of certain items in the set is changed based on the user's decisions.

First, result set mode is entered with function sqlsrs ("start result set"):

```
sqlsrs (cur)    /* start result set */
```

Then a query establishing the initial result set and the outer bounds of subsequent queries is compiled and executed:

```
SELECT * FROM ITEM WHERE NUMSOLD < 1000
```

The next query addresses the ITEM table, but in effect ranges over only the rows in the result set of the previous query. In this query, you specify a supplier:

```
SELECT * FROM ITEM WHERE SUPPLIER = :1
```

The statement is compiled, output buffers are set, the supplier name is bound, the statement is executed, and rows are fetched. These rows are a subset of the rows in the result set of the first SELECT statement. All ITEMS returned are items in which the number sold is less than 1000 and the supplier is the supplier bound to :1. The rows are displayed on the screen in a scrollable fashion to permit the user to browse through them to select rows for update. A function (sqlprs) is available to position the cursor at any given row, which then becomes the current row. At this point an UPDATE statement can be executed to change the price of the row currently pointed to by the cursor.

When processing on the result set is completed, the (sqlcrs) function closes the result set and returns to the normal mode of processing.

A result set can be saved prior to closing and then restarted in result set mode again.

Data Consistency and Multiple Users

A number of issues arise when database access is shared among several users. One issue—who has the right to look at what—is addressed by implementing a scheme of authority levels and privileges, as discussed in Part 1. Another equally important issue has to do with ensuring that data remains consistent. Without some provision for safeguarding the consistency of the data in the face of changes made by multiple users, we would quickly come to grief.

Suppose, for instance, that two successive instructions are issued to change the price of cinnamon, currently priced at 45 cents. The first change involves raising the price by 7 cents; the second involves reducing it by 3 cents. The net change should be an increase of 4 cents so that the cinnamon is finally priced at 49 cents.

John receives the first instruction. He queries table INVENTORY to find the current price but does not immediately put through the update. In the meantime, Marsha receives the second instruction. She queries the table, sees the current price of 45 cents and updates this, reducing it 3 cents to 42 cents.

Finally, John does his update. His information is that cinnamon costs 45 cents, so he updates the price to 52 cents and commits the transaction.

But look what has happened. Because John queried the table *before* Marsha did her update, he based his update on information that became obsolete when Marsha made her change. And when John committed his update, he unwittingly committed it on top of Marsha's, overwriting hers. The net effect is as if Marsha's update never took place: the final price of cinnamon stands at 52 cents when it should be 49 cents.

When John determined that an increase of 7 cents should result in a new price of 52 cents, he was operating on the basis of data (from his query) that was no longer consistent with data in the database.

Locking

To prevent this kind of situation and its consequences, multiuser systems use various *locking* schemes. The locking scheme used by SQLBase and described here is modeled on that of DB2 and is similar to the schemes adopted by the majority of SQL implementations.

Depending on the implementation, locks are placed on individual rows (also called *records*) or on database *pages*. The size of a database page can vary with the implementation: in SQLBase, a page is 1024 bytes.

A page can contain any sort of data, including indexes and data from the system catalog. In systems with page-level locking, if a row is almost the size of a database page, only that row is locked. If a row is much smaller than a page, then a group of adjacent records that together more nearly make up a physical page are placed under the same lock.

In systems with record-level locking, only individual rows are locked.

Locking is automatic. An application program does not have to issue explicit locking calls to the engine; the engine itself issues the calls.

When a record is locked, whether the row is accessible to other users depends on the type of lock employed. There are two types, shared and exclusive.

With a *shared lock* (sometimes referred to as an S-lock) on a record, more than one user at a time can lock the record. A shared lock is placed on a record when the record is read (that is, during a SELECT). With an *exclusive lock* (X-lock), only one user at a time can use or lock the record. Exclusive locks are placed when a record will be modified (for example, during an UPDATE, INSERT or DELETE). Other users cannot open the record even for reading when an exclusive lock is in place.

If the system used by John and Marsha in the example featured locking, Marsha's update could be kept from vanishing. A shared lock would be placed on the row for cinnamon when John issued his query. Because the lock is a *shared* lock, Marsha could query the same row (and place her own shared lock on the row, incidentally) while John's lock is in place, but she could not modify the row.

Isolation Levels

How long a lock remains in place depends on the *level of isolation*, which can be chosen by the user. The different levels of isolation represent different levels or orders of stringency in the locking scheme. Their purpose is to address the fact that provisions you make to maintain consistency of data are likely to interfere with keeping the resources of the system easily and efficiently available to multiple users.

For example, suppose that John chooses a level of isolation such that locks are maintained for the duration of a transaction. Suppose, too, that instead of querying the table *before* John does his update, Marsha does not try to access the table until afterward. Now, when John does his update, an exclusive lock is placed on the record both he and Marsha need. This lock prevents Marsha from even querying that record, let alone updating it, until John commits. If John is slow to do this, Marsha could be made to wait some time.

The ease with which a system can be shared among users is commonly called *concurrency*. Striving for absolute data consistency costs you concurrency, so you have to balance the two virtues. The various levels of isolation let you strike this balance at different points.

The SQLBase-DB2 scheme of locking offers three levels of isolation: Read Repeatability (RR), Cursor Stability (CS), and Read Only (RO). These reflect different levels in the degree to which one user's activity in a database is isolated from other users'.

Read Repeatability

The highest level of isolation is called *Read Repeatability* (RR). With this level, locks are maintained during the entire transaction.

This isolation level derives its name from the fact that, with this level, however many times the same record of data is read (that is, queried) over the course of a transaction, the data is guaranteed not to change. Other readers of the data cannot update any records that have been read by the RR transaction while that transaction remains in progress. The last example, in which Marsha had to wait for John to commit, describes a situation that is possible with a Read Repeatability transaction.

This level of isolation ensures that data remains consistent until the user placing the lock is done, but it offers lower concurrency than may be practical for many multiuser situations.

Cursor Stability

Cursor Stability (CS) is so named because a record retains a shared lock only while the record is being read—that is, while the cursor is actually on the record. In this sense, the data at the cursor is stable. Shared locks are dropped, however, when the cursor leaves the record. Exclusive locks are retained for the entire transaction, as in the case of Read Repeatability.

If John reads record A and then reads record B, the shared lock on record A is released under Cursor Stability and Marsha can update the record. However, if John updates a row on record A, Marsha will still not be able to access that record until John has issued a COMMIT, regardless of which record John's cursor is currently on. This is because record A acquires an exclusive lock from the update, and exclusive locks are only released when a transaction is committed.

Cursor Stability provides higher concurrency but a lower likelihood of consistency than Read Repeatability because data that has been read as part of a transaction can be changed by other users of the system as each new record is read. Consequently, this isolation level still makes it possible for an update to be undone, as in the example. However, many implementations, including SQLBase, provide mechanisms for discovering whether data already read during a transaction has been updated by another user.

The Cursor Stability level is adequate for most applications dealing with data entry. In such applications, each data entry screen represents a single record, and although it is important to ensure that the record on the screen is locked (that is, remains stable) while it is read and modified, it usually is not necessary to maintain the lock after the user moves to the next record.

Read Only

Read Only (RO) is a special isolation level that involves no locking and therefore no waiting. It is used only for reading data, never for updating.

The Read Only level gives a user a snapshot view of the entire database, with all data as it existed as of the moment the Read Only transaction began. This level is especially useful when, for instance, a long report needs to be printed but the user does not want to delay other users who may want to update the database. If Read Repeatability is specified, other users cannot modify the records while they are being printed. If Cursor Stability is specified, the report might print records that are inconsistent with one another. With Read Only, the user is guaranteed consistent data, but the data may not be current to the last second.

Deadlocks

A *deadlock* occurs when two transactions are waiting for each other to release a shared lock on the same records so that they can place an exclusive lock on the records.

For example, if after querying and thus adding her shared lock to John's, Marsha waited for John to release his lock, John would find Marsha's lock when he went to update, and so John and Marsha would end up waiting for each other to release their locks.

Unless a condition like this is detected, the two transactions could wait indefinitely. For this reason, most implementations employ a mechanism to detect and deal with such situations. SQLBase, for instance, handles deadlocks by rolling back the transaction whose most recent request caused the problem. SQLBase then returns an error message to the application program, which must retry the transaction.

More on Rollbacks and Locking

In SQLBase, you can include data-definition and data-control statements, such as CREATE, DROP, and GRANT, in multistatement transactions without immediately following them with a COMMIT. In some implementations, however, you must issue a COMMIT after each of these statements, to end the transaction. Then, if a rollback happens later, the object of the CREATE, DROP or GRANT remains.

With SQLBase, the object of these statements is rolled back along with the rest of the transaction.

The issue here is that a rollback of a transaction containing uncommitted data-definition or data-control statements can lock other users out of records in the system catalog. These statements place locks on these records, and the locks are likely to remain if a transaction containing such statements is rolled back. Most of the time, therefore, you should commit after executing CREATE, DROP, ALTER or GRANT statements, even if you are not required to by the implementation.

Summary

This chapter discussed topics that go beyond the basic stages in the database access cycle. Special arrangements for reading and writing LONG data were mentioned. The chapter also described the provision in standard SQL—implemented by SQLBase—for querying just the rows in the result set of a preceding query, without reiterating the search conditions used by that query to select those rows.

The chapter closed with an examination of the issues of locking and concurrency for multiuser systems.

CHAPTER 16

Using a Precompiler Interface

As you saw in Chapter 14, "Using a Function Call Interface," when you program for a function call interface to a SQL database management system, you must provide function calls for every step in the processing of the embedded SQL statements. You do not have the luxury of letting the interface handle such clerical chores as setting output buffers and fetching successive rows as you did when you issued SQL statements interactively with the SQLTalk interface in Part 1, "Using the SQL Language."

Anyone wistful for those simpler arrangements will be glad to learn that there is an easier way to embed SQL. This approach combines much of the straightforwardness of an interactive interface with the power of function calls and is suitable for virtually all programming situations. The key is to use a precompiler.

What Is a Precompiler?

A *precompiler* (also called a *preprocessor*) is a program that analyzes another program and replaces higher-level source code with lower-level source code for a particular system.

For example, a SQL precompiler replaces SQL statements in a program with function calls for the particular SQL implementation that supports that precompiler. But precompilers are not unique to the SQL language. There are other kinds of precompilers as well, for other languages and systems—for the COBOL language itself, for instance. With a COBOL precompiler, you can write abbreviated, higher-level COBOL statements—just as with a SQL precompiler you can write higher-level SQL statements. The COBOL precompiler replaces the higher-level statements with lower-level COBOL code.

Every SQL implementation offers SQL precompilers for various popular programming languages, such as COBOL or C. A COBOL SQL precompiler replaces SQL statements with function calls in COBOL programs; a C SQL precompiler replaces SQL statements with function calls in C programs; and so forth.

As you have seen, in order for the database engine to process a SQL statement, the engine must be issued appropriate step-by-step instructions in the form of function calls. A SQL precompiler lets us write programs for performing database operations without having to code function calls ourselves. Rather, we merely issue SQL statements in the program, and sometimes some special precompiler statements too. We set these off with a special syntax to flag them for the precompiler.

Then we run the program through the precompiler, which *precompiles* it— that is, substitutes appropriate function calls for any SQL statements. Precompiling a program is thus an extra step we must take before we run the program, if we write for a precompiler. We cannot run the program without first precompiling it because the program lacks function calls until they are inserted by the precompiler. After the program is precompiled, though, it is just like the sort of program discussed in Chapter 14, "Using a Function Call Interface," and Chapter 15, "Advanced Programming with a Function Call Interface." The program contains function call code and is ready to run.

Think of a precompiler as being like the automatic dialing buttons on a telephone. To reach a number, you might have to enter a long-distance telephone service number, an access or security number, the area code, and the telephone number itself. You could easily make mistakes entering all these numbers manually, and it is tedious to do, besides. With an automatic dialer, you can enter the entire sequence by pressing perhaps just a single key.

Similarly with a precompiler. Instead of issuing function calls in your source program manually, you save trouble and reduce the risk of error by having a precompiler issue them for you.

Note, though, that using a precompiler is an alternative to using function calls only in a narrow sense. You are not circumventing the need for function calls when you use a precompiler any more than you are circumventing the need to enter all the appropriate digits when you use an automatic dialer. Both function calls and digits still need to be provided; you are just using a way of providing them automatically. Like an automatic dialer, a precompiler only does work that could be, and would otherwise have to be, done by hand.

Advantages of Precompilers

The main advantage of using a precompiler is that we do not have to code function calls manually. However, other advantages follow from this: because you do not have to code function calls, your programs can be shorter and you can write them more easily and in less time.

Consider, for example, the following COBOL program. This program uses the SQLBase COBOL function call interface to find the number of employees in a particular department:

```
SET PTR TO ADDRESS OF SELECT-STATEMENT.
CALL "MFSQLCOM" USING SQL-CURSOR, PTR, LEN, SQL-RETURN-CODE.

IF   SQL-RETURN-CODE NOT = ZERO
THEN MOVE "SELECT COMPILE" TO FAILURE-MSG
     GO TO 900-COMMON-ERROR-ROUTINE.

SET PTR TO ADDRESS OF EMP-COUNT.
MOVE 1 TO ITEM-NO.
CALL "MFSQLSSB" USING SQL-CURSOR, ITEM-NO, SQLPUIN, PTR, PDL,
                      SCALE, CVL, FSC, SQL-RETURN-CODE.

IF   SQL-RETURN-CODE NOT = ZERO
THEN MOVE "SET SELECT BUFFER" TO FAILURE-MSG
     GO TO 900-COMMON-ERROR-ROUTINE.

CALL "MFSQLEXE" USING SQL-CURSOR, SQL-RETURN-CODE.

IF   SQL-RETURN-CODE NOT = ZERO
THEN MOVE "EXECUTING SELECT" TO FAILURE-MSG
     GO TO 900-COMMON-ERROR-ROUTINE.

CALL "MFSQLFET" USING SQL-CURSOR, SQL-RETURN-CODE.

IF   SQL-RETURN-CODE = ZERO
THEN DISPLAY "EMPLOYEES IN DEPT 1: ", EMP-COUNT.

IF   SQL-RETURN-CODE NOT = 1
THEN MOVE "FETCH" TO FAILURE-MSG
     GO TO 900-COMMON-ERROR-ROUTINE.
```

By writing for a COBOL SQL precompiler, you can achieve the same result with the following few lines of code:

```
EXEC SQL
   SELECT COUNT(*) INTO :EMP-COUNT WHERE DEPT = 1
END-EXEC

DISPLAY "EMPLOYEES IN DEPT 1: ", EMP-COUNT.
```

Note the SQL statement set off for the precompiler with the elements EXEC SQL and END-EXEC.

How much code you can save by writing for a precompiler depends to some extent on the precompiler and the application, but a 50 percent reduction is common. This reduction obviously leads to comparable reductions in development time and coding errors.

The example also shows how much more easily you can keep track of what the program is supposed to be doing when you write for a precompiler. The higher-level, less fine-grained coding you do when you write for a precompiler better allows you to keep perspective on the overall logic of the program: you are less likely to lose sight of the woods for the trees.

These advantages are especially helpful to less experienced programmers, and that is in itself another advantage: precompilers enable less experienced programmers to do work that otherwise they could not do.

Another major advantage of coding for a precompiler is that the resulting programs are more portable—that is, they run more easily in, or can be ported to, different environments. Programs written for a precompiler can run unchanged on a wider range of computers, even on machines using different operating systems and different implementations of SQL. Programs written for a particular function call interface can run only with the SQL implementation that supports that interface and, generally speaking, only on computers of the same kind.

Every SQL implementation has a unique set of function calls. The calls in each set do much the same sorts of things but in different ways, and they work only with the implementation for which they were designed.

For example, SQLBase provides the `sqlfet` function call for fetching a row of data. Other implementations have function calls that fetch a row of data, too, but these function calls have different names and do not necessarily work the same way as `sqlfet`. At a minimum, to use a program containing the SQLBase call `sqlfet` on a different system, you have to change `sqlfet` and any other SQLBase calls to function calls appropriate to the other system.

But a program written for the SQLBase COBOL SQL precompiler, for example, is portable: it can be used as is with COBOL SQL precompilers for a variety of other SQL database systems. Each precompiler processes the program in the same way, replacing precompiler statements—SQL statements embedded in the program using the special precompiler syntax—with function calls. But which function calls are substituted depends on the precompiler. Each precompiler substitutes function calls appropriate to its particular system; the result is a version of the program adapted to run on the system for that precompiler. Thus, a program written for a precompiler can be used with many systems.

This portability of programs written for precompilers is possible because there is a de facto standard syntax for writing precompiler statements. If precompilers differed as much in their syntax requirements as function call interfaces do in their function calls, no advantage in portability would be gained by writing for precompilers. In fact, though, virtually all SQL precompilers use the syntax of the IBM DB2 SQL precompilers.

IBM supports the same SQL precompiler syntax for the programming languages COBOL, FORTRAN, PL/I, and assembly. Identical precompiler statements can be embedded in programs written in any of these languages. In fact, the influence of this syntax is so widespread that the syntax is often adopted even for precompilers designed for programming languages other than the four supported by IBM.

Because this syntax has acquired the status of a de facto standard, programs using this syntax for a SQL precompiler will be highly portable—at least as far as the SQL-related code goes. The language in which a program is written affects portability too though. Some programming languages are inherently more portable than others. COBOL and C, for instance, were designed to be very portable, and programs written in these languages transfer well from one environment to another. Other languages, such as FORTRAN and assembly, are more machine-dependent. Even assuming that translating the precompiler statements in programs written in these languages poses no difficulties, such programs likely will need other revisions before they can work in a new environment.

Limitations of Precompilers

Precompilers are not perfect. Because they generate code in a general-purpose, mechanical fashion, the result is not always as graceful as what you might produce doing the work yourself. For instance, code supplied by a precompiler may distort alignment or use cryptic naming conventions.

Potentially more serious is a precompiler's handling of SELECT, INSERT, UPDATE, and DELETE statements containing program variables, or *host variables*, as these variables are generally called in the context of precompilers. As we explained in Chapter 13, "SQL Programming Concepts," a major benefit of using program variables in SQL statements is that you can compile these statements once and then, without recompiling, use a looping procedure to execute them as many times as you have sets of new values to substitute. You do not have to compile the statement again for each new set of values.

A precompiler, however, may specify function call interface code to compile such statements again for each substitution. The precompiler "knows" only that a SQL statement must be compiled and executed, so it does both for each substitution. The precompiler is not sophisticated enough to specify a single compile operation and then set up a loop for multiple executions. As a result, an applications program that could benefit by using loops may run slower if it is written for a precompiler.

Fortunately, there are ways to solve this problem. One way is to use an advanced precompiler feature called *dynamic SQL*. Precompilers with this feature have two additional precompiler statements, PREPARE and PERFORM, for separating the compile and execute operations.

When a SQL statement is embedded in an application program with the PREPARE statement, the precompiler supplies code only for compiling the statement, not for executing it. Function calls for executing the statement are given only when the precompiler encounters an EXECUTE statement. Thus, for multiple executions without recompiling, you can code a single PREPARE statement and put the PERFORM statement in a loop to execute the compiled statement once for each substitution of values.

Another way to avoid redundant compiles is to manually code function calls and a looping procedure for any SQL statements containing program variables, and then use precompiler statements everywhere else. This approach works because the precompiler cares only about precompiler statements, which it replaces with function call code. Everything else, including any function call code you have written yourself, the precompiler leaves unchanged. The function call code you write may make the program less portable, but you are no worse off for that than if you did not have a precompiler in the first place, and you remain a good deal better off in other respects.

The next chapter describes the specifics of coding for a precompiler and the syntax for writing precompiler statements. Because COBOL is the most popular programming language for writing for a SQL precompiler, we use a SQL precompiler for the COBOL language.

Summary

Precompilers are an alternative to manually coding function calls in a SQL applications program. You can code higher-level precompiler statements, consisting of SQL statements coded using a special precompiler syntax. The SQL precompiler replaces these statements with appropriate function calls.

In addition to being easier to write, programs written for a precompiler are shorter, require less development time, are easier to understand and revise, and are less likely to contain errors. They also are more portable and can be run more easily in different environments.

CHAPTER 17

Using a COBOL SQL Precompiler

This chapter explains how to code for a precompiler that uses the IBM DB2 precompiler syntax. This syntax has become a virtual standard for all sorts of SQL precompilers; as a result, application programs written using the IBM DB2 syntax can be run with precompilers for different SQL systems. We describe the principal operations that must be provided for when you code for this type of precompiler, and we also describe some important conventions and resources.

For reference and to dramatize how much simpler it can be to write applications for precompilers, two functionally equivalent programs—one written using the SQLBase function call interface for COBOL and one written for the SQLBase SQL/Preprocessor for COBOL—are included in Appendix C, "Sample COBOL Programs," for readers to compare. In this chapter, selections of code that list line numbers (for example, 007500) are excerpted from the precompiler program in Appendix C.

Syntax of Precompiler Statements

This section describes three matters relating to syntax: delimiting SQL statements in code so that the precompiler can recognize them as such; delimiting COBOL statements; and using the SELECT * formulation to specify all columns of a table in the SELECT list. A fourth matter, when to precede host variables with a colon, is discussed in the section on host variables. (*Host variables* are what program variables occurring in SQL statements are customarily called in precompiler literature. We adopt that usage in this chapter.)

For the precompiler to be able to identify the SQL statements for which it is to supply function calls in a COBOL application program, these statements must be set off or *delimited* in some way. The strings EXEC SQL and END-EXEC are used for this purpose: EXEC SQL marks the beginning of a SQL statement, and END-EXEC marks the end. Each of these delimiters should appear on its own line. For example:

```
EXEC SQL
  UPDATE EMP
  SET EMP_SAL = EMP_SAL * (1 + :raise)
  WHERE EMP_NO = :employee
END-EXEC.
```

The precompiler converts each delimited SQL statement, including the delimiters, to a comment and follows this with the SQL statement's equivalent in function call code.

Note the trailing period after the END-EXEC delimiter in the example. This period marks the end of the preceding *COBOL* statement. When multiple SQL statements are coded with no COBOL statements in between, this period must be present after the trailing END-EXEC of each SQL statement.

If only one SQL statement occurs between two COBOL statements, however, then a terminating period may or may not be necessary, depending on the scope you want the preceding COBOL statement to have.

For instance, if you do not code a trailing period on the END-EXEC (line 008500) in the following example, then the next line of code (line 008700) will fall within the scope of the IF/THEN clause. This will cause PRT-HOURLY-PAY to be updated only when HOURLY-PAY is greater than $4 per hour. You need to put a period after line 008500, as shown, to restrict the scope of the IF/THEN so that updating PRT-HOURLY-PAY does not depend on HOURLY-PAY being greater than 4.

```
007900     IF    HOURLY-PAY > 4
008000     THEN MOVE "FIRED!" TO PRT-REMARKS
008100          MOVE 0        TO HOURLY-PAY
008200          EXEC SQL
008300             DELETE FROM EMP
008400                WHERE CURRENT OF FETCUR
008500          END-EXEC.
008600
008700     MOVE HOURLY-PAY TO PRT-HOURLY-PAY.
```

Another issue related to syntax is the use of the asterisk as a shorthand for "all columns" in the SELECT list.

In the discussion of interactive SQL, we introduced the convention of using an asterisk in the SELECT list of queries to select from all columns of a single table named in the FROM clause. Using the asterisk in that context is equivalent to listing the names of all columns in the table in the order in which they are defined in the table.

Using the SELECT * syntax is allowed in application programs for a precompiler too, but is best avoided, for several reasons.

In the first place, if you change a table's definition—add a new column, for instance—you might have to modify any program that used a SELECT * against the table. The SELECT * would automatically retrieve the additional column, but the program would lack provisions for handling the extra column of output. If you name columns in the SELECT list rather than use an asterisk, you do not have to revise the program.

Second, listing the columns in the SELECT list makes it easier to see the relationship between the columns being selected and the host variables named in the INTO clause. In other words, avoiding the SELECT * usage makes applications more self-documenting.

Finally, using SELECT * slightly slows performance because internally SQL has to translate the asterisk into the appropriate column names.

All told, it is best not to use SELECT * with application programs, but only with an interactive interface. This is how SELECT * is intended to be used.

Connecting to a Database

As we remarked in the last chapter, COBOL SQL precompilers tend to be closely modeled on the DB2 precompiler. But DB2 does not presently support either multiple connections or multiple databases. This makes it unnecessary in DB2 either to use handles (which identify different simultaneous connections) or to specify the database we want to connect to. In DB2, there is only *the* database, and connections are made automatically, using a user's operating system ID, when a SELECT or other SQL statement is issued. There is no provision for issuing an explicit CONNECT statement.

As a result, other SQL systems need to depart from the DB2 model to provide for multiple connections or to connect to a particular database with a precompiler application program.

One approach is to make available a precompiler statement for generating code in the application program to establish a connection. SQLBase, for instance, offers the CONNECT TO statement:

```
EXEC SQL
  CONNECT TO database_name/user_name/password
END-EXEC
```

The CONNECT TO statement is peculiar to SQLBase, however, so including it in an application program prevents you from using the application with a precompiler for another system (such as DB2).

Alternatively, you can specify your user name, your password, and the name of the database you want to connect to as parameters on the command line when you run the precompiler. This causes the precompiler to generate appropriate code in the precompiler output without your having to code statements specific to a particular implementation. The precompiler application in Appendix C, "Sample COBOL Programs," which contains no provision for connecting, could be run as is by this method.

SELECT Statements that Return Multiple Rows

For a query to retrieve a result set consisting of more than one row, you need to declare a cursor and then perform a fetch. You must provide for both these operations in an application program for a precompiler just as you do when you code for a function call interface. For a precompiler application, however, the mechanics are much simpler. We describe these mechanics in this and the next few sections.

As explained in Chapter 1, when a query that retrieves multiple rows is executed, the database engine positions a cursor on the first, or current, row to be retrieved and awaits an instruction to fetch the row.

Using the cursor to keep track of your row position in the result set, you can sequentially fetch each row one at a time. The first fetch in the application reads the first row in the result set, the second fetch reads the second row in the result set, the third fetch reads the third row, and so on, until you get a NOT FOUND condition, signifying that there are no more rows to be fetched. At this point, you close the cursor.

Depending on the SQL implementation, an application program may even be able to use multiple cursors simultaneously on different queries. Having multiple active cursors makes possible simultaneous queries and sophisticated update and delete operations performed on the rows picked out by the respective cursors as the rows are retrieved. Simultaneous operations of this sort are discussed in Chapter 15, "Advanced Programming with a Function Call Interface."

In any case, in a precompiler application as in a function call application, each cursor used must be declared with a DECLARE CURSOR statement, opened with an OPEN statement, read with a FETCH statement (most often in a looping process), and closed with a CLOSE statement.

This section next shows some examples that illustrate the logic of a program that declares and uses a cursor to process a set of rows. The complete program that is the source of all the excerpts used with numbered lines is in Appendix C, "Sample COBOL Programs."

In this program, the cursor is used to process a set of rows from a table of employees, EMP. The name of each employee from Department 2 is selected and printed in a report. Additionally, any employee earning less than $2 per hour is given a raise and any employee earning more than $4 per hour is fired. Any salary adjustments or dismissals are reported in a remarks area in the report.

The first operation is to define the cursor. This is done with a DECLARE CURSOR statement, which names the cursor and specifies the SELECT statement with which the cursor will be associated:

```
003900     EXEC SQL
004000       DECLARE FETCUR CURSOR FOR
004100         SELECT EMPNO, FIRST_NAME, INITIAL, LAST_NAME,
004200              FIRST_DAY, HRLY_PAY
004300         FROM EMP
004400         WHERE DEPT = 2
004500         FOR UPDATE OF HRLY_PAY
004600     END-EXEC.
```

The DECLARE CURSOR statement names the cursor FETCUR. The SELECT statement defines the set of rows that the cursor will retrieve—in this case, all employees in Department 2.

Notice the FOR UPDATE OF clause at the end of the query. Most SQL systems (although not SQLBase) require a FOR UPDATE OF clause in the SELECT statement (as shown in the example) if an update will be performed using the cursor position in the result set of the query. The FOR UPDATE OF clause names any columns that the program may intend to update. If a column is not named in the FOR UPDATE OF clause, the column cannot be updated and you get an error code if you try.

The FOR UPDATE OF clause is appended to the end of a SELECT statement. In general, the precompiler syntax for a query whose result set will be used to do updates is

```
EXEC SQL
  DECLARE cursorname CURSOR FOR
    SELECT column names
    FROM table(s) or view(s)
    WHERE search condition
  FOR UPDATE OF column names
END-EXEC.
```

The column names in the FOR UPDATE OF clause can be different from the column names specified in the SELECT list. The updates will be performed as a separate operation using a CURRENT OF *cursor* phrase, as you will see.

SELECT statements that include the SQL keyword DISTINCT, a UNION operator, an aggregate or other function, a GROUP BY clause, a HAVING clause, or an ORDER BY clause are considered read-only and cannot be used with FOR UPDATE OF or the CURRENT OF *cursor* phrase. SELECT statements also are considered read-only if the FROM clause lists more than one table or uses a view that cannot be updated.

After declaring the cursor, the program can use it to process the first row of the set of rows. But first the program needs to open it. You open a cursor just as you would open a sequential file: with an OPEN statement. The following code opens cursor FETCUR:

```
004800     EXEC SQL
004900        OPEN FETCUR
005000     END-EXEC.
```

In executing this code, the application program tells SQL to process the SELECT statement defined in the DECLARE CURSOR statement. Processing this statement positions the cursor at the first row in the result set.

The WHENEVER Statement

Now the program is almost ready to enter the fetch loop. But first we need to provide a way to let the program escape from the loop after it enters. One way is to supply code that directs the program, after each fetch, to check an area in the program called the SQL Communication Area, or SQLCA, to see whether the cursor has reached the end of the data.

The SQLCA contains several fields with information to help the programmer track how SQL is performing. The SQLCODE field, for instance, is updated every time a SQL statement is processed and indicates whether the statement was processed successfully. A value of 100 in the SQLCODE field means that no more rows were found. You can make use of this field by coding the following after the FETCH statement to get the program out of the fetch loop:

```
IF   SQLCODE = 100
THEN GO TO 800-CLOSE-CURSOR.
```

Actually, the SQLBase engine returns a value of 1 to indicate end of data. DB2, however, returns a value of 100. For the sake of consistency with DB2 usage, the SQLBase precompiler accepts code specifying 100 and translates this to 1 for the engine. In writing for the precompiler, therefore, you specify 100 as the value of SQLCODE to indicate end of data.

Another way to escape the fetch loop, the WHENEVER statement, is offered by the precompiler itself.

The WHENEVER statement uses the SQLCA too, checking to see whether one of three possible conditions is met. If the condition is not met, the program continues processing; if it is met, the program branches to a specified routine.

You can specify one of three conditions for the WHENEVER statement to flag: NOT FOUND, SQLERROR, and SQLWARNING. Each reflects a certain value in a different field in the SQLCA.

The NOT FOUND condition alerts you when the engine cannot find a (further) row to satisfy the SQL statement. Because this condition is true whenever SQLCODE equals 100, a WHENEVER statement specifying this condition has the same effect as the sample code just listed.

The second condition available for use in a WHENEVER statement, SQLERROR, indicates that SQL has discovered an error while attempting a SQL operation.

The third condition, SQLWARNING, occurs when SQL has flagged a warning when executing a SQL statement.

To let the program escape from a fetch loop, we want to code a WHENEVER NOT FOUND statement, as follows:

```
005200      EXEC SQL
005300          WHENEVER NOT FOUND
005400              GO TO 800-CLOSE-CURSOR
005500      END-EXEC.
```

The SQL Communication Area

As we said, the SQL Communications Area contains a number of fields with useful information about the system.

The SQLCA is defined in a COBOL application as follows:

```
01  SQLCA.
    05 SQLCAID       PIC X(8) VALUE "SQLCA".
    05 SQLCABC       PIC S9(9) COMP VALUE 136.
    05 SQLCODE       PIC S9(9) COMP.
    05 SQLERRM.
        49 SQLERRML  PIC S9(4) COMP.
        49 SQLERRMC  PIC X(70).
    05 SQLERRP       PIC X(8).
    05 SQLERRD       OCCURS 6 TIMES PIC S9(9) COMP.
    05 SQLWARN.
        10 SQLWARN0  PIC X(1).
        10 SQLWARN1  PIC X(1).
        10 SQLWARN2  PIC X(1).
        10 SQLWARN3  PIC X(1).
        10 SQLWARN4  PIC X(1).
        10 SQLWARN5  PIC X(1).
        10 SQLWARN6  PIC X(1).
        10 SQLWARN7  PIC X(1).
    05 SQLEXT        PIC X(8).
```

Many precompilers require an application program to include this code. Some precompilers, among them the SQLBase precompiler, for instance, automatically generate the code if it is not provided.

The SQLCA is a useful tool for debugging a SQL application program, and it is a good idea to provide a routine for viewing the various components of the SQLCA. In particular, it is important to track the return code (SQLCODE), the number of rows that SQL inserted, updated, or deleted (SQLERRD(3)), and whether any warning flags have been turned on (SQLWARN0).

The following fields make up the SQLCA, as implemented by the COBOL DB2 precompiler. Precompilers of other SQL systems use the same fields but sometimes implement them differently and generally do not implement them all.

SQLCAID: A header string that identifies this structure as the SQL Communication Area. The value of this field should always be "SQLCA".

SQLCABC: The length of the SQL Communication Area. The value of this field should always be 136.

SQLCODE: The return code reflecting the results of the previous SQL statement. As we mentioned, a value of 0 means that the statement executed successfully, a negative number means that an error occurred, and a positive number means that the statement executed but an exception has occurred. A value of 100 in this field is a special case indicating that a fetch did not find the first or next row or that an INSERT, UPDATE, or DELETE statement failed to add, change, or remove any rows because no rows satisfied the search condition.

SQLERRM: A variable-length string describing an error condition. As with all variable length fields, the first element (SQLERRML) tells you the length of the string and the second element (SQLERRMC) contains the data.

SQLERRP: Unused character string.

SQLERRD: An array of six numeric fields. The third field, SQLERRD(3), is the only field of any importance to an application. The value in SQLERRD(3) tells you how many rows were just inserted, updated, or deleted.

SQLWARN: This is a group item made up of the elementary fields SQLWARN0 through SQLWARN7, described as follows:

SQLWARN0: Set to *W* if any of the following warning fields have been flagged with a warning.

SQLWARN1: Set to *W* if truncation occurred when data was moved to a host variable. Normally, this means that the declared width of the host variable was insufficient to handle the data. This condition may be acceptable, depending on the circumstances.

SQLWARN2: This third warning field, like the others, indicates a condition that may not be an error but could be important for the programmer to know about. If set to *W*, this field indicates that one or more null values were disregarded when functions such as AVG, SUM, MIN, or MAX were computed.

SQLWARN3: Set to *W* if the number of host variables in a SQL statement is not equal to the number of columns in the table or view.

SQLWARN4: Set to *W* if the application program attempts to execute an UPDATE or DELETE statement that does not contain a WHERE clause, if the statement was compiled with a dynamic SQL PREPARE statement.

SQLWARN5: Set to *W* if the application program attempts to use a SQL statement that is valid only in a SQL/DS environment.

SQLWARN6: Set to *W* if SQL adjusts a derived date or TIMESTAMP value to account for the last day of the month.

SQLWARN7: Reserved.

SQLEXT: Unused character string.

The WHENEVER option gives you a way to check the fields in the SQLCA without extensive coding. You can specify two types of actions with a WHENEVER condition. You can issue a CONTINUE statement directing the application program to continue its execution, or you can code a GO TO statement. A WHENEVER statement affects all subsequent source SQL statements until another WHENEVER statement is encountered.

Fetching

Now we are ready to issue a FETCH statement.

The SELECT statement defined by the DECLARE CURSOR statement identifies the rows of the result set but does not by itself bring any data into the application program. When we issue a FETCH in the application program, SQL uses the previously opened cursor to point at the next row in the result set. This next row becomes the current row. SQL then moves the contents of this row into the host variables specified in the INTO clause of the FETCH statement:

```
006000     EXEC SQL
006100        FETCH FETCUR
006200          INTO :EMPLOYNO, :FIRST-NAME, :MIDDLE-INITIAL,
006300               :LAST-NAME, :START-DATE, :HOURLY-PAY
006400     END-EXEC.
```

This fetch operation retrieves into the specified host variables the columns named earlier in the SELECT statement associated with the FETCUR cursor when FETCUR was declared.

SQL maintains the position of the current row until the application program issues another FETCH. Knowing that the cursor is still on that row enables you to issue an UPDATE or DELETE for the row, using the CURRENT OF *cursor* phrase. This phrase applies the UPDATE or DELETE to the row currently under the cursor.

For example, in the sample program, we update the employee's hourly pay if the employee's rate is less than $2 per hour:

```
007000      IF   HOURLY-PAY < 2
007100      THEN MOVE "PAY INCREASE" TO PRT-REMARKS
007200           MOVE 2               TO HOURLY-PAY
007300           EXEC SQL
007400             UPDATE EMP
007500               SET HRLY_PAY = 2
007600               WHERE CURRENT OF FETCUR
007700           END-EXEC.
```

An UPDATE or DELETE with a CURRENT OF *cursor* phrase differs from other updates and deletes in that it updates only one row—the row that the cursor is on.

The following example shows a DELETE statement using the CURRENT OF *cursor* phrase. In this example, any employee who has an hourly pay greater than $4 per hour is dismissed:

```
007900      IF   HOURLY-PAY > 4
008000      THEN MOVE "FIRED!" TO PRT-REMARKS
008100           MOVE 0          TO HOURLY-PAY
008200           EXEC SQL
008300             DELETE FROM EMP
008400               WHERE CURRENT OF FETCUR
008500           END-EXEC.
```

After the current row is updated or deleted, it cannot be updated or deleted again because it no longer exists as such. To establish a new current row, we must issue another FETCH.

When the program has fetched beyond the last row, the WHENEVER statement causes the program to branch to the paragraph named 800-CLOSE-CURSOR. Now the cursor must be closed. The following code from the sample program closes the FETCUR cursor:

```
009100 800-CLOSE-CURSOR.
009200      EXEC SQL
009300        CLOSE FETCUR
009400      END-EXEC.
```

Whenever the application program either completes or aborts a transaction—that is, if the program issues either a COMMIT or a ROLLBACK—all open cursors are automatically closed by SQL. After a cursor is closed, any row position marked by that cursor is lost. If you want to issue a COMMIT (or ROLLBACK) before you have fetched all rows that you want to process, you have to arrange in the program to reestablish cursor positions before you can resume fetching where you left off.

The SELECT INTO Statement

The precompiler makes available an additional clause—the INTO clause—that you can use with SELECT statements you do not expect to return more than one row. The clause goes after the SELECT clause and before the FROM clause in a query:

```
EXEC SQL
   SELECT column names
   INTO host variables
   FROM table(s) or view(s)
   WHERE search condition
END-EXEC
```

The clause, like the INTO clause used with the FETCH statement, lists the host variables into which you want to put the values retrieved by the SELECT.

For convenience, we sometimes refer to a SELECT statement that contains an INTO clause as a SELECT INTO statement.

Singling out SELECT statements that return only one row for different treatment from SELECT statements that return multiple rows saves some work. As we said, for a query to return *more* than one row in its result, you have to institute a fetch procedure, which entails declaring a cursor and associating it with the particular SELECT statement, opening the cursor, fetching the result set of rows one at a time, and finally closing the cursor when you are done.

SQL can return *a single row*, however, without your having to declare a cursor or do a fetch. You can use a SELECT INTO statement to have SQL do this for you. With a SELECT INTO statement, you still must specify what you want done with the row (analogous to specifying host variables in the INTO clause of a FETCH), but you do not have to code DECLARE CURSOR, OPEN, CLOSE, or FETCH statements.

In the INTO clause, you indicate what you want done with the result row. You can either specify a host variable for each item in the SELECT list, or you can simply name the host structure where all the variables you want to use are listed. (Host structures are discussed later in this chapter.)

When you list host variables in the INTO clause of a SELECT INTO statement, the value of the first item in the SELECT list is returned into the first host variable you specify, the value of the second column is returned into the second host variable, and so on, just as with the INTO clause of a FETCH.

In the following SELECT statement, the employee's name, EMP_NAME, is fetched and returned into the host variable :employee:

```
EXEC SQL
  SELECT EMP_NAME
  INTO :employee
  FROM EMP
  WHERE EMP_NO = :emp-no
END-SQL
```

We expect this SELECT statement to return at most one row because we know that every employee is supposed to have a unique employee number. Perhaps we have a unique index on EMP_NO, enforcing uniqueness for all rows in that column.

If the WHERE clause allows more than one row to be returned, SQL returns an error code in the SQLCODE field of the SQLCA and does not retrieve any rows.

Host Variables

Host variables were mentioned in several contexts in this chapter; here we say a few words about them in their own right.

A host variable is a field defined in an application program and used by SQL statements in one of three ways. A host variable can be the *destination* for data retrieved from the database—the output buffers described in Chapter 13, "SQL Programming Concepts." A host variable can be the *source* of data to be entered into the database—the input buffers mentioned in Chapter 13. And finally, a host variable can be used in a *search condition* (that is, in a WHERE clause).

We have already shown host variables used as the destination for data that was output by the database in the INTO clauses of FETCH and SELECT INTO statements. Here is an example of a host variable—department, preceded by a colon—used in a WHERE clause:

```
EXEC SQL
  DECLARE FETCUR CURSOR FOR
    SELECT EMPNO, FIRST_NAME, INITIAL, LAST_NAME,
           FIRST_DAY, HRLY_PAY
    FROM EMP
    WHERE DEPT = :department
    FOR UPDATE OF HRLY_PAY
END-EXEC.
```

Making the department number in the WHERE clause a host variable rather than a constant saves us from having to write a similar program for every department in the company. Rather, we can run the same query for any department just by specifying a different value for the variable.

The next example, using an UPDATE statement, shows a host variable used as the source of data to be entered into the database. The example is based on a passage in the sample precompiler program in Appendix C, "Sample COBOL Programs." There the code uses constants to update an employee's hourly pay to $4 per hour if the employee previously earned less than $2 per hour. By making the minimum salary a host variable instead of using the constant value of $2 per hour, we can generalize the program:

```
007000      IF    HOURLY-PAY < minimum-hourly-pay
007100      THEN MOVE "PAY INCREASE"        TO PRT-REMARKS
007200           MOVE minimum-hourly-pay    TO HOURLY-PAY
007300      EXEC SQL
007400         UPDATE EMP
007500            SET HRLY_PAY = :minimum-hourly-pay
007600            WHERE CURRENT OF FETCUR
007700      END-EXEC.
```

Notice that the program data name minimum-hourly-pay is used three times. The first two times (lines 007000 and 007200), it is used as a COBOL variable name and is not preceded by a colon. The third time (line 007500), it is used as a SQL host variable preceded by a colon. All three instances refer to the same variable.

Host variable names in SQL statements do not necessarily have to be preceded by a colon. Whether they do depends on the context. For instance, you can omit the colon with host variables in an INTO clause. The precompiler understands that whatever follows the INTO keyword in a SELECT INTO statement must be a host variable, so theoretically you can leave out the colon.

Nevertheless, it is good programming practice to use a colon with every occurrence of a host variable in a SQL statement. There is no good reason *not* to use a colon in these situations, and using one improves clarity and saves having to keep in mind some rather technical rules.

On the other hand, you must not use colons with variables that appear in COBOL code proper—that is, code that is not a part of a SQL statement—even if the variable is the same as one also used (and preceded by a colon) in a SQL statement. SQL precompilers understand colons, but COBOL does not.

The following example shows host variables used in an INSERT statement:

```
100-INSERT-DATA.
    READ INPUT-FILE INTO IN-REC
      AT END CLOSE INPUT-FILE
          GO TO 900-MAIN-EXIT.
    EXEC SQL
      INSERT INTO EMP VALUES
        (:IN-FIRST-NAME, :IN-INITIAL, :IN-LAST-NAME,
         :EMP-NO, :DEPTNO, :IN-START-DATE, :HOURLY-PAY)
    END-EXEC.
    GO TO 100-INSERT-DATA.
```

Whatever values are read from the sequential file INPUT-FILE into the host variables are inserted into the database.

Host variables can be used only in place of data values, by the way. They cannot be used to substitute table names, view names, or column names. For example, we *cannot* use host variables in the following fashion, even though the prospect of creating what amounts to a generic query may look tempting:

```
EXEC SQL
  SELECT :column1, :column2, :column3, :column4
    INTO :field-1, :field-2, :field-3, :field-4
    FROM :tablename
    WHERE :fieldname = :search-field
END-EXEC.
```

Assignment rules cover the use of host variables, whether for doing a FETCH or SELECT of a column value *into* a host variable or for doing an INSERT or UPDATE using values *from* a host variable. In general, assignment rules are similar from one SQL implementation to another, but they vary in the flexibility they allow in data conversions. In DB2, for example, numeric fields and character fields are incompatible, and data from a host variable with a CHAR data type cannot be inserted in a SQL column defined as INTEGER, say. SQLBase, on the other hand, will convert the character data to numeric if the data in the character field is made up entirely of digits.

COBOL Host Structures

In INTO clauses and in the VALUES clause of an INSERT statement, you will often want to use a number of host variables. There is a labor-saving alternative to listing all the host variables in the clause itself: you can define a *host structure* where they are listed once and then refer to them collectively (in the order they are listed) simply by naming the host structure.

A *host structure* is a group of host variables used collectively as the source or destination for a set of selected values—for example, as a set of values to be inserted into or selected from the columns of a row. Here, for example, is a host structure called EMPLOYEE-ADDRESS:

```
01 EMPLOYEE-INFORMATION.
   02 EMPLOYEE-ADDRESS.
      03 EMPLOYEE-STREET  PIC X(20).
      03 EMPLOYEE-CITY    PIC X(20).
      03 EMPLOYEE-STATE   PIC X(02).
      03 EMPLOYEE-ZIP     PIC X(10).
```

In the example, the EMPLOYEE-ADDRESS host structure appears as a substructure of another structure, EMPLOYEE-INFORMATION. The host structure itself has two levels, one listing the name of the structure, and one consisting of four elementary data items, or host variables. Host structures ordinarily are limited to a maximum of two levels.

When you refer in a SQL statement to names of host variables for which a host structure has been defined, you can either give just the name of the host variable, or you can give the name of the host variable qualified (that is, preceded) by the name of the structure followed by a period: for example, EMPLOYEE-ADDRESS.EMPLOYEE-STREET. This STRUCTURE.FIELD naming convention allows us to uniquely pick out a host variable name that may be duplicated in another structure. The convention, borrowed from the PL/I language and similar to the OF clause in COBOL, is valid in COBOL only when it is used within a SQL statement.

After you have defined a host structure, you can refer to the host structure rather than having to name each host variable individually.

For example, suppose that you have defined the following structure:

```
01  EMPLOYEE-DATA.
    02  EMPLOYEE-FIRST-NAME      PIC X(20).
    02  EMPLOYEE-MIDDLE-INITIAL  PIC X(01).
    02  EMPLOYEE-LAST-NAME       PIC X(20).
```

You can now use the following SQL statement to retrieve the name of a particular employee into the host structure just defined. Because you have defined the structure, you do not have to name all the host variables in the INTO clause of the SQL statement itself:

```
EXEC SQL
  SELECT FIRST_NAME, INITIAL, LAST_NAME
    INTO :EMPLOYEE-DATA
    FROM EMP
    WHERE EMPNO = :employee
END-EXEC.
```

Declaring Table and View Definitions

COBOL SQL application programs are not required to provide table or view definitions—the name, length and data type of every column the table contains—describing each table or view the program uses, but there are a couple of advantages to giving them anyway.

First, a program that declares this information is more self-documenting. It is convenient to be able to refer to this information in the DECLARE statement as you code.

Second, including this information helps avoid compile errors. When a declaration of the tables and views is included, the precompiler uses it to verify that you have coded correct column names and used correct data types in your SQL statements.

Many precompilers, in fact, include a programming tool called a *declaration generator* that automatically produces the DECLARE statements that should be included in the application program.

The DB2 precompiler, for instance, has a declaration generator program called DCLGEN. The DCLGEN program reads the SQL system tables and produces the complete SQL DECLARE statement for any table or view specified. DCLGEN also creates a Data Division structure that matches the table or view column data types.

If you do not have a declaration generator, you can declare table and view definitions manually by writing a DECLARE TABLE statement in the application program's Data Division. To code a DECLARE TABLE, you indicate the table's name and then list each column name with the column data type.

Even if the table is a view, you code DECLARE *name* TABLE, not DECLARE *name* VIEW. The precompiler always looks for the keyword TABLE as the third token.

An example of the DECLARE TABLE statement for the EMP employee table follows:

```
EXEC SQL
   DECLARE EMP TABLE
      (FIRST_NAME CHAR(20),
       INITIAL    CHAR(01),
       LAST_NAME  CHAR(20),
       EMPNO INTEGER,
           DEPT       INTEGER,
           FIRST_DAY  DATE,
           HRLY_PAY   DECIMAL(5,2))
   END-EXEC.
```

Summary

This chapter covered the principal operations that must be coded when you write for a precompiler. Topics included coding for SELECT statements that use a cursor to return multiple rows; how to run a query and simultaneously perform updates and deletes using the CURRENT OF *cursor* phrase; alternatives for coding a way out of a fetch loop; and, with queries that return only a single row, using an INTO clause so that you do not have to declare a cursor and do a fetch.

Host variables also were discussed, and how to set up a host structure to define a set of host variables all at once.

CHAPTER 18

Using a dBASE Interface

We have looked at two ways to use SQL in application programs written in a procedural language: by embedding SQL function calls and by embedding SQL statements for a precompiler. With the advent of Ashton-Tate's dBASE IV and the dBASE-language dBXL and Quicksilver interfaces from WordTech, a third way of using SQL has emerged: now it is possible to embed SQL in applications written in the dBASE language, or even to write SQL applications in dBASE-language code without overtly using SQL at all.

Because the new dBASE-language products work with different SQL engines, the decision which to choose may depend to some degree on the choice of a SQL DBMS. The dBASE IV product, for instance, is for use with Ashton-Tate's new SQL engine; the new WordTech/SQL dBXL and Quicksilver products come in different versions for SQLBase, ORACLE, and Novell. Except where they differ in the dBASE or SQL extensions that they offer, however, the products generally are similar in their syntax and use SQL in much the same way.

The appearance of these dBASE/SQL products is noteworthy for at least a couple of reasons. One, it further underscores SQL's growing dominance as the standard language for database management; two, by adding the dBASE language to the list of procedural languages in which SQL applications can be written, the new dBASE-language products make SQL accessible to thousands of dBASE programmers.

The dBASE language differs from C and COBOL in some important respects. dBASE is a higher-level language: operations do not have to be specified in the same detail. The dBASE language has the programming control structures of a procedural language, but it also has an English-like syntax and many built-in provisions specifically designed for retrieving and managing data and for creating user interface screens. These features have contributed to the dBASE language's longstanding popularity as a language for database management and application programming for microcomputers.

SQL lacks programming structures, so it must be embedded in order to be used in applications. But SQL is more powerful and efficient than the dBASE language when it comes to managing data. SQL code is more compact than dBASE-language code to do the same thing, and indeed with SQL we can do more things. By using the two languages together, dBASE users get the best of both worlds: the familiar programming structures and ease of use of the dBASE language, and the superior data management capabilities of SQL.

Besides being a higher-level language than either C or COBOL, the dBASE language differs from these languages in another way: it was designed to be used with an *interpreter* rather than with a *compiler*.

An interpreter translates a line of higher-level dBASE-language source code into lower-level executable code and runs the line immediately. An interpreter is thus especially suited for situations in which code will be entered interactively. SQLTalk, for instance, is an interpreter. Programs can be written for an interpreter, but they take longer to execute because the source code is translated only at run time, as the program is run.

With a compiler, an entire program of source code can be translated in advance. The compiled version then can be loaded into memory and run without time having to be spent on translation along the way. Nor does the program have to be recompiled to be run again. An interpreter, on the other hand, produces no complete, translated version that can be saved, and therefore must translate each line over again each time the program is run.

Until the appearance of WordTech's dBIII Compiler (the predecessor of Quicksilver), the only way to translate dBASE-language code was to use an interpreter. Now, though, with the development of dBASE-language compilers and dBASE-language interfaces designed to work with a SQL engine, the dBASE language has become a viable alternative medium in which to write SQL applications.

In fact, the dBASE language offers a number of attractive features. Not only is the language a higher-level language than either C or COBOL (and therefore in some ways easier to use), but there are fewer operations involved in processing a dBASE-language application program. For instance, you do not specifically need to provide for setting variables, compiling, and executing, as you do when you use a function call interface. In this respect, using the dBASE language is like coding for a precompiler.

But processing a SQL application written in the dBASE language even saves a step over using a precompiler: there is no precompile stage. A precompiler application must first be precompiled, then compiled, and then run. An application written using the dBASE language is just compiled, without preliminaries, if you are using a dBASE compiler such as Quicksilver. Or you can even omit the compile stage and just use an interpreter such as dBXL, in which case you can run the program as soon as you finish writing it. The dBASE-language code is translated, and the SQL statements are SQL-compiled and executed when the program is run.

Because SQL function calls cannot be interspersed in the code the way they can when you write for a precompiler, it is possible that the dBASE language may give you less ability to fine-tune an application than if you were using C or COBOL. But the ease of use of the language and its being specially tailored for database applications are significant advantages.

As we said earlier, the WordTech dBXL product is being released in a version designed to be used with SQLBase. Because SQLBase is used for the examples in this book, dBXL is used for the examples in this chapter. Except for a few dBASE-language extensions found only in the WordTech products and noted as such in the text, the differences from dBASE IV are minimal.

Invisible and Embedded SQL

dBXL offers two types of SQL interface: *embedded SQL*, which is similar to the SQL interface offered by dBASE IV, and a WordTech extension called *invisible SQL*.

With some generally minor syntactical differences, dBASE-language embedded SQL is like the embedded SQL used with a precompiler: entire SQL statements, rather than function calls, are embedded in the dBASE-language code.

With dBXL invisible SQL, no SQL code appears. Rather, a special command— SET DATASERVER ON—is issued to indicate that subsequent lines of dBASE-language code are addressed to the SQL engine and refer to SQL tables, not to dBASE databases (as dBASE "tables" are called). This allows you to work with SQL tables entirely using dBASE-language code. The code is translated to SQL statements automatically when the program is interpreted or compiled. When you want to work with a dBASE database again, you issue the SET DATASERVER OFF command.

Whether you use invisible or embedded SQL, you must do two things in dBXL at the outset of any program (or interactive session): you must specify the SQL engine you want to work with, and you must connect to a database.

You use the command SET DATASERVER TO to specify the SQL engine. For example, to specify SQLBase, you say:

```
SET DATASERVER TO SQLBASE
```

To connect to a database, you issue a SQL CONNECT command. In SQLBase, you specify the database name, user name, and password with the following command:

```
CONNECT databasename/username/password
```

Let's look now at each type of interface.

Invisible SQL

The dBXL invisible SQL interface lets you use the dBASE language to work with tables in a SQL database exactly as if they were dBASE databases. You do not directly use SQL at all.

For instance, the following code uses the dBASE-language LIST command, analogous to the SQL SELECT command, to list a SQL table's contents. The use of the SET DATASERVER ON command in the first line indicates that you want to access SQL tables:

```
SET DATASERVER ON
USE Guests
LIST
```

The result looks like this:

Record#	NAME	SEX	BUILD	HEIGHT
1	BETTE MIDRIFF	F	M	66
2	MARCELLO HISTRIONI	M	M	66
3	JEAN-PAUL ROTUNDO	M	L	70
4	MICHAEL JOHNSON	M	L	71
5	CLINT WESTWOOD	M	M	73

You can use the dBASE-language SET FILTER command to restrict the rows listed to only those rows satisfying the filter condition (analogous to using a WHERE clause):

```
SET FILTER TO Name = "BETTE MIDRIFF"
LIST
```

Only one row satisfies the filter condition:

Record#	NAME	SEX	BUILD	HEIGHT
1	BETTE MIDRIFF	F	M	66

Similarly, you can perform all other operations on SQL tables, using dBASE-language code. You can add and edit data, analogous to using SQL INSERT, UPDATE, or DELETE statements. You can alter a table's structure and even add columns that behave like columns of the special dBASE MEMO and LOGICAL data types. And, you can transfer data between SQL tables and dBASE databases.

For example, the following code first specifies that you are addressing SQL, indicates the particular table, and then uses the dBASE-language COPY command to copy the contents of the table to a new dBASE database GUESTS2 created by the COPY command itself:

```
SET DATASERVER ON
USE Guests
SET DATASERVER OFF
COPY TO Guests2
```

You issue the SET DATASERVER OFF command before you do the copy to establish that you are no longer addressing SQL. You need to use SET DATASERVER only when you want to create or open a SQL table. After a SQL table is opened in a work area, you can use dBASE-language commands to work with the table without having to issue the SET DATASERVER command first each time. In this instance, turning DATASERVER off ensures that the table is copied as a dBASE database. If you had not turned off DATASERVER, COPY would have created a second SQL table.

You can even *join* a dBASE database and a SQL table, using the dBASE-language SET RELATION command. The procedure is just like the one for using SET RELATION on two dBASE databases except you use SET DATASERVER to gain access to SQL.

The following example shows the code you would enter to join a SQL table GUEST_WT (having a column NAME) with a dBASE database GUESTS. The table and database are joined on the column NAME that each contains. The SELECT command is the dBASE-language SELECT, not the SQL SELECT; the command selects the current dBASE work area.

```
SET DATASERVER ON
USE Guest_wt
SELECT 2
SET DATASERVER OFF
USE Guests
INDEX ON Name TO Gname
SELECT Guest_wt
SET RELATION TO Name INTO Guests
LIST Name, Weight, When, B->Build, B->Height FOR Name = "BETTE MIDRIFF"
```

Here is the result:

```
Record#  NAME            WEIGHT  WHEN      B->BUILD   B->HEIGHT
     1   BETTE MIDRIFF   150     06/14/88  M          66
     2   BETTE MIDRIFF   148.5   06/16/88  M          66
```

In short, with the invisible SQL interface, you can perform all operations on SQL tables using dBASE-language code. This allows you to use SQL tables even if you do not know SQL.

If you do know SQL, however, you generally will want to use SQL directly to manage the data stored in SQL tables. For this, you use embedded SQL.

Embedded SQL

Assuming that you are familiar with the SQL language, there are two major reasons for using embedded SQL rather than invisible SQL to access data stored in SQL tables. One is the greater power and economy of SQL as a data management language; the other is that embedded SQL runs faster. With embedded SQL, the interpreter does not need to translate instructions from the dBASE language into SQL. The time saved improves the speed of performance.

Both dBXL and dBASE IV support all standard SQL keywords. However, SQL can be used only to address SQL tables; it cannot be used with dBASE databases. To use SQL with data stored in dBASE databases, these databases must first be converted to SQL tables. dBXL and Quicksilver, for instance, offer a special utility, DBTOSQL, for this purpose.

In many respects, using embedded SQL in the dBASE language is like using embedded SQL for a precompiler. But there are differences, and some interesting effects can be achieved by using SQL with special dBASE-language features.

For example, dBXL-embedded SQL, like precompiler-embedded SQL, supports use of the SELECT statement with an INTO clause. In both cases, the clause lists the memory variables into which the result columns of a query returning only a single row will be stored. The purpose of the clause, in dBXL as with precompilers, is to allow us to omit declaring a cursor and doing a fetch for SELECT statements that return only one row. Rather, we can SELECT the row directly INTO variables specified in the SELECT statement itself.

A difference, though, between the precompiler and dBASE-language use of SELECT with an INTO clause is that the precompiler version yields an error if the SELECT in fact returns more than one row; the dBXL version, however, returns the first row and stores it in the variables.

The following example shows a SELECT...INTO statement embedded in dBASE-language code. The query returns the employee name, salary, manager, and department number for the employee number specified interactively by the user. The dBASE @...SAY...GET command is used to display the information, appropriately labeled, in an on-screen form, with the value of each column appearing in an editable field. When the user is done editing these fields, the values as they appear on-screen are stored again to the memory variables and used with a SQL UPDATE statement to update that row in the table.

The fact that there should be at most one employee having a given employee number means that the query should return only one row.

Neither a dBXL SET DATASERVER command nor a precompiler-style EXEC SQL delimiter is required to mark the beginning of an embedded SQL statement in the dBASE language. The engine determines by the syntax of the embedded SQL statements that the intention is to access SQL. The semicolon at the end of some lines has here a dBASE function, not the SQL function: it signifies that the line in question wraps and is continued on the succeeding line:

```
STORE SPACE(4) TO empno
@ 3,5 SAY "Enter employee number: " GET empno
READ
SELECT Ename, Empsal, Mgr, Deptno FROM Emp WHERE Empno = m->empno ;
    INTO ename, empsal, mgr, deptno
    @ 5,5 SAY CENTER("EMPLOYEE NUMBER " + STR(m->empno))
    @ 6,5 SAY "Employee name:         " GET m->ename
    @ 7,5 SAY "Salary:                " GET m->empsal
    @ 8,5 SAY "Manager:               " GET m->mgr
    @ 9,5 SAY "Department:            " GET m->deptno
READ
UPDATE Emp SET Ename = m->ename, Empsal = m->empsal, ;
    Mgr = m->mgr, Deptno = m->deptno WHERE Empno = m->empno
```

A SELECT statement with an INTO clause selects just a single row and requires no cursor. dBXL also offers another clause—the SAVE TO clause—that you can use with a SELECT statement without declaring a cursor. This clause, which must be used if you want to do a report on data returned using embedded SQL, retrieves an entire multiple-row result set. Instead of being fed to variables a row at a time for processing, as would be the procedure using a FETCH, the entire set of rows is stored in a temporary .dbf file that exists as long as the program executes. As a .dbf file, the result then can be processed using a dBASE report form. For example:

```
SELECT Empno, Ename, Empsal, Mgr, Deptno FROM Emp ;
    SAVE TO Employee
SET DATASERVER OFF
USE Employee
INDEX ON Empno TO Empno
REPORT FORM Empform TO PRINT
```

Here we turn off DATASERVER after the query because we want to go back to dBASE. The new .dbf file—`Employee`—which contains the result, is a dBASE file, and `Empform` is a dBASE report form.

We could also have stored the .dbf file permanently rather than temporarily by appending the keyword KEEP after the file name in the SAVE TO clause.

Many dBASE users will find it an advantage that they can continue using their existing dBASE report forms to process data retrieved with SQL. For instance, you might use a SELECT with a SAVE TO clause to download data from DB2 by way of the SQLBase DB2 interface. The data, originating in DB2 but stored now in a .dbf file, could be processed just like dBASE data.

Another advantage of the SAVE TO clause is that the tables addressed by the query do not have to remain locked to other users while data is fetched and processed. By the time processing begins on the .dbf file all the data has been fetched, so the locks can be removed.

Another interesting feature of dBASE-language interfaces is that they implement the dBASE macro substitution function in a way that amounts to a new SQL extension.

In the dBASE language, macro substitution allows the substitution of a character-string memory variable for keywords, other memory variable names or even parts of names, and field names. In applying macro substitution to SQL in dBXL, several standard SQL restrictions on the use of variables in SQL statements were dropped.

Thus, in standard SQL, variable substitution is permitted only in a WHERE clause, an INTO clause, or a SET clause; it is not permitted in table names, view names, or column names. But dBXL *allows* these substitutions in SQL, just as analogous substitutions are allowed in dBASE. Consequently, generic queries like the following example are actually acceptable in dBXL.

This example is similar to the one we gave in Chapter 17, "Using a COBOL SQL Precompiler," to illustrate types of substitutions forbidden with precompiler code. Macro substitution variables are prefixed with an ampersand (&):

```
SELECT &column1, &column2, &column3, &column4
FROM &tablename
```

Macro substitution gives programmers greater freedom to build general-purpose SQL statements, leaving actual specification of the values of the variables until the user fills them in just before the statement is run.

The following code, for instance, uses macro substitution to supply a database name and the program user's user name and password, entered in response to prompts, in a SQL CONNECT statement. The information is substituted only when the statement is executed. To ensure confidentiality, the dBASE-language SET COLOR TO command temporarily configures the editable field for the password to black characters on a black background. The second occurrence of the command returns the screen to its default setting:

```
STORE SPACE(8) TO dbname, username, password
@ 3,5 SAY "Enter database name:  " GET dbname
@ 5,5 SAY "Enter your user name: " GET username
@ 6,5 SAY "Enter your password:  "
SET COLOR TO N/N,N/N
@ 6,28 GET password
SET COLOR TO
READ
CONNECT &dbname/&username/&password
```

Cursor Operations

The two uses of the SQL SELECT statement described so far have not required cursors. SELECT with an INTO clause retrieves only a single row; SELECT with a SAVE TO clause can retrieve a multirow result set but does not use SQL to process those rows one at a time. Rather, the rows are simply dumped into a .dbf file.

Whenever you want to retrieve multiple rows and process them one at a time in SQL, you have to use cursors. With a dBASE interface, in which report-writing is taken care of with dBASE functions, you are most likely to want to do SQL row-at-a-time processing in connection with an UPDATE or DELETE statement. Typically, a SELECT statement is associated with a cursor and used to define the set of rows you want. These rows are then retrieved one at a time by using a programming loop to reiterate a FETCH statement, with each FETCH retrieving the row currently under the cursor. Each row as it is retrieved is displayed, perhaps in a form, with the values of the various columns appearing in editable fields. As the fields are edited, the new values are plugged into the SET clause of an UPDATE statement, and the row currently picked out by the cursor and identified with a WHERE CURRENT OF *cursor* clause is updated in the table.

From the standpoint of the SQL code, the procedure for doing row-at-a-time processing in the dBASE language is virtually identical to that for using cursors with a precompiler.

First a DECLARE statement associates a cursor with the SELECT statement. If the SELECT statement will be used with an UPDATE or DELETE statement, you must add a FOR UPDATE clause naming the columns to be edited. If you omit this clause, the result of the SELECT is read-only and you will not be able to update it.

When you are ready to execute the query, you issue an OPEN statement to open the cursor, and then you issue the first FETCH statement, retrieving one row into variables. When the program user is done editing the contents of these, the current values of the variables are fed to an UPDATE statement. You continue this process until a FETCH generates a return code of 1 for SQLCODE, one of the fields in the SQL Communication Area of the program (see Chapter 17, "Using a COBOL SQL Precompiler"). With SQLBase, a return code of 1 indicates that there are no more rows to fetch. At this point, you CLOSE the cursor.

The following example embodies all the steps just described. Note the use of the AUTOMEM keyword in the FETCH statement. This keyword is a dBASE-language extension of dBXL that automatically creates and initializes a memory variable for each column in the SELECT list. The keyword saves having to name the variables into which the row will be fetched.

```
STORE SPACE(20) TO job
@ 10,10 SAY "Enter job title: " GET job
READ
DECLARE Jobedit CURSOR FOR ;
    SELECT Name, Address, Job, Dept, Salary ;
    FROM Employee ;
    WHERE Job = :job ;
    FOR UPDATE OF Address, Job, Dept, Salary
OPEN Jobedit
FETCH Jobedit INTO AUTOMEM
DO WHILE SQLCODE() <> 1
```

```
        CLEAR
        @ 2,0 SAY CENTER("Employee Name: " + Name)
        @ 5,5 SAY "Address: " GET m->address
        @ 10,5 SAY "Job: " GET m->job
        @ 20,40 SAY "Department: " GET m->dept
        @ 15,30 SAY "Current Salary: " GET m->salary
        READ
        UPDATE Employee ;
     SET Address = :address, Job = :job, Department = :dept, ;
            Salary = :salary ;
        WHERE CURRENT OF Jobedit
        FETCH Jobedit INTO AUTOMEM
ENDDO
CLOSE Jobedit
```

Quicksilver and dBASE IV also allow you to make C function calls. Instead of fetching data into variables and then using these with SQL UPDATE and DELETE statements, you can send a variable as a parameter to a C function for processing. Ashton-Tate's dBASE Tools for C offers a selection of routines that can be used this way. Quicksilver also supports the dBASE Tools for C and lets you use original C routines of your own as well.

Two complete sample programs are given in Appendix E, "Sample dBASE Programs."

Summary

This chapter described using SQL with one of the new dBASE-language interfaces to SQL, such as dBASE IV and dBXL. These interfaces allow applications to be written using dBASE-language program-control structures but employing SQL to manage data stored in a SQL database.

The dBXL and Quicksilver SQL interfaces not only permit access to SQL tables by way of embedded SQL but also enable these tables to be addressed with dBASE-language code. This second type of interface to SQL is called invisible SQL.

dBASE-language embedded SQL is generally similar to embedded SQL for a precompiler. Two features that are special to dBASE-language embedded SQL, however, are macro substitution and use of the SELECT statement with a SAVE TO clause that saves SQL query results to a .dbf file.

Part III

Looking Ahead

CHAPTER 19

Promising Developments and Extensions

Up to now we have talked about the SQL language as it is—in other words, as it has actually been implemented by various vendors—and we have focused on features that are offered fairly universally. In this chapter, we depart from this rule and describe some features and extensions of SQL *not* yet widely implemented—or implemented at all in some cases—but that seem likely to be.

In general, the new standard SQL features this chapter discusses have a common theme or tendency—to more nearly automate certain jobs that users currently must do themselves. To the extent that the new features are implemented, they will make applications easier and faster to write, and several of them improve safeguards for maintaining the integrity of data. Until they *are* implemented, though, the features merely reflect provisions in the specifications for a standard SQL.

The chapter also looks at two promising extensions, CONNECT BY and COMPUTE, which are not part of the proposed extensions of SQL, but that seem likely to be implemented by more vendors.

The DEFAULT Clause

Whenever a field is left blank—in the course of an insert, for instance—the field is assigned a null value. A null in a field means that the value of that field is not specified—in other words, the value is unknown.

Because nulls behave rather strangely, they can make life difficult in SQL. They are, however, a necessary evil. Still, although it may be impossible to dispense

233

with nulls entirely, you can take steps to minimize their use. You could, for instance, adopt a convention of replacing nulls with a nonnull value such as 0, −1, spaces, or "unknown", depending on the context.

A new feature of SQL lets you replace nulls this way automatically. This feature is a DEFAULT clause. The clause can be added to column definitions in a CREATE TABLE statement. For instance:

```
CREATE TABLE GUEST_ROSTER (NAME VARCHAR(25) NOT NULL,
    ROOM VARCHAR(3), TRAINER VARCHAR(8) DEFAULT 'Unassign',
    ARRIVAL DATE NOT NULL, DEPARTURE DATE, DISCOUNT DECIMAL(2,2))
```

The DEFAULT clause `DEFAULT 'Unassign'` has been added to the definition of column TRAINER. With the addition of the DEFAULT clause, whenever a null would otherwise be generated for column TRAINER, the character string `'Unassign'` is automatically inserted instead. (The default cannot be 'Unassigned' rather than 'Unassign' because the length of column TRAINER is only 8 characters; at 10 characters, 'Unassigned' will not fit.

The DEFAULT clause offers several other options as well that make the feature useful for speeding up data entry. Rather than specify a literal value, such as the 'Unassign' string in the example, you can specify one of three keywords— CURRENT, USER, or NULL. The first two keywords cause a column to default to a context-dependent value: the CURRENT keyword causes the value of the column to default to the current date and time; USER causes the value of the column to default to the authorization ID of the user issuing the SQL statement. The NULL keyword causes the column to default to null.

For example, you could specify DEFAULT CURRENT for columns ARRIVAL and DEPARTURE in table GUEST_ROSTER. This would save having to fill in the date and time when a new guest signs in or checks out at the desk. Assuming that the current date and time are what you want to enter, you could simply leave the appropriate field blank and let the DEFAULT clause insert the information for you.

You might use a DEFAULT USER clause if the table contains a column for the desk clerk's name. SQL would then automatically insert the authorization ID of the clerk currently on duty whenever the clerk performs an insert and leaves that field blank.

The CHECK Constraint

Part 1 described how to use a CHECK option with a CREATE VIEW statement. Using the CHECK option ensures that inserts or updates of a view do not violate the defining characteristic of the view, as stated in the WHERE clause of the subquery in the CREATE VIEW statement. For example:

```
CREATE VIEW PREFERRED_GUESTS AS
   SELECT NAME, DISCOUNT
   FROM GUEST_ROSTER
   WHERE DISCOUNT !< .15
   WITH CHECK OPTION
```

Use of the CHECK option in the statement prevents the view from being inserted into or updated in such a way that it would contain rows with a value of less than .15 in DISCOUNT.

Now SQL permits a similar CHECK constraint to be added directly to CREATE TABLE statements. The syntax of the new CHECK constraint is slightly different from the syntax of the CHECK option for views, but the net effect is the same: the CHECK constraint specifies a search condition that must be satisfied for any insert or update to the table in question.

A CHECK constraint can be added to a CREATE TABLE statement in either of two ways: a constraint can be made part of the column definition of the column constrained, or constraints can be added at the end of the CREATE TABLE statement.

The following example shows the first way. A CHECK constraint is added to the column definition of DISCOUNT in the CREATE TABLE statement that defines table GUEST__ROSTER. The clause prevents any row from containing a value for DISCOUNT that is greater than .2:

```
CREATE TABLE GUEST_ROSTER (NAME VARCHAR(25) NOT NULL,
    ROOM VARCHAR(3), TRAINER VARCHAR(8), ARRIVAL DATE NOT NULL,
    DEPARTURE DATE, DISCOUNT DECIMAL(2,2) CHECK (DISCOUNT !> .2))
```

When you use a CHECK constraint this way, as part of a column definition, you are restricted to naming in the constraint only the column being defined. At the end of the CREATE statement, however, you can add separate CHECK constraints that are not part of any column definition, and these constraints can refer to more than one column of the table.

For example, the following CREATE TABLE statement includes a CHECK constraint referring to the two columns DISCOUNT and TRAINER. The constraint ensures that only Serena's guests receive a 20 percent discount. Because two columns are named, the constraint cannot appear as part of a column definition; it must be placed as a separate clause at the end of the statement:

```
CREATE TABLE GUEST_ROSTER (NAME VARCHAR(25) NOT NULL,
    ROOM VARCHAR(3), TRAINER VARCHAR(8), ARRIVAL DATE NOT NULL,
    DEPARTURE DATE, DISCOUNT DECIMAL(2,2) CHECK (DISCOUNT !> .2))
    CHECK (DISCOUNT < .2 OR TRAINER = 'SERENA')
```

The CHECK constraint for table definitions is a welcome new feature of standard SQL. As it is implemented, it will relieve you of having to go the roundabout route of creating and working through a view whenever you want to use a CHECK constraint with a table.

Integrity Constraints

Part 1 introduced the concept of the primary key—the column or group of columns whose job it is to contain uniquely identifying attributes for each row in a table.

To enable a primary key to do what it is supposed to do, namely, identify particular rows, it is important that the primary key contain no nulls or duplicate values—values that are the same for more than one row. You can ensure that a primary key column contains no nulls by specifying NOT NULL in the column definition, as we have done for columns NAME and ARRIVAL in the table definition of GUEST_ROSTER in the previous example. But until recently the only way in standard SQL to keep out duplicate *nonnull* values was to perform the extraneous operation of creating a unique index on the primary key. Clearly, it would be better if you could ensure the integrity of the primary key directly, in the table definition itself.

ANSI-standard SQL now provides for doing this by allowing the use of the keyword phrase PRIMARY KEY to specify primary key columns in the CREATE TABLE statement. If the primary key consists of a single column, the phrase can be made a part of that column's definition. For example, ROOM is the single-column primary key of table ROOMS:

```
CREATE TABLE ROOMS (ROOM VARCHAR(3) PRIMARY KEY, NAME VARCHAR(15),
    RATE FLOAT, DESCRIPTION LONG VARCHAR)
```

If a table has a composite primary key, made up of two or more columns, a PRIMARY KEY *clause* can be added to list the columns. This ensures that no two rows are permitted to be the same across all values in the primary key columns:

```
CREATE TABLE GUEST_ROSTER (NAME VARCHAR(25) NOT NULL,
    ROOM VARCHAR(3), TRAINER VARCHAR(8) DEFAULT 'Unassign',
    ARRIVAL DATE NOT NULL, DEPARTURE DATE, DISCOUNT DECIMAL(2,2),
    PRIMARY KEY (NAME, ARRIVAL))
```

Another keyword, UNIQUE, is now available too. This keyword has exactly the same effect as PRIMARY KEY—to forbid duplicate values—but it can be applied to columns that are not part of the primary key. UNIQUE can be appended to any individual column definition or, like PRIMARY KEY, used in a clause that lists the appropriate columns collectively, following the column definitions in the CREATE TABLE statement.

In the following example, the room number by itself is the primary key. But because we want to ensure that no two rooms are given the same name, we use the keyword UNIQUE on column NAME to prevent duplicate values in that column:

```
CREATE TABLE ROOMS (ROOM VARCHAR(3) PRIMARY KEY, NAME
    VARCHAR(15) NOT NULL UNIQUE, RATE FLOAT, DESCRIPTION LONG VARCHAR)
```

Referential Integrity Constraints

Often a table contains a column (or columns) based on the primary key of either that same table or, more frequently, some other table. Column ROOM of table GUEST_ROSTER is an example. This column lists the rooms assigned to current guests. The column is based on column ROOM in table ROOMS, which lists the room numbers of all the spa's rooms: only room numbers also appearing in ROOMS.ROOM belong in GUEST_ROSTER.ROOM. Breaking this rule would be like assigning a guest to a nonexistent room.

ROOMS.ROOM is a primary key column of ROOMS. Column GUEST_ROSTER.ROOM is called a *foreign key*: given the purpose of the column, every value in GUEST_ROSTER.ROOM should either be null (for example, in the case of a guest not assigned a room) or match some value in the primary key ROOMS.ROOM from which the foreign key column derives. The nonnull values of foreign key GUEST_ROSTER.ROOM should be a subset of the values of primary key ROOMS.ROOM: there should be no nonnull values in GUEST_ROSTER.ROOM that fail to match a value in ROOMS.ROOM.

This special relationship between primary key and foreign key columns is called *referential integrity*; properly maintaining it is a job that currently devolves for the most part on the user.

The integrity of the special relationship between primary and foreign keys can be violated in two ways. One is by inserting into or updating a foreign key column so that it is made to contain a value that does not match any value in the primary key—assigning someone a nonexistent room in GUEST_ROSTER, for instance. The other way is by updating or deleting from the primary key without making a coordinate adjustment in foreign keys—removing the room from ROOMS without reassigning its occupants, for example.

The result is the same in either case: the foreign key is left containing values not matched in the primary key.

A new feature of standard SQL enables you to close off the second of these avenues by which referential anomalies can materialize, namely, through isolated deletes or updates on the primary key end. ANSI-standard SQL now provides for building into the table definitions a *referential constraint* that automatically reflects changes to a primary key in any foreign keys.

The new referential constraint takes the form of a FOREIGN KEY clause, one or more of which can be added to the CREATE TABLE statement for any table containing a foreign key. The clause specifies the columns that are foreign keys and declares which primary key columns they refer to. You can then append to this clause two rules: an *update rule*, which describes how any update of the primary key will affect a foreign key, and a *delete rule*, which describes how any delete on the primary key will be reflected.

For instance, you could attach a referential constraint to the definition of table GUEST_ROSTER, as follows:

```
CREATE TABLE GUEST_ROSTER (NAME VARCHAR(25) NOT NULL,
    ROOM VARCHAR(3), TRAINER VARCHAR(8) DEFAULT 'Unassign',
    ARRIVAL DATE NOT NULL, DEPARTURE DATE, DISCOUNT DECIMAL(2,2),
    PRIMARY KEY (NAME, ARRIVAL))
FOREIGN KEY (ROOM) REFERENCES ROOMS (ROOM)
    ON UPDATE CASCADE
    ON DELETE CASCADE
```

By choosing CASCADE as the desired action in an update on ROOMS.ROOM, you are directing that, for any value which is updated, all matching values in GUEST_ROSTER.ROOM will be updated in the same way: that the effects of the update will *cascade* to the foreign key.

Similarly with the delete rule: you are directing that, for any value in ROOMS.ROOM which is deleted, all rows in GUEST_ROSTER having a matching value in column GUEST_ROSTER.ROOM will be deleted too.

Although the example shows instances of both the update and the delete rule, either rule could have been omitted. In fact, you probably would not want a delete from ROOMS.ROOM to delete the entire row for a guest assigned that room in GUEST_ROSTER.

The other two options besides CASCADE with these two rules are SET NULL and SET DEFAULT.

Using either rule with the SET NULL option—for example, ON DELETE SET NULL—directs that, for any update or delete performed on the primary key, matching values in the foreign key are set to null. Using either rule with SET DEFAULT sets matching values in the foreign key to whatever is defined for them in an appropriate DEFAULT clause.

Incidentally, in the example, the FOREIGN KEY clause is attached at the end of the CREATE TABLE statement. Because only one column is listed as a foreign key, the clause and accompanying rules could just as well have been added to the definition of the foreign key column GUEST_ROSTER.ROOM. But whenever you want to declare more than one foreign key column at a time, the clause must be placed at the end, as in the example.

Scroll Cursors

So far we have always spoken of the embedded SQL fetch operation as applying to the *next* row of the result set of a query. Fetching has been depicted as a matter of always dealing from the top of the deck: the cursor is positioned at the first row of the result set, and successive rows are retrieved from the top of the set down, in response to successive FETCH statements. This is in keeping with what, until lately, has been the ANSI-standard procedure for fetching.

In 1987, ANSI standards were modified to accept a new variation on the embedded SQL DECLARE CURSOR statement, which was discussed briefly in Part 2. ANSI-standard SQL now supports the use of a new SCROLL keyword with this statement, as follows:

```
DECLARE cursor name SCROLL CURSOR
```

A *scroll cursor* is different from an ordinary cursor in that it permits scrolling—the application can range freely through the result set, up or down, and fetch any specified row instead of always having to fetch the *next* row. New keywords—NEXT, PRIOR, FIRST, LAST, ABSOLUTE (*row position*), and RELATIVE (*row position*)—are available for use with FETCH statements associated with a cursor declared to be a scroll cursor. These keywords are necessary to specify the row that will be fetched, in that this row does not always need to be the next row with a scroll cursor. For example:

```
FETCH PRIOR FETCUR
    INTO :EMPLOYNO, :FIRST-NAME, :MIDDLE-INITIAL,
         :LAST-NAME, :START-DATE, :HOURLY-PAY
```

The advantage of scroll cursors is that they make it much easier for applications to provide for browsing. This feature is increasingly popular for applications and is outright essential if you have Windows-based applications with scroll bars.

If SQL makes no provision for scroll cursors, the application must. In practice, this has meant that, when an application wants to permit fetching of some row preceding the next row, the application has to somehow note the row and then rerun the query in order to approach the row from the top of the result set. Scroll cursors permit an application simply to specify the row in the FETCH statement, and the row is retrieved without rerunning the query. Therefore, not only is programming made easier but performance also is improved.

The new SQL standard for scroll cursors uses them only with read-only result sets. That is, according to the standard, a result table retrieved using a scroll cursor cannot be updated; you would not be allowed to use a query containing a FOR UPDATE OF clause with a DECLARE SCROLL CURSOR statement.

Scroll cursors have in effect already been implemented for SQLBase by way of the result set mode feature, described in Chapter 15, "Advanced Programming with a Function Call Interface." This feature, incidentally, extends SQL by *permitting updates of result sets retrieved in result set mode*. The result set mode feature works by internally storing row identifiers of the rows retrieved in such a way that these rows can be retrieved again—and operated on—without rerunning the query.

An implementation must, however, guard against a certain pitfall when it allows updates of result sets in a multiuser environment. This pitfall may explain why the new SQL standard prescribes that result tables retrieved with scroll cursors shall be read-only.

The problem is that, unless you choose an isolation level comparable to the stringent SQLBase Read Repeatability level (which locks other users out of all rows in the result set until the transaction is committed), then another user could update a result set row without your noticing. You might then update the row yourself under the mistaken impression that it still contained the values it had when you first saw it.

For example, suppose that you have used a scroll cursor, or SQLBase result set mode, to retrieve a result table of 225 rows. You are browsing through the table and currently can see rows 201 through 225 on-screen. If your isolation level is Read Repeatability, then all other users are locked out of all 225 rows until you commit, because with this isolation level you maintain an exclusive right to change any of the rows until you are done with the transaction. Here no problem can arise.

Nor is there a problem if the isolation level is Read Only. This case is like the situation envisioned by the ANSI standards for all uses of scroll cursors. Because you do not reserve a right to update any of the rows, you are not in danger of updating them incorrectly.

The case is different, however, if you have chosen an isolation level comparable to the SQLBase level of Cursor Stability. To maximize access to the data, this level maintains locks only while you are actually using the rows. Consequently, someone could update row 199 when it is off your screen. If you fail to notice the change when you scroll back to row 199, you could change the row again yourself and put in incorrect data.

To prevent this sort of accident, any implementation that permits updates of rows retrieved with a scroll cursor must do something similar to what SQLBase does—notify the user if a row in the result set he or she is working with has been changed. SQLBase does this by returning a special fetch status code that either identifies a particular row as having been updated or, in the case of a delete, announces that the row cannot be found.

The CONNECT BY Clause

SQL does not do a good job of representing hierarchical relationships. In this type of relationship, you want to know, for instance, the names of all employees immediately reporting to a certain officer in a company, the names of any employees reporting to any of these employees, the names of any employees reporting to any of these employees, and so on. You could again have reason to represent this type of relationship if you were doing a genealogy or processing bills of materials for parts assemblies that contain other assemblies, which contain other assemblies, and so on.

Chapter 19: Promising Developments and Extensions

A SQL query can be used to return all the information needed to trace such relationships; the problem is that with standard SQL you cannot retrieve the information in an order that organizes the information hierarchically.

For example, an organizational chart showing who reports to whom in a company might look like figure 19.1:

Fig. 19.1. Organizational flow chart.

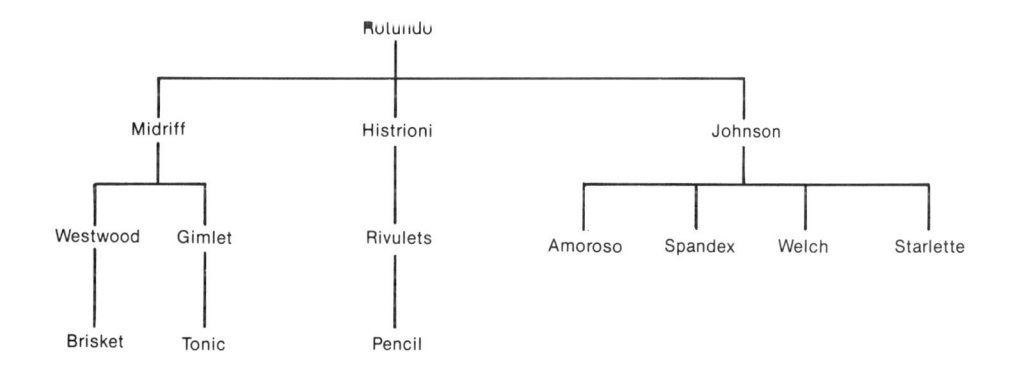

```
                        Rotundo
           ┌───────────────┼───────────────┐
        Midriff         Histrioni        Johnson
        ┌───┴───┐          │       ┌──────┬───┴───┬──────┐
     Westwood Gimlet    Rivulets Amoroso Spandex Welch Starlette
        │       │          │
     Brisket  Tonic      Pencil
```

Given a suitable table EMP, you can use the following query to retrieve all the information necessary to construct the diagram:

```
SELECT ENAME, EMPNO, MGR, DEPTNO
FROM EMP
ORDER BY DEPTNO;

ENAME        EMPNO    MGR     DEPTNO
=========    =====    ====    ======
ROTUNDO      6145
WESTWOOD     6378     6134      10
MIDRIFF      6134     6145      10
BRISKET      6121     6378      10
TONIC        6119     6265      10
GIMLET       6265     6134      10
HISTRIONI    6154     6145      20
PENCIL       6266     6283      20
RIVULETS     6283     6154      20
AMOROSO      6191     6286      30
JOHNSON      6286     6145      30
STARLETTE    6789     6286      30
SPANDEX      6256     6286      30
WELCH        6143     6286      30

14 ROWS SELECTED
```

All the information needed to create this diagram is in the table, but the ordering of the information is not itself hierarchical: apart from being grouped by department number, the rows appear haphazardly.

The Oracle DBMS addresses this situation with an interesting extension that makes it possible to use a query to retrieve rows in a *tree-structured* order. This order is specified by using two special clauses, CONNECT BY and START WITH, and a new keyword, PRIOR. The CONNECT BY clause indicates the columns that will define the structure of the tree—in other words, the columns whose relationship determines the hierarchy—EMPNO and MGR, in this case. The placement of the PRIOR keyword determines the direction in which the ordering will proceed, whether from top to bottom as specified in the following example, or from bottom to top. The START WITH clause indicates the row where you want the tree to begin.

This is a case in which a picture is worth a thousand words:

```
SELECT ENAME, EMPNO, MGR, DEPTNO
FROM EMP
CONNECT BY PRIOR EMPNO = MGR
START WITH ENAME = 'ROTUNDO'
ORDER BY DEPTNO;
```

ENAME	EMPNO	MGR	DEPTNO
ROTUNDO	6145		
MIDRIFF	6134	6145	10
WESTWOOD	6378	6134	10
BRISKET	6121	6378	10
GIMLET	6265	6134	10
TONIC	6119	6265	10
HISTRIONI	6154	6145	20
RIVULETS	6283	6154	20
PENCIL	6266	6283	20
JOHNSON	6286	6145	30
AMOROSO	6191	6286	30
STARLETTE	6789	6286	30
SPANDEX	6256	6286	30
WELCH	6143	6286	30

14 ROWS SELECTED

The hierarchy starts with the row for ROTUNDO. The CONNECT BY clause specifies (essentially) that the next row shall be one in which MGR lists the EMPNO of a prior row—ideally, of the immediately prior row, but failing that, of the row listed by the immediately prior row; or failing that, of the row listed by the row listed by the immediately prior row; and so on. Thus MGR for MIDRIFF lists ROTUNDO's EMPNO; MGR for WESTWOOD, who reports to MIDRIFF, is MIDRIFF's EMPNO; MGR for BRISKET, who reports to WESTWOOD, is WESTWOOD's EMPNO; and so on.

The tree-structured order of the result can be highlighted by using a special LEVEL keyword in the SELECT list to add a result column giving the tree level of each row, and by using report-writing functions to indent the ENAME column of each row according to its level. For example (omitting the query this time):

```
ENAME          LEVEL    EMPNO    MGR     DEPTNO
=========      =====    =====    ====    ======
ROTUNDO          1      6145
  MIDRIFF        2      6134     6145      10
    WESTWOOD     3      6378     6134      10
      BRISKET    4      6121     6378      10
    GIMLET       3      6265     6134      10
      TONIC      4      6119     6265      10
  HISTRIONI      2      6154     6145      20
    RIVULETS     3      6283     6154      20
      PENCIL     4      6266     6283      20
  JOHNSON        2      6286     6145      30
    AMOROSO      3      6191     6286      30
    STARLETTE    3      6789     6286      30
    SPANDEX      3      6256     6286      30
    WELCH        3      6143     6286      30

14 ROWS SELECTED
```

You can also start with a different row—MIDRIFF, for instance—in which case only the rows for MIDRIFF and her staff are retrieved. And, you can use the LEVEL keyword in interesting ways. For instance:

```
SELECT LEVEL, AVG(SAL)
FROM EMP
CONNECT BY PRIOR EMPNO = MGR
START WITH ENAME = 'ROTUNDO'
GROUP BY LEVEL
ORDER BY LEVEL;

LEVEL    AVG(SAL)
=====    ========
  1      6,000.00
  2      4,583.23
  3      3,295.45
  4      1,279.98

4 ROWS SELECTED
```

The ability to order data hierarchically in this fashion can be very useful. We should not be surprised to see the feature implemented more widely in the future.

The COMPUTE Clause

One particularly irksome limitation of standard SQL is the inability to retrieve both detail and summary rows in the same result. For example, you can either *list* the names of all guests assigned to trainers Julio or Michael, as follows:

```
SELECT TRAINER, NAME
FROM GUEST_ROSTER
WHERE TRAINER = 'MICHAEL'
OR TRAINER = 'JULIO'
ORDER BY TRAINER, NAME;

TRAINER   NAME
=======   =========================
JULIO     JEAN-PAUL ROTUNDO
JULIO     MARLON SPANDEX
JULIO     MICHAEL JOHNSON
MICHAEL   BETTE MIDRIFF
MICHAEL   CLINT WESTWOOD
MICHAEL   JANE FYUNDAI
MICHAEL   JOAN TONIC
MICHAEL   OLYMPIA WELCH
```

or you can *count* them:

```
SELECT TRAINER, COUNT(NAME)
FROM GUEST_ROSTER
WHERE TRAINER = 'MICHAEL'
OR TRAINER = 'JULIO'
GROUP BY TRAINER;

TRAINER   COUNT(NAME)
=======   ===========
JULIO               3
MICHAEL             5
```

You cannot, however, list *and* count in the same result:

```
SELECT TRAINER, NAME, COUNT(NAME)
FROM GUEST_ROSTER
WHERE TRAINER = 'MICHAEL'
OR TRAINER = 'JULIO'
GROUP BY TRAINER, NAME;

TRAINER   NAME                       COUNT(NAME)
=======   =========================  ===========
JULIO     JEAN-PAUL ROTUNDO                    1
JULIO     MARLON SPANDEX                       1
JULIO     MICHAEL JOHNSON                      1
MICHAEL   BETTE MIDRIFF                        1
MICHAEL   CLINT WESTWOOD                       1
MICHAEL   JANE FYUNDAI                         1
MICHAEL   JOAN TONIC                           1
MICHAEL   OLYMPIA WELCH                        1
```

When you try to list and count in the same result, the aggregate function regards every row having a distinct set of values (that is, different from every other row) for TRAINER and NAME as a group unto itself. Consequently, the number of names—namely, one—in each of these groups is counted, when you actually want to count the total number of names assigned to each trainer. This is the fault of the GROUP BY clause. But you have to use a GROUP BY clause whenever you include in the SELECT list aggregate functions with anything that is *not* an aggregate function. If you omit the GROUP BY clause, you get an error; if you omit NAME from the SELECT list, you do not get a list of the guests you want to count but only the count by itself, as we have already shown.

Sybase Inc. supports an extension of standard SQL that lets you have your cake and eat it too. Essentially, the extension integrates a report-writing feature into the SELECT statement in the form of an additional, optional clause—a COMPUTE clause. Using this clause, you can have summary values of aggregate functions appear as additional rows in the result of a query whose SELECT list contains only column names, as follows. For example:

```
SELECT TRAINER, NAME
FROM GUEST_ROSTER
WHERE TRAINER = 'MICHAEL'
OR TRAINER = 'JULIO'
ORDER BY TRAINER, NAME
COMPUTE COUNT(NAME);

TRAINER   NAME
========  =========================
JULIO     JEAN-PAUL ROTUNDO
JULIO     MARLON SPANDEX
JULIO     MICHAEL JOHNSON
MICHAEL   BETTE MIDRIFF
MICHAEL   CLINT WESTWOOD
MICHAEL   JANE FYUNDAI
MICHAEL   JOAN TONIC
MICHAEL   OLYMPIA WELCH
                                   COUNT
          =========================
          8
```

This example shows the total number of guests assigned to either Julio or Michael. If you want to break down this total, you can use a special keyword BY with one or more of the column names from the ORDER BY clause (required when the BY keyword is used). This causes a summary row to appear at every point at which the BY column or columns change, as follows:

```
SELECT TRAINER, NAME
FROM GUEST_ROSTER
WHERE TRAINER = 'MICHAEL'
OR TRAINER = 'JULIO'
ORDER BY TRAINER, NAME
COMPUTE COUNT(NAME) BY TRAINER;

TRAINER   NAME
========  =========================
JULIO     JEAN-PAUL ROTUNDO
JULIO     MARLON SPANDEX
JULIO     MICHAEL JOHNSON
                                   COUNT
          =========================
```

```
                  3
MICHAEL    BETTE MIDRIFF
MICHAEL    CLINT WESTWOOD
MICHAEL    JANE FYUNDAI
MICHAEL    JOAN TONIC
MICHAEL    OLYMPIA WELCH
                              COUNT
                   =========================
                  5
```

It is possible to use several *instances* of the same kind of aggregate function in the COMPUTE clause, but only one *kind* of aggregate function can be used. For instance, the example below uses the MAX aggregate function twice in the same COMPUTE clause. To use two different aggregate functions—for example, MAX and AVG, as in the following example—you must use more than one COMPUTE clause.

```
SELECT TRAINER, NAME, DISCOUNT, ARRIVAL
FROM GUEST_ROSTER
WHERE TRAINER = 'MICHAEL'
OR TRAINER = 'JULIO'
ORDER BY TRAINER, NAME
COMPUTE MAX(DISCOUNT), MAX(ARRIVAL) BY TRAINER;

TRAINER   NAME                         DISCOUNT      ARRIVAL
=======   ==========================   ==========    ===========
JULIO     JEAN-PAUL ROTUNDO            .2            15-JUN-1988
JULIO     MARLON SPANDEX               .05           16-JUN-1988
JULIO     MICHAEL JOHNSON                            15-JUN-1988
                                       MAX           MAX
                                       ==========    ===========
                                       .2            16-JUN-1988

MICHAEL   BETTE MIDRIFF                              14-JUN-1988
MICHAEL   CLINT WESTWOOD               .15           25-JUN-1988
MICHAEL   JANE FYUNDAI                 .1            19-JUN-1988
MICHAEL   JOAN TONIC                   .05           23-JUN-1988
MICHAEL   OLYMPIA WELCH                .1            22-JUN-1988
                                       MAX           MAX
                                       ==========    ===========
                                       .15           25-JUN-1988
```

The following example shows the COMPUTE clause used with two different aggregate functions—MAX and AVG. Because the functions are not the same, they must go in separate COMPUTE clauses:

```
SELECT TRAINER, NAME, DISCOUNT, ARRIVAL
FROM GUEST_ROSTER
WHERE TRAINER = 'MICHAEL'
OR TRAINER = 'JULIO'
ORDER BY TRAINER, NAME
COMPUTE AVG(DISCOUNT) BY TRAINER
COMPUTE MAX(ARRIVAL) BY TRAINER;
```

```
TRAINER   NAME                       DISCOUNT       ARRIVAL
========  =========================  ==========   ===========
JULIO     JEAN-PAUL ROTUNDO             .2         15-JUN-1988
JULIO     MARLON SPANDEX                .05        16-JUN-1988
JULIO     MICHAEL JOHNSON                          15-JUN-1988
                                        AVG
                                    ==========
                                    .125000000
                                                       MAX
                                                 ===========
                                                  16-JUN-1988
MICHAEL   BETTE MIDRIFF                            14-JUN-1988
MICHAEL   CLINT WESTWOOD                .15        25-JUN-1988
MICHAEL   JANE FYUNDAI                  .1         19-JUN-1988
MICHAEL   JOAN TONIC                    .05        23-JUN-1988
MICHAEL   OLYMPIA WELCH                 .1         22-JUN-1988
                                        AVG
                                    ==========
                                    .100000000
                                                       MAX
                                                 ===========
                                                  25-JUN-1988
```

The COMPUTE clause is not a feature of standard SQL, but it is an attractive extension. It may well begin appearing in other implementations.

Summary

This chapter described several features and extensions that recently have been incorporated into the SQL standard or appear to be promising candidates for wider implementation. They include

- ❏ A DEFAULT clause that lets you automatically replace nulls resulting from, for instance, a field's being left blank in the course of an insert, with a default value specified in the column definition for the field.

- ❏ A CHECK clause, added to column definitions in the CREATE TABLE statement, to ensure that inserts or updates of the table do not violate conditions specified in the clause.

- ❏ Integrity constraints consisting of the keywords PRIMARY KEY and UNIQUE that can be added to a CREATE TABLE statement to prevent duplicate values from appearing in specified columns and to allow for foreign key references from other tables.

- ❏ Referential integrity constraints in the form of a FOREIGN KEY clause with several options. The clause lists columns that are foreign keys and declares which primary key columns they refer to. Either of two rules can be given with the clause to specify which of several possible effects an update or delete of an indicated primary key will have on the foreign key.

- Scroll cursors, offered by Gupta Technologies, allowing a fetch to retrieve any specified row of a result set rather than being confined to retrieving only the next row. Scroll cursors make it easier for applications to provide for browsing.
- A CONNECT BY clause, offered by Oracle, that makes it possible to use a query to retrieve rows in a hierarchical, *tree-structured* order.
- A COMPUTE clause, offered by Sybase, that makes it possible to retrieve in the same result both individual detail rows and summary values from **aggregate functions**.

CHAPTER 20

SQL: Where We've Been and Where We're Going

You have now had a fairly thorough introduction to the way the SQL language works, its basic features, and some of its most popular or promising extensions. You have also seen some of the variety of ways that SQL can be used in writing database application programs. For instance, SQL API function calls and precompiler code can be embedded in programs written in virtually any procedural language. Also, with the advent of such front-end tools as dBXL and Quicksilver, SQL now can be used even with languages—notably the dBASE interface language—initially designed for non-SQL (indeed, nonrelational) database management systems.

Many of the more recent SQL developments have related to improving procedures for using SQL in application programs or for running these programs in a straightforward way on different machines or with different database products. This line of development has grown so important lately that it may come as a surprise to learn that fitting out SQL for use with database applications has not always had the high priority it has now. Initially, in fact, this use of SQL was scarcely envisioned.

Looking briefly at how SQL came to be used as it is today will help you gain perspective on the direction SQL development is taking. This chapter, and this book, conclude with an assessment of what the future appears to hold.

The Origins of SQL

SQL began with a paper published in 1970 by E.F. Codd, a mathematician working at the IBM Research Laboratory in San Jose, California. In this paper, "A Relational Model of Data for Large Shared Data Banks" (*Communications of the ACM*, Vol. 13, No. 6, June 1970), Codd formulated the principles of a relational system for managing data in a database and described a relational algebra for organizing the data in tables.

The paper caused a considerable stir and spurred a number of people to begin researching the possibility of designing a system based on Codd's relational model. Out of this activity came another important paper: "SEQUEL: A Structured English Query Language" (*Proceedings of the 1974 ACM SIGMOD Workshop on Data Description, Access and Control*, May 1974) by D.D. Chamberlin and R.F. Boyce, both (like Codd) researchers at IBM's San Jose Research Laboratory. Their paper defined a language, the original ancestor of SQL, designed to meet the requirements of Codd's relational algebra. Two years later, Chamberlin and others developed a revised version of the language, SEQUEL/2, and shortly thereafter IBM built a prototype system, System R, which implemented most of its features.

None of these inventors of SQL had it principally in mind to create a tool for application programmers, much less a tool that allowed programmers to port their applications easily from machine to machine, and so on. Their first concern was just to implement a language to manage a relational database. The inventors envisioned using the language chiefly as a tool for doing ad hoc queries and analysis. In this regard, one of the main virtues of SQL was its relative ease of use: with SQL, you could work with the data in a database *without* being a programmer. SQL (the name was changed around 1980) was equipped with fetches and program variables, but they were not provided with an eye to using them in applications so much as for the interactive capabilities they made possible.

Meanwhile, IBM was not alone in pursuing research to develop a SQL-based database. In fact, the first relational database product, appearing even before those from IBM, was released by Oracle Corporation (then called Relational Software Inc.). The interface to this system was UFI (User Friendly Interface), an interactive interface similar to SQLTalk. This interface had some provision for applications to be written for it, but applications were not its main focus. The product was really designed to be used interactively.

At the same time that System R was being implemented, parallel work was proceeding at the University of California, Berkeley. This work, also stemming from Codd's paper, led to the development of a relational language called QUEL that is broadly similar to SQL. The products of Relational Technologies Inc. and Britton-Lee descend from this branch of research. Relational Technologies' INGRES, for instance, initially was based on QUEL, although it now has essentially shifted or is in the process of shifting to a SQL engine.

Over the next few years, many companies started implementing SQL, and SQL began to be available for a variety of machines, both mainframes and microcomputers. In 1981 IBM came out with SQL/DS for the DOS/VSE operating system, and then, in 1983, with DB2 for MVS. Data General Corporation, Digital Equipment Corporation, Hewlett-Packard Company, and Tandem all developed SQL products at about the same time, too, adding to the number of SQLs on the market—all of them somewhat different. For while all the implementations derived from the same original papers, to some extent each vendor steered development in a different direction. Thus the pattern was already being set for the variety of embellishments and extensions that still distinguish the different products today.

Gradually the programmatic capabilities of SQL began to be fleshed out. Oracle produced a forms interface that allowed some manipulation of data by filling in fields in forms instead of by having to issue SQL statements, and applications could be written using this interface. The precompiler interface also appeared and, practically speaking, became part of the SQL language as a result of being incorporated into the DB2 and SQL/DS manuals. Then the function call interface as developed in ORACLE and INGRES appeared in the marketplace, and people began to realize that the potential of SQL went beyond its usefulness as an end-user language.

This was just as well for the fortunes of SQL, for it was becoming apparent that as an end-user language SQL was not going to succeed. Initially, SQL may have appeared easy to use insofar as it permitted queries and so forth to be issued without programming, but SQL never credibly established itself as easy to use in any more absolute sense. The emphasis shifted to using embedded SQL in applications programs.

Encouraging this line of development was the fact that the performance of SQL products kept improving. The faster they got, the more attractive they became for doing applications. The result was that relational databases moved more from being interesting ad hoc query tools to being production-oriented database management systems.

Only then did there begin to be a premium on *portability*—the ability to run one and the same application on a variety of machines. Now it was possible to write powerful applications using SQL, the pinch was that the usefulness of an application was all too often confined to a particular environment. This limitation was the next major focus of attention from vendors, who began offering broadly compatible families of products that ran on different machines. Oracle Corporation, for instance, ported their database engine from its original VAX/VMS environment to IBM's VM operating system for mainframes and to various UNIX platforms, allowing users to run the same application, with minor changes, in several environments. Oracle's example was followed by Relational Technologies Inc. and then by other companies, all of which came out with implementations of their original engine and interfaces, designed for new environments.

With progress in making applications more portable, the next area that began to receive vendors' attention was the difficulty in communicating *between* different environments. After it became possible to port applications from one machine to another, people began to want to run an application in one environment—on a PC, for instance—and address a database in a different environment—on a mainframe, perhaps. The ability to physically separate the interface (or *front end*) of a database system from the engine (or *back end*) in this fashion—or even to use SQL simultaneously among many front ends and many back ends—came to be called *connectivity*, or *connectability*. It is fair to say that Gupta Technologies was a pioneer in this development of SQL: not only was SQLBase (1986) the first SQL database server for PC LANs (local area networks), but SQLWindows (1988) was the first engine-independent front end for SQL databases.

A Universal SQL?

It would be nice if we could end the progress report by saying that SQL has reached the point at which an application written for one SQL product will run with all of them. Unfortunately, we can't and it won't. Every vendor has differentiated his or her engine in minor, and in some cases, major ways. Even IBM's several products—DB2, SQL/DS, and OS/2 Extended Edition, for instance—differ from each other. As a result, SQL implementations are only imperfectly compatible with one another, and the question about how to get more portability and more connectivity is still a critical one.

Part of the problem is that effecting complete compatibility involves more than just having all vendors agree on a certain set of features to offer. Besides incompatibilities that stem from vendors' offering different extensions, incompatibilities are possible even among vendors offering exactly the same features and extensions.

Incompatibilities can appear at several levels. The outermost is the SQL language itself—the level of such SQL statements as SELECT, UPDATE, and INSERT. Although different implementations agree in the main on these, they tend—as you have seen—to add clauses of their own for special purposes, or even to add entirely new types of statements. Or the syntax of the statements may vary to some extent among different systems.

For these reasons, implementations of SQL belonging to different vendors sometimes are referred to as *dialects*: they differ in essentially the same way that dialects of a natural language do. By and large, "speakers" of the various dialects can understand each other, but there are minor differences in pronunciation, and perhaps not all words are shared.

At another level, differences can exist in the function call interface (also called the API—"application programming interface") or even in the precompiler syntax.

The analogy here is to *written* as opposed to spoken language: even when a spoken language is shared, different communities may write the language differently. One might write *color* and another write *colour*. For one SQL system, the function call to connect to a database might be ORACON; for another it might be SQLCON or SQLCONNECT. Or arguments might appear in a different order: *user name, database name, password* versus *password, database name, user name*. Differences such as these can persist at the programmatic level even in the face of standardization at the level of SQL statements. And in fact standardization at this level does not receive as much attention as the standardization of SQL statements themselves.

When there are differences at either of these levels, the incompatibilities interfere with the ability to connect front ends and back ends of different vendors and to run an application on a variety of machines.

As users, we might try to address this by fixing on one vendor's products for all environments, but even doing this does not necessarily yield complete portability. IBM's OS/2 Extended Edition for the PC is not entirely compatible with IBM's own DB2 for the mainframe, for example. Portability thus can be problematical even within one vendor's product line.

Then, too, programming languages themselves are not entirely standardized. COBOL on a mainframe is not necessarily the same as COBOL on a microcomputer or COBOL on a minicomputer. And here again we may encounter incompatibilities arising from the fact that different versions of the language are offered by different vendors.

Even if we go so far as to confine ourselves not only to one SQL vendor's SQL but also to one COBOL vendor's COBOL, we may find that we are paying an unacceptable price in other respects, for all vendors' products do not *perform* the same. One vendor's SQL may perform well on a minicomputer but miserably on a mainframe. Or the product may do very well on a mainframe or minicomputer but require so much memory that it is terribly slow on a PC.

So, as things stand, the goal of complete portability has not been met except in the special case in which we may be willing to use a single vendor's SQL engine and a single vendor's language for all machines. And, this solution is not always either workable or desirable.

Which leads us to the question, What is the outlook for the future?

Prospects

Complete standardization of the SQL language is unlikely if this standardization is meant to imply that all versions would then offer exactly the same features and use exactly the same syntax. There is no reason to think that developers will stop having ideas for interesting new features such as those mentioned in Chapter 19, "Promising Developments and Extensions." Standardization is always bound to lag behind such new developments: no matter how much the boundaries of standard SQL continue to expand, encompassing a greater and greater body of features, the frontier is likely to keep expanding too. And, on the frontier we will always find diversity.

But even though the vision of a perfectly unified SQL may be a mirage, we can still expect to see continual gains in portability and connectivity as new features are added to the standard.

For application programmers this means that there is a substantial and growing subset of the SQL language that they can use with confidence that their applications will work with other engines. This is especially true if programmers write for a precompiler interface, but even directly coding function calls is likely to have less and less of an adverse effect on portability. Comparable function calls belonging to different systems tend to differ, as we said earlier, only in minor syntactic details. This means that, unless the application calls a feature not supported by the engine in which the application is supposed to run, a one-to-one translation from one set of function calls to another is easy to bring about.

Another development that will tend to minimize the problem of portability is the appearance of application development tools that include a fourth-generation language. These development tools allow applications to be built virtually or entirely without coding and with little or no attention paid to tailoring them to a particular engine. Rather, the application is assembled from the menus and options of the tool, which comes with a selection of SQL drivers. The drivers—also called translators or routers—enable applications to run with many different SQL engines.

We can expect to see vendors of front ends supplying drivers to allow their products to run against different SQL engines. As a result, lack of portability should largely cease to be a problem except when we want to use extensions to the SQL language or API that are peculiar to a certain engine.

Summing Up

Here, then, is a summary of our predictions for the future:

No static SQL standard is likely to emerge; vendors will continue to provide new extensions. But at the same time, implementations will converge on the more established features, and the number of standard features will grow even as the frontier of development continues to expand.

Even though standardization is likely to occur at the level of the SQL language, we are less likely to see standardization at the API level, except perhaps in the case of the precompiler interface. This should become standardized and useful for most of the purposes for which an application is needed—for example, accounting, reporting, and querying. But there will always be specialized applications, such as ad hoc query tools and graphic-based systems, that require better performance and a greater degree of control over interactions between a front end and a back end than a precompiler interface can provide. These more demanding applications will keep function call interfaces from becoming obsolete. And although function calls are unlikely to be significantly standardized, translating from one to another is not a major headache.

We probably will continue to see many SQL engines, and the choice among them will hinge not on the completeness of the implementation of the SQL language—because every vendor will offer essentially everything in that regard—but on the relative performance of the engine in the chosen environment.

We can expect to see more and more cases of front ends divorced from back ends. So far they have been offered together, but advances in the ability to operate one vendor's front end with another's engine will result in more front ends offered by vendors who do not even make a back end. These separately marketed front-end tools will come with drivers for a variety of back ends, thus easing the problem of portability.

APPENDIX A

Sample C Program

The following program, SAMPLE.C, is written in the C programming language. It was constructed, with some additions, from the sample code in Chapter 14, "Using a Function Call Interface." Some of the additions illustrate operations described in Chapter 15, "Advanced Programming with a Function Call Interface."

The program covers three transactions. The first transaction creates a table. The next transaction inserts data into the table. The third transaction, a multihandle operation, shows a query and an UPDATE statement working in tandem. As each row of the result set of the query is fetched from a table, it is updated (or not) based on user input. In the example, the data used is contained in the program itself.

SAMPLE.C

```c
#include "stdio.h"
#include "sql.h"
#include "errsql.h"
/* data for sample table           */
    struct item {
        char desc[26];
        char price[6];
    } tabdata[]= {"CINNAMON", "1.00",
                  "SAGE", ".95",
                  "BASIL", ".89",
                  "OREGANO",".89",
                  "SAFFRON","3.00",
                  "GINSENG","4.59",
                  "", "" };
/* The default database name "demo" and default password is used for this */
/* sample program. */
```

257

```
        static   char note[]="sample.txt";
        static   char dbnam[] = "demo";
        static   char crtitem [] =     /* CREATE ITEM table command */
        "CREATE TABLE ITEM (ITEM_NO NUMBER NOT NULL, DESCRIPTION CHAR(25),\
PRICE DECIMAL (5,2), NOTES LONG VARCHAR)";

        static char insitem[] =
        "INSERT INTO ITEM VALUES (:1,:2,:3,:4)";

        static char selitem [] =
        "SELECT * FROM ITEM";

        static char updprice[] =
        "UPDATE ITEM SET PRICE = :1 WHERE CURRENT OF C1";

        SQLTCUR cur1;              /* first handle          */
        SQLTCUR cur2;              /* second handle         */
        short ret;                 /* return code           */
        char notebuf[200];         /* buffer for long note */
        uint itemno;               /* item number           */
        char pricebuf[25];         /* price area            */
        char itembuf[26];          /* item area             */
main()
{
        int len;                   /* length of bound data */
        int cols;                  /* bind variable number */
/* Connect to demo database       */
        if (ret = sqlcnc (&cur1, dbnam,0))
                        failure(ret ,"CONNECT");
        if (ret = sqlcnc (&cur2, dbnam,0)) /*second handle*/
                        failure(ret,"CONNECT 2");
/* Create the ITEM table */
        if (sqlcex (cur1, crtitem, 0))
                failure(cur1, "CREATE TABLE error");
        if (sqlcmt(cur1))          /* Commit DDL transaction    */
                failure (cur1,"ON CREATE COMMIT");
        itemins();                 /* Insert the ITEM data    */
        if (sqlcmt(cur1))          /* Commit the transaction   */
                failure (cur1,"ON INSERT COMMIT");
        priceupd ();               /* Select and update prices */
        if (sqlcmt (cur1))         /* Commit update transaction */
                failure (cur1,"ON UPDATE COMMIT");
        discnct(); /* Disconnect handle */
}
itemins()
{
        FILE *fp;
        int col;
        struct item *datap;        /* pointer to input data */
        short maxitem = 0;         /* highest item number   */
/* Open the file for getting the LONG text */
        if ((fp = fopen(note, "r")) == NULL)
                failure (cur1, "OPEN FILE ERROR");
```

```c
        /* Compile insert statement */
        if (sqlcom (cur1, insitem, 0))
                failure(cur1, "COMPILE ERROR");
/* Bind three LONG columns to the area that contains data */
        if (sqlbnn(cur1,1,&maxitem,sizeof(int),0,SQLPUIN) ||
           sqlbnn (cur1, 2, itembuf, 0, 0, SQLPSTR) ||
           sqlbnn(cur1,3,pricebuf,0,0,SQLPSTR))
                failure(cur1, "SQLBNN ERROR ");
        datap = &tabdata[0];            /* Point to data   */
        while (*(datap->desc) != '\0')  /* Insert rows     */
        {
                maxitem++;              /* Get new item number        */
                strcpy(itembuf, datap->desc);  /* Copy description */
                strcpy(pricebuf,datap->price); /* Copy price      */
/* Bind the LONG column */
                if (sqlbln (cur1, 4))
                        failure (cur1, "ERROR ON SQLBLN");
                wrtlong(fp);            /* Write the long field */
                if (sqlexe (cur1))      /* Execute the insert   */
                        failure(cur1,"ERROR ON EXECUTE");
                datap++;                /* Next item to insert  */
        }
        fclose (fp);
        printf ("out of insert loop\n");
}

/* The routine fetches each row, including LONG data, asks for user input */
/* regarding new price, and updates the price if indicated.  */
priceupd ()
{
                int len;
                short frc;              /* Fetch return code   */
                char newprice[25];
                                        /* Length of data read */
                char line[80];
                                        /* Output buffer       */
                if (sqlcom (cur1, selitem, 0)) /* Compile select */
                        failure(cur1, "SELECT COMPILE");
                if (sqlscn (cur1, "C1", 2)) /* Name cursor C1    */
                        failure(cur1, "SET CURSOR NAME");
                if (sqlcom (cur2, updprice, 0)) /* Compile UPDATE */
                        failure(cur2, "COMPILE ERROR");
/*      Bind price buffer for update statement  */
                if (sqlbnn(cur2,1,newprice,0,0,SQLPSTR))
                        failure(cur2, "SQLBNN ERROR ");
/* Set buffers for the character columns. Not necessary for last column, */
/* which is a LONG. */
        if (sqlssb(cur1, 1, SQLPUIN, &itemno, sizeof(itemno),
                0,SQLNPTR, SQLNPTR)
                || sqlssb(cur1, 2,SQLPSTR, itembuf, sizeof (itembuf),
                  0,SQLNPTR, SQLNPTR)
                ||sqlssb(cur1, 3,SQLPSTR, pricebuf, sizeof (pricebuf),
```

```
                        0, SQLNPTR, SQLNPTR))
                    failure (cur1, "ERROR on SET SELECT BUFFER");
        if (sqlexe (cur1))
                    failure (cur1, "Execute error");
        while (!(frc = sqlfet(cur1)))   /* Fetch one at a time*/
        {
            printf("\n\n\n");
            sprintf (line, "%d   %s   %s\n", itemno, itembuf,pricebuf);
            printf ("%s\n", line);        /* Display data on the screen */
/* Read the LONG column and display      */
            for (; ;)
            {
                    memset (line, '\0', 80);
                    if (ret = sqlrlo(cur1, 4, line, 79, &len))
                       failure (cur1, "Error on read long");
                    else
                       printf ("%s", line); /* Display the data */
                    if (len == 0)       /* No more data for that row */
                    {
                       if (ret = sqlelo (cur1))/* End long */
                           failure (cur1, "Error on end long");
                       else
                       printf("\n");
                         break;
                            /* Done processing LONG */
                    }
            }

        /* Update the price according to user input */
            for (; ;)
            {
printf ("Enter new price for %s; or return if no price
        change ", itembuf);
                /* Get user input */
                *gets (newprice);
                if (*newprice == '\0')
                    break;        /* No input */
                strcpy (pricebuf,newprice);
                printf ("newprice=%s\n",newprice);
                if (ret = sqlexe (cur2))
                        failure (cur2, "update execute error");
            }
        }
        if (frc != 1)     /* If not end of fetch    */
                failure (cur1, "Error on Fetch");
}
/* This routine writes the LONG column using data from SAMPLE.TXT. */
wrtlong (fp)
FILE *fp;
{
        char col = 4;
        int count;
```

```
/* Open the SAMPLE.TXT file, which contains the LONG data. Each record entry */
/* for this sample program is delineated with a line containing a single     */
/* backslash. When this is reached, end the LONG operation, move the         */
/* other LONG data into its data area, and execute the insert.               */
        for (; ;)
        {
                memset (notebuf,'\0',200);
                if ((fgets(notebuf,200,fp)) == NULL)/* Read file       */
                        break;          /* End of file                 */
                if (notebuf[0] == '\\')
                        break;                  /* No more row data    */
                count = strlen(notebuf);        /* How many bytes to write */
                if (sqlwlo(cur1,notebuf,count))  /* Write LONG          */
                        failure(cur1, "Error on WRITE LONG\n");
        }
        if (sqlelo(cur1))  /* End LONG operation*/
                failure(cur1, "Error on End long");
        printf ("after end long routine\n");
}
failure (cur, p)
SQLTCUR cur;                            /* handle                      */
char  *p;                               /* message string              */
{
        SQLTEPO    epo;                 /* error position              */
        char errmsg [SQLMERR];          /* error text                  */

        sqlerr(ret, errmsg);            /* get error text              */
        if (cur1 || cur2)               /* handle connected?           */
        {
           sqlrcd (cur, &ret);
           sqlepo(cur, &epo);           /* get error position  */
           sqlcex(cur, "DROP TABLE ITEM",0);    /* drop table for testing */
        }
        printf("%d %s, %s %d\n", ret,p, errmsg, epo);
        discnct ();                     /* disconnect handles */
        exit(1);
}
discnct ()
{
    if (cur1)
        sqldis(cur1);
    if (cur2)
        sqldis(cur2);
}
```

SAMPLE.TXT

The file SAMPLE.TXT consists of entries separated by backslashes (\). For example:

```
Sage is good in eggs, meat, and fish.
\
Basil is good in tomato sauce and pesto.
```

```
\
Oregano is good in tomato sauce.
\
Saffron comes from Spain. It is expensive because each flower is handpicked.
It is a delicious and delicate spice used in paella.
\
Ginseng is considered by some to have magical properties. Used in tea.
```

APPENDIX B

SQLBase API Function Calls

This appendix lists the SQLBase API functions.

Name	Function
sqlarf	Apply roll-forward journal
sqlbkp	Network backup of database
sqlbld	Bind LONG data
sqlbln	Bind LONG data (by number)
sqlbnd	Bind data variables
sqlbnn	Bind data variables (by number)
sqlcex	Compile and execute
sqlcmt	Commit a transaction
sqlcnc	Connect to a cursor or database
sqlcnr	Connect to a cursor or database without recovery
sqlcom	Compile a SQL statement
sqlcon	Connect to a cursor and database
sqlcpy	Copy from table to table
sqlcrs	Close (and save) result set
sqlcty	Get the command type
sqldes	Describe an item in a SELECT statement

sqldin	Deinstall a database
sqldir	Get directory of available databases
sqldis	Disconnect from a cursor and database
sqldon	Terminate use of Windows API dynamic library
sqldrs	Drop result set
sqldsc	Describe the items in a SELECT list
sqldst	Drop a stored SQL statement
sqlebk	End network backup
sqlefb	Enable fetch backward
sqlelo	End of LONG read or write operation
sqlepo	Get error position in statement
sqlerf	End roll-forward journal
sqlerr	Get error message text
sqlers	End network restore
sqlexe	Execute a SQL statement
sqlexp	Show query execution plan
sqlfbk	Fetch backward a row
sqlfer	Get full SQLBase error message line
sqlfet	Fetch the next result row
sqlfqn	Get fully qualified column name from SELECT list
sqlgfi	Get fetch information
sqlgls	Get size of LONG column
sqlgnr	Get number of rows in a table
sqlims	Set input message size
sqlini	Initialize API library under Microsoft Windows
sqlins	Install a database
sqllab	Get label information for item in SELECT list
sqllsk	Seek position in LONG data
sqlnbv	Return number of program variables
sqlnrr	Return number of rows in result set
sqlnsi	Return the number of SELECT items

Appendix B: SQLBase API Function Calls

sqloms	Set output message size
sqlprs	Position cursor in result set
sqlrbf	Get the rollback flag
sqlrbk	Rollback a transaction
sqlrcd	Get the return code
sqlrdc	Read database chunk for network backup
sqlres	Restore file backed up with network backup
sqlret	Retrieve a stored SQL statement
sqlrlo	Read LONG data
sqlrow	Get the number of rows affected
sqlrrd	Recover restored database
sqlrrs	Restart result set
sqlscn	Set cursor name
sqlscp	Set number of cache pages
sqlsil	Set isolation level
sqlslp	Set log parameters
sqlspr	Stop restriction mode
sqlsrf	Start roll-forward journal
sqlsrs	Start result set mode
sqlssb	Set SELECT buffer
sqlsss	Set sort buffer size
sqlsta	Get disk I/O statistics
sqlsto	Store a compiled SQL statement
sqlstr	Start restriction mode
sqlsys	Get database system information
sqltio	Set timeout on waiting for a lock
sqlurs	Undo a result set
sqlwdc	Write database chunk of network backup file
sqlwlo	Write LONG data
sqlxad	Add two numbers in SQLBase internal format
sqlxcn	Convert string to SQLBase internal number

sqlxda	Add *n* days to an internal SQLBase date
sqlxdp	Convert date using picture formats
sqlxdv	Divide two internal numbers
sqlxml	Multiply two internal numbers
sqlxnp	Convert SQLBase internal number using picture formats
sqlxpd	Convert string to internal date
sqlxsb	Subtract two internal numbers

APPENDIX C

Sample COBOL Programs

This appendix contains two COBOL application programs. Both use a cursor to perform update and delete operations. The first program is written for a function call interface. The second program is written for a precompiler.

Program for a Function Call Interface

The following application program was written for a SQLBase SQL/API COBOL function call interface:

```
000100 IDENTIFICATION DIVISION.
000200 PROGRAM-ID.     EXAMPLE1.
000300
000400
000500
000600
000700 REMARKS.        This program demonstrates using the SQL
000800                 application programming function call interface.
000900                 The program uses a cursor to process a set
001000                 of rows from the EMP employee table. Any
001100                 employee earning less than $2 an hour is given
001200                 a raise, and any employee earning more than
001300                 $4 an hour is fired.
001400
001500 ENVIRONMENT DIVISION.
001600 DATA DIVISION.
001700 WORKING-STORAGE SECTION.
001800 77  CUR1            PIC 9(04) COMP-5 VALUE 0.
001900 77  RCD1            PIC 9(04) COMP-5 VALUE 0.
002000 77  CUR2            PIC 9(04) COMP-5 VALUE 0.
002100 77  RCD2            PIC 9(04) COMP-5 VALUE 0.
```

```
002200 77  DB-NAME           PIC X(04)         VALUE "DEMO".
002300 77  CURNAME           PIC X(06)         VALUE "FETCUR".
002400 77  EMPLOYNO          PIC S9(08) COMP-5.
002500 77  HOURLY-PAY        PIC S9(3)V99 COMP-3.
002600 77  PTR               USAGE POINTER.
002700 77  LEN               PIC X(04) COMP-5 VALUE 4.
002800 77  SELECT-ITEM-NO    PIC 9(02) COMP    VALUE 0.
002900 77  PDL               PIC 9(02) COMP    VALUE 0.
003000 77  SCALE             PIC 9(02) COMP    VALUE 0.
003100 77  PDT               PIC X(01)         VALUE SPACES.
003200 77  SQLPBUF           PIC X(01)         VALUE X"01".
003300 77  SQLPSLO           PIC X(01)         VALUE X"08".
003400 77  SQLPSPD           PIC X(01)         VALUE X"0E".
003500 77  SQLNPTR           USAGE POINTER.
003600 77  NULL-VALUE        PIC X(01)         VALUE X"00".
003700
003800 01  SELECT-STATEMENT.
003900     02  FILLER        PIC X(90) VALUE "SELECT EMPNO, FIRST_NAME,
004000-        "INITIAL, LAST_NAME, FIRST_DAY, HRLY_PAY FROM EMP WHERE
004100-        "DEPT = 2".
004200     02  FILLER        PIC X(01) VALUE X"00".
004300
004400 01  UPDATE-STATEMENT.
004500     02  FILLER        PIC X(51) VALUE
004600         "UPDATE EMP SET HRLY_PAY = 2 WHERE CURRENT OF FETCUR".
004700     02  FILLER        PIC X(01) VALUE X"00".
004800
004900 01  DELETE-STATEMENT.
005000     02  FILLER        PIC X(39) VALUE
005100         "DELETE FROM EMP WHERE CURRENT OF FETCUR".
005200     02  FILLER        PIC X(01) VALUE X"00".
005300
005400 01  PRINT-LINE.
005500     02  PRT-EMPNO       PIC Z(02).
005600     02  FILLER          PIC X(01).
005700     02  PRT-FIRST-NAME  PIC X(10).
005800     02  FILLER          PIC X(01).
005900     02  MIDDLE-INITIAL  PIC X(01).
006000     02  FILLER          PIC X(01).
006100     02  PRT-LAST-NAME   PIC X(10).
006200     02  FILLER          PIC X(01).
006300     02  START-DATE      PIC X(10).
006400     02  FILLER          PIC X(01).
006500     02  PRT-HOURLY-PAY  PIC ZZZ.99.
006600     02  FILLER          PIC X(01).
006700     02  PRT-REMARKS     PIC X(20).
006800
006900 01  ERROR-LINE.
007000     02  FILLER        PIC X(11) VALUE "EXAMPLE1 : ".
007100     02  ERROR-MSG     PIC X(30) VALUE SPACES.
007200     02  FILLER        PIC X(02) VALUE " (".
007300     02  ERROR-CODE    PIC 9(06) VALUE ZERO.
007400     02  FILLER        PIC X(02) VALUE ") ".
007500
```

```
007600 01  SSB-ERROR-MSG.
007700     02  FILLER          PIC X(16) VALUE "FAILURE ON SSB #".
007800     02  SSB-ERR-NO      PIC 9(01).
007900/
008000 PROCEDURE DIVISION.
008100     CALL "MFGLUE".
008200     CALL "MFSQLAPI".
008300
008400******************************************************************
008500*                                                                *
008600*    CONNECT TO DATABASE:                                        *
008700*                                                                *
008800*    Two cursors are necessary. One cursor is to be used         *
008900*    for fetching from the database, and the second cursor       *
009000*    is used to do updates or deletes as necessary.              *
009100*                                                                *
009200******************************************************************
009300
009400     SET PTR TO ADDRESS OF DB-NAME.
009500
009600     CALL "MFSQLCNC" USING CUR1, PTR, LEN, RCD1.
009700
009800     IF  RCD1 NOT = ZERO
009900     THEN MOVE "FAILURE ON CONNECT OF CURSOR1" TO ERROR-MSG
010000          MOVE RCD1                            TO ERROR-CODE
010100          DISPLAY ERROR-LINE
010200          GO TO 800-CLOSE-CURSOR.
010300
010400     CALL "MFSQLCNC" USING CUR2, PTR, LEN, RCD2.
010500
010600     IF  RCD2 NOT = ZERO
010700     THEN MOVE "FAILURE ON CONNECT OF CURSOR2" TO ERROR-MSG
010800          MOVE RCD2                            TO ERROR-CODE
010900          DISPLAY ERROR-LINE
011000          GO TO 800-CLOSE-CURSOR.
011100
011200******************************************************************
011300*                                                                *
011400*    NAME FIRST CURSOR:                                          *
011500*                                                                *
011600*    The first cursor is named "FETCUR" so that the              *
011700*    second cursor can reference the first cursor. The second    *
011800*    cursor references the first cursor doing updates and        *
011900*    deletes with the CURRENT OF cursor clause.                  *
012000*                                                                *
012100******************************************************************
012200
012300     SET PTR TO ADDRESS OF CURNAME.
012400     MOVE 6  TO LEN.
012500
012600     CALL "MFSQLSCN" USING CUR1, PTR, LEN, RCD1.
012700
012800     IF  RCD1 NOT = ZERO
012900     THEN MOVE "FAILURE SETTING CURSOR NAME" TO ERROR-MSG
013000          MOVE RCD1                          TO ERROR-CODE
```

```
013100          DISPLAY ERROR-LINE
013200          GO TO 800-CLOSE-CURSOR.
013300
013400**********************************************************
013500*                                                        *
013600*    COMPILE THE SELECT STATEMENT                        *
013700*                                                        *
013800*    The compile of the SELECT statement verifies syntax,*
013900*    checks to see that the user has been granted authority *
014000*    to fetch the data from the table, and does access path *
014100*    analysis to figure out the best way of retrieving the  *
014200*    requested data.                                     *
014300*                                                        *
014400**********************************************************
014500
014600      SET  PTR  TO ADDRESS OF SELECT-STATEMENT.
014700      MOVE ZERO TO LEN.
014800      CALL "MFSQLCOM" USING CUR1, PTR, LEN, RCD1.
014900
015000      IF   RCD1 NOT = ZERO
015100      THEN MOVE "FAILURE ON SELECT COMPILE" TO ERROR-MSG
015200           MOVE RCD1                        TO ERROR-CODE
015300           DISPLAY ERROR-LINE
015400           GO TO 800-CLOSE-CURSOR.
015500
015600**********************************************************
015700*                                                        *
015800*    SET UP SELECT BUFFERS                               *
015900*                                                        *
016000*    A SELECT buffer needs to be set up for each column being *
016100*    selected from the database. In this case, we are   *
016200*    selecting six columns. This process tells SQL where to *
016300*    put data when retrieving it from the database, how much *
016400*    space is provided, and the input data-type conversion. *
016500*                                                        *
016600**********************************************************
016700
016800      SET  SQLNPTR TO ADDRESS OF NULL-VALUE.
016900      MOVE 1       TO SELECT-ITEM-NO.
017000      SET  PTR     TO ADDRESS OF EMPLOYNO.
017100      MOVE SQLPSLO TO PDT.
017200      MOVE 8       TO PDL.
017300      PERFORM 700-SET-SELECT-BUF THRU 790-SET-SELECT-BUF-EXIT.
017400
017500      MOVE 2       TO SELECT-ITEM-NO.
017600      SET  PTR     TO ADDRESS OF PRT-FIRST-NAME.
017700      MOVE SQLPBUF TO PDT.
017800      MOVE 10      TO PDL.
017900      PERFORM 700-SET-SELECT-BUF THRU 790-SET-SELECT-BUF-EXIT.
018000
018100      MOVE 3       TO SELECT-ITEM-NO.
018200      SET  PTR     TO ADDRESS OF MIDDLE-INITIAL.
018300      MOVE SQLPBUF TO PDT.
018400      MOVE 1       TO PDL.
018500      PERFORM 700-SET-SELECT-BUF THRU 790-SET-SELECT-BUF-EXIT.
```

```
018600
018700          MOVE 4         TO SELECT-ITEM-NO.
018800          SET  PTR       TO ADDRESS OF PRT-LAST-NAME.
018900          MOVE SQLPBUF TO PDT.
019000          MOVE 10        TO PDL.
019100          PERFORM 700-SET-SELECT-BUF THRU 790-SET-SELECT-BUF-EXIT.
019200
019300          MOVE 5         TO SELECT-ITEM-NO.
019400          SET  PTR       TO ADDRESS OF START-DATE.
019500          MOVE SQLPBUF TO PDT.
019600          MOVE 10        TO PDL.
019700          PERFORM 700-SET-SELECT-BUF THRU 790-SET-SELECT-BUF-EXIT.
019800
019900          MOVE 6         TO SELECT-ITEM-NO.
020000          SET  PTR       TO ADDRESS OF HOURLY-PAY.
020100          MOVE SQLPSPD TO PDT.
020200          MOVE 5         TO PDL.
020300          MOVE 2         TO SCALE.
020400          PERFORM 700-SET-SELECT-BUF THRU 790-SET-SELECT-BUF-EXIT.
020500
020600***************************************************************
020700*                                                             *
020800*    EXECUTE SELECT STATEMENT                                 *
020900*                                                             *
021000*    The execution of the SELECT statement establishes        *
021100*    the set of rows to be fetched.                           *
021200*                                                             *
021300***************************************************************
021400
021500          CALL "MFSQLEXE" USING CUR1, RCD1.
021600
021700          IF   RCD1 NOT = ZERO
021800          THEN MOVE "FAILURE SELECT EXECUTE" TO ERROR-MSG
021900               MOVE RCD1                    TO ERROR-CODE
022000               DISPLAY ERROR-LINE
022100               GO TO 800-CLOSE-CURSOR.
022200
022300***************************************************************
022400*                                                             *
022500*    FETCH THE DATA                                           *
022600*                                                             *
022700*    The following loop fetches a row of data at a time.      *
022800*    If the employee's hourly pay is less than $2 per         *
022900*    hour, an update using the second cursor occurs. If the   *
023000*    employee's hourly pay is greater than $4 per hour,       *
023100*    a delete using the second cursor occurs.                 *
023200*                                                             *
023300***************************************************************
023400
023500 100-FETCH-A-ROW.
023600          CALL "MFSQLFET" USING CUR1, RCD1.
023700
023800          IF   RCD1 = 1
023900          THEN GO TO 800-CLOSE-CURSOR.
024000
```

```
024100      IF  RCD1 NOT = ZERO
024200      THEN MOVE "FAILURE ON FETCH" TO ERROR-MSG
024300           MOVE RCD1                TO ERROR-CODE
024400           DISPLAY ERROR-LINE
024500           GO TO 800-CLOSE-CURSOR.
024600
024700      IF  HOURLY-PAY < 2
024800      THEN MOVE "PAY INCREASE" TO PRT-REMARKS
024900           MOVE 2              TO HOURLY-PAY
025000           SET PTR  TO ADDRESS OF UPDATE-STATEMENT
025100           CALL "MFSQLCEX" USING CUR2, PTR, LEN, RCD2
025200      IF   RCD2 NOT = ZERO
025300      THEN MOVE "FAILURE ON UPDATE" TO ERROR-MSG
025400           MOVE RCD2                TO ERROR-CODE
025500           DISPLAY ERROR-LINE
025600           GO TO 800-CLOSE-CURSOR.
025700
025800      IF  HOURLY-PAY > 4
025900      THEN MOVE "FIRED!" TO PRT-REMARKS
026000           MOVE 0             TO HOURLY-PAY
026100           SET PTR  TO ADDRESS OF DELETE-STATEMENT
026200           CALL "MFSQLCEX" USING CUR2, PTR, LEN, RCD2
026300      IF   RCD2 NOT = ZERO
026400      THEN MOVE "FAILURE ON DELETE" TO ERROR-MSG
026500           MOVE RCD2                TO ERROR-CODE
026600           DISPLAY ERROR-LINE
026700           GO TO 800-CLOSE-CURSOR.
026800
026900      MOVE EMPLOYNO    TO PRT-EMPNO.
027000      MOVE HOURLY-PAY TO PRT-HOURLY-PAY.
027100      DISPLAY PRINT-LINE.
027200      MOVE SPACES TO PRINT-LINE.
027300      GO TO 100-FETCH-A-ROW.
027400
027500*****************************************************************
027600*                                                               *
027700*    ROUTINE TO PERFORM SET SELECT BUFFER FUNCTION CALL         *
027800*                                                               *
027900*****************************************************************
028000
028100 700-SET-SELECT-BUF.
028200     CALL "MFSQLSSB" USING CUR1, SELECT-ITEM-NO, PDT, PTR, PDL,
028300                           SCALE, SQLNPTR, SQLNPTR, RCD1.
028400
028500      IF  RCD1 NOT = ZERO
028600      THEN MOVE SELECT-ITEM-NO                 TO SSB-ERR-NO
028700           MOVE "FAILURE SETTING SELECT BUFFER" TO ERROR-MSG
028800           MOVE RCD1                           TO ERROR-CODE
028900           DISPLAY ERROR-LINE
029000           DISPLAY SSB-ERROR-MSG
029100           GO TO 800-CLOSE-CURSOR.
029200 790-SET-SELECT-BUF-EXIT.
029300     EXIT.
029400
```

```
029500***********************************************************
029600*                                                          *
029700*    END OF JOB ROUTINE THAT DISCONNECTS THE CURSOR         *
029800*                                                          *
029900***********************************************************
030000
030100 800-CLOSE-CURSOR.
030200     IF   CUR1 = ZERO
030300     THEN GO TO 850-CLOSE-2ND-CURSOR.
030400
030500     CALL "MFSQLDIS" USING CUR1, RCD1.
030600
030700     IF   RCD1 NOT = ZERO
030800     THEN MOVE "FAILURE ON DISCONNECT OF CURSOR1" TO ERROR-MSG
030900          MOVE RCD1                              TO ERROR-CODE
031000          DISPLAY ERROR-LINE.
031100
031200 850-CLOSE-2ND-CURSOR.
031300     IF   CUR2 = ZERO
031400     THEN GO TO 900-MAIN-EXIT.
031500
031600     CALL "MFSQLDIS" USING CUR2, RCD2.
031700
031800     IF   RCD2 NOT = ZERO
031900     THEN MOVE "FAILURE ON DISCONNECT OF CURSOR2" TO ERROR-MSG
032000          MOVE RCD2                              TO ERROR-CODE
032100          DISPLAY ERROR-LINE.
032200
032300 900-MAIN-EXIT.
032400     STOP RUN.
```

Program for Precompiler

The following application program was written for the SQLBase SQL/Preprocessor for COBOL, a COBOL SQL precompiler:

```
000100 IDENTIFICATION DIVISION.
000200 PROGRAM-ID.      EXAMPLE2.
000300
000400
000500
000600
000700 REMARKS.         This program demonstrates how to use a SQL
000800                  precompiler interface. The program uses a
000900                  cursor to process a set of rows from
001000                  the EMP employee table. Any employee
001100                  earning less than $2 an hour is given a
001200                  raise, and any employee earning more than
001300                  $4 an hour is fired.
001400
001500 ENVIRONMENT DIVISION.
001600 DATA DIVISION.
001700 WORKING-STORAGE SECTION.
```

```
001800 77  EMPLOYNO            PIC S9(05) COMP.
001900 77  FIRST-NAME          PIC X(20).
002000 77  LAST-NAME           PIC X(20).
002100 77  HOURLY-PAY          PIC S9(3)V99.
002200
002300 01  PRINT-LINE.
002400     02  PRT-EMPNO        PIC Z(02).
002500     02  FILLER           PIC X(01).
002600     02  PRT-FIRST-NAME   PIC X(10).
002700     02  FILLER           PIC X(01).
002800     02  MIDDLE-INITIAL   PIC X(01).
002900     02  FILLER           PIC X(01).
003000     02  PRT-LAST-NAME    PIC X(10).
003100     02  FILLER           PIC X(01).
003200     02  START-DATE       PIC X(10).
003300     02  FILLER           PIC X(01).
003400     02  PRT-HOURLY-PAY   PIC ZZZ.99.
003500     02  FILLER           PIC X(01).
003600     02  PRT-REMARKS      PIC X(20).
003700
003800 PROCEDURE DIVISION.
003900     EXEC SQL
004000       DECLARE FETCUR CURSOR FOR
004100         SELECT EMPNO, FIRST_NAME, INITIAL, LAST_NAME,
004200                FIRST_DAY, HRLY_PAY
004300         FROM EMP
004400         WHERE DEPT = 2
004500         FOR UPDATE OF HRLY_PAY
004600     END-EXEC.
004700
004800     EXEC SQL
004900       OPEN FETCUR
005000     END-EXEC.
005100
005200     EXEC SQL
005300       WHENEVER NOT FOUND
005400         GO TO 800-CLOSE-CURSOR
005500     END-EXEC.
005600
005700 100-FETCH-A-ROW.
005800     MOVE SPACES TO PRINT-LINE.
005900
006000     EXEC SQL
006100       FETCH FETCUR
006200         INTO :EMPLOYNO, :FIRST-NAME, :MIDDLE-INITIAL,
006300              :LAST-NAME, :START-DATE, :HOURLY-PAY
006400     END-EXEC.
006500
006600     MOVE EMPLOYNO   TO PRT-EMPNO.
006700     MOVE FIRST-NAME TO PRT-FIRST-NAME.
006800     MOVE LAST-NAME  TO PRT-LAST-NAME.
006900
```

```
007000       IF    HOURLY-PAY < 2
007100       THEN MOVE "PAY INCREASE" TO PRT-REMARKS
007200            MOVE 2              TO HOURLY-PAY
007300            EXEC SQL
007400               UPDATE EMP
007500                  SET HRLY_PAY = 2
007600                  WHERE CURRENT OF FETCUR
007700            END-EXEC.
007800
007900       IF    HOURLY-PAY > 4
008000       THEN MOVE "FIRED!" TO PRT-REMARKS
008100            MOVE 0          TO HOURLY-PAY
008200            EXEC SQL
008300               DELETE FROM EMP
008400                  WHERE CURRENT OF FETCUR
008500            END-EXEC.
008600
008700       MOVE HOURLY-PAY TO PRT-HOURLY-PAY.
008800       DISPLAY PRINT-LINE.
008900       GO TO 100-FETCH-A-ROW.
009000
009100 800-CLOSE-CURSOR.
009200       EXEC SQL
009300          CLOSE FETCUR
009400       END-EXEC.
009500
009600 900-MAIN-EXIT.
009700       STOP RUN.
```

APPENDIX D

Sample Database

This appendix is for readers who want to try examples of SQL statements like those used in Part 1, "Using SQL Interactively." The appendix contains SQL statements and data to re-create the five principal tables of the SPA database addressed by these examples.

To re-create the database, you use your system's interactive data manager interface to load the SQL statements from this appendix into a freshly initialized SQL-based database.

Readers who have Gupta Technologies' SQLBase can enter the statements exactly as they appear in this appendix through SQLTalk. Even readers who have a different DBMS probably can enter the statements—with one exception—verbatim through their own interactive data manager interface, although slight changes may have to be made.

The statements can be entered either by typing them directly in the interactive interface or by typing them first in an editor and then, in the interactive interface, running the resulting file as a batch file (see, for example, the SQLTalk RUN command).

The one statement, just alluded to, that is likely to require revising in order to be entered in a system other than SQLBase is the INSERT statement that supplies data for table ROOMS.

The first row of data associated with this statement contains text for the LONG VARCHAR column DESCRIPTION of the ROOMS table. Conventions for entering LONG data vary widely among different systems. In the case of this first row of data, two syntactical features are peculiar to SQLTalk: the long keyword preceding the LONG text for the DESCRIPTION column, and the pair of slashes (//) that terminate the text.

For readers not using SQLBase, the simplest remedy is just to omit entering the LONG text. You edit the row by following these steps:

1. Delete the $long keyword and replace it with a single comma, as shown in this example:

   1,ANNATTO RM,300,,

2. Delete the text describing the room and the pair of slashes terminating the text.

Alternatively, of course, the row can be edited in accordance with the applicable rules for entering LONG data on the system being used.

```
CREATE TABLE GUEST_ROSTER (NAME VARCHAR(25) NOT NULL,
ROOM VARCHAR(3), TRAINER VARCHAR(8), ARRIVAL DATE NOT NULL,
DEPARTURE DATE, DISCOUNT DECIMAL(2,2))
/
INSERT INTO GUEST_ROSTER
VALUES(:1, :2, :3, :4, :5, :6)
\
JEAN-PAUL ROTUNDO,3,JULIO,15-JUN-1988,17-JUN-1988,.2
BETTE MIDRIFF,1,MICHAEL,14-JUN-1988,16-JUN-1988,,
MARCELLO HISTRIONI,2,TODD,26-JUN-1988,,.1
MICHAEL JOHNSON,4,JULIO,15-JUN-1988,19-JUN-1988,,
CLINT WESTWOOD,5,MICHAEL,25-JUN-1988,,.15
SEAN PENCIL,6,TODD,15-JUN-1988,20-JUN-1988,.05
HETAERA,7,SERENA,24-JUN-1988,,,
JOANNIE RIVULETS,8,SERENA,25-JUN-1988,,.15
WARREN AMOROSO,9,TODD,16-JUN-1988,23-JUN-1988,.2
MARLON SPANDEX,10,JULIO,16-JUN-1988,23-JUN-1988,.05
OLYMPIA WELCH,11,MICHAEL,22-JUN-1988,27-JUN-1988,.1
HEATHER STARLETTE,12,SERENA,22-JUN-1988,,.05
DOLLY BRISKET,13,SERENA,22-JUN-1988,,,
JOAN TONIC,14,MICHAEL,23-JUN-1988,,.05
SEAN PENCIL,9,TODD,23-JUN-1988,,.1
MEL GIMLET,15,YVETTE,17-JUN-1988,24-JUN-1988,,
DON JACKSON,16,TODD,17-JUN-1988,25-JUN-1988,.1
HETAERA,10,SERENA,14-JUN-1988,20-JUN-1988,.2
ROBERT DINERO,17,YVETTE,18-JUN-1988,25-JUN-1988,.1
JANE FYUNDAI,18,MICHAEL,19-JUN-1988,26-JUN-1988,.1
DYAN HOWITZER,19,YVETTE,19-JUN-1988,26-JUN-1988,,
BIANCA JOGGER,20,TODD,20-JUN-1988,27-JUN-1988,.15
/
CREATE TABLE GUESTS (NAME VARCHAR(25) NOT NULL, SEX VARCHAR(1),
BUILD VARCHAR(1), HEIGHT INTEGER)
/
INSERT INTO GUESTS
VALUES(:1, :2, :3, :4)
\
BETTE MIDRIFF,F,M,66,
MARCELLO HISTRIONI,M,M,66,
JEAN-PAUL ROTUNDO,M,L,70,
MICHAEL JOHNSON,M,L,71,
CLINT WESTWOOD,M,M,73,
```

```
JOANNIE RIVULETS,F,S,65,
WARREN AMOROSO,M,M,70,
MARLON SPANDEX,M,M,71,
OLYMPIA WELCH,F,L,70,
HEATHER STARLETTE,F,M,66,
DOLLY BRISKET,F,S,61,
JOAN TONIC,F,M,62,
MEL GIMLET,M,M,70,
DON JACKSON,M,M,70,
ROBERT DINERO,M,L,69,
JANE FYUNDAI,F,L,65,
DYAN HOWITZER,F,S,68,
BIANCA JOGGER,F,S,61,
ENGLEBERT HUMPTYDUMPTY,M,L,72,
SHIRLEY O'SHADE,F,M,64,
SHARE,F,S,71,
STELLA SHIELDS,F,M,65,
SEAN PENCIL,M,S,65,
HETAERA,F,S,63,
/

CREATE TABLE ROOMS (ROOM VARCHAR(3), NAME VARCHAR(15),
RATE FLOAT, DESCRIPTION LONG VARCHAR)
/
INSERT INTO ROOMS (ROOM, NAME, RATE, DESCRIPTION)
VALUES (:1, :2, :3, :4)
\
1,ANNATTO RM,300,$long
One of our most attractive rooms, the Annatto Room is spacious and well
appointed in the luxurious La Bamba style. It includes its own complete gym,
jacuzzi, Olympic-size bath, and 36-inch television. Every surface is done in
delightful shades of annatto.
//
2,CARMINE RM,300,,
3,CERISE RM,250,,
4,CHERRY RM,250,,
5,MAROON RM,250,,
7,PEACH RM,250,,
8,MARIGOLD SUITE,325,,
9,GOLD RM,250,,
10,AMBER RM,250,,
11,BEIGE RM,250,,
12,SAND RM,250,,
13,JADE SUITE,325,,
14,MYRTLE SUITE,325,,
15,TURQUOISE RM,250,,
18,DAHLIA SUITE,325,,
19,OLIVE SUITE,375,,
20,PEARL SUITE,425,,
6,PUCE RM,250,,
16,MARINE RM,250,,
17,INDIGO RM,250,,
/

CREATE TABLE GUEST WT (GUEST VARCHAR(25) NOT NULL, WEIGHT DECIMAL(4,1),
WHEN DATE)
```

```
/
INSERT INTO GUEST_WT
VALUES(:1,:2,:3)
\
BETTE MIDRIFF,150,1988-06-14
BETTE MIDRIFF,148.5,1988-06-16
MARCELLO HISTRIONI,158,1988-06-26
MARCELLO HISTRIONI,157.5,1988-06-27
JEAN-PAUL ROTUNDO,190,1988-06-15
JEAN-PAUL ROTUNDO,189,1988-06-17
MICHAEL JOHNSON,186,1988-06-15
MICHAEL JOHNSON,183,1988-06-19
CLINT WESTWOOD,180,1988-06-25
CLINT WESTWOOD,178.5,1988-06-27
SEAN PENCIL,148,1988-06-15
SEAN PENCIL,150,1988-06-20
SEAN PENCIL,152,1988-06-23
SEAN PENCIL,149,1988-06-27
HETAERA,130,1988-06-14
HETAERA,128,1988-06-20
HETAERA,130,1988-06-24
HETAERA,129,1988-06-27
JOANNIE RIVULETS,115,1988-06-25
JOANNIE RIVULETS,116,1988-06-27
WARREN AMOROSO,168,1988-06-16
WARREN AMOROSO,162.5,1988-06-23
MARLON SPANDEX,171,1988-06-16
MARLON SPANDEX,165,1988-06-23
OLYMPIA WELCH,165,1988-06-22
OLYMPIA WELCH,159,1988-06-27
HEATHER STARLETTE,147,1988-06-22
HEATHER STARLETTE,143,1988-06-27
DOLLY BRISKET,125,1988-06-22
DOLLY BRISKET,122,1988-06-27
JOAN TONIC,136,1988-06-23
JOAN TONIC,133,1988-06-27
MEL GIMLET,166,1988-06-17
MEL GIMLET,163,1988-06-24
DON JACKSON,165,1988-06-17
DON JACKSON,159,1988-06-25
ROBERT DINERO,195,1988-06-18
ROBERT DINERO,185,1988-06-25
DYAN HOWITZER,125,1988-06-19
DYAN HOWITZER,128,1988-06-26
BIANCA JOGGER,113,1988-06-20
BIANCA JOGGER,109,1988-06-27
JANE FYUNDAI,165,1988-06-19
JANE FYUNDAI,160,1988-06-26
/

CREATE TABLE WEIGHT_CHART (HEIGHT INTEGER, SEX CHAR(1),
BUILD CHAR(1),MIN_WT DECIMAL(3,0), MAX_WT DECIMAL(3,0))
/
INSERT INTO WEIGHT_CHART VALUES(:1,:2,:3,:4,:5)
\
```

```
61,M,S,123,129
62,M,S,125,131
63,M,S,127,133
64,M,S,129,135
65,M,S,131,137
66,M,S,133,140
67,M,S,135,143
68,M,S,137,146
69,M,S,139,149
70,M,S,141,152
71,M,S,144,155
72,M,S,147,159
73,M,S,150,163
74,M,S,153,167
75,M,S,157,171
61,M,M,126,136
62,M,M,128,138
63,M,M,130,140
64,M,M,132,143
65,M,M,134,146
66,M,M,137,149
67,M,M,140,152
68,M,M,143,155
69,M,M,146,158
70,M,M,149,161
71,M,M,152,165
72,M,M,155,169
73,M,M,159,173
74,M,M,162,177
75,M,M,166,182
61,M,L,133,145
62,M,L,135,148
63,M,L,137,151
64,M,L,139,155
65,M,L,141,159
66,M,L,144,163
67,M,L,147,167
68,M,L,150,171
69,M,L,163,175
70,M,L,156,179
71,M,L,159,183
72,M,L,163,187
73,M,L,167,192
74,M,L,171,197
75,M,L,176,202
57,F,S,99,108
58,F,S,100,110
59,F,S,101,112
60,F,S,103,115
61,F,S,105,118
62,F,S,108,121
63,F,S,111,124
64,F,S,114,127
65,F,S,117,130
66,F,S,120,133
```

```
67,F,S,123,136
68,F,S,126,139
69,F,S,129,142
70,F,S,132,145
71,F,S,135,148
57,F,M,106,117
58,F,M,108,120
59,F,M,110,123
60,F,M,112,126
61,F,M,115,129
62,F,M,118,132
63,F,M,121,135
64,F,M,124,138
65,F,M,127,141
66,F,M,130,143
67,F,M,133,147
68,F,M,136,150
69,F,M,139,153
70,F,M,142,156
71,F,M,145,159
57,F,L,115,128
58,F,L,117,131
59,F,L,119,134
60,F,L,122,137
61,F,L,125,140
62,F,L,128,144
63,F,L,131,148
64,F,L,134,152
65,F,L,137,156
66,F,L,140,160
67,F,L,143,164
68,F,L,146,167
69,F,L,149,170
70,F,L,152,173
71,F,L,155,176
/
```

APPENDIX E

Sample dBASE Programs

This appendix contains two sample application programs using SQL statements embedded in dBASE-language code.

The first program, Sample Program 1, creates an EMPLOYEE table and displays an on-screen form with an editable field for each column in the table. The user can fill in these fields with new values. When the user is done, the values on-screen are relayed to an INSERT statement to be inserted into a new row. The user is prompted, if necessary, not to leave the fields Soc_sec_no and Lastname empty. The program stops when the user leaves the on-screen fields blank.

The second program, Sample Program 2, declares a cursor for a query having a FOR UPDATE clause and fetches each row into variables. If the values of the variables satisfy either of two specified conditions, the values are relayed to the appropriate UPDATE statement—there are two—and used to update the row currently under the cursor.

Sample Program 1

```
* Initialize memory variables for user name and password.
STORE SPACE(8) TO dbname, username, password
@ 3,5 SAY "Enter your user name: " GET username
READ
@ 5,5 SAY "Enter your password: "
* Change the display color for GET areas to hide the user's password.
SET COLOR TO N/N, N/N
@ 5,27 GET password
READ
SET COLOR TO
```

```
@ 7,5 SAY "Enter database name: " GET dbname
READ
* The following command, to select the SQLBase server, is a WordTech extension.
SET DATASERVER TO SQLBASE
* Log onto the SQL data server.
CONNECT &dbname/&username/&password
* Create the Employee table. Use of semicolons follows dBASE usage, not SQL,
* and indicates that the line of code wraps.
CREATE TABLE Employee ( Soc_sec_no DECIMAL(9,0) NOT NULL, ;
                        Lastname   CHAR(15) NOT NULL, ;
                        Firstname  CHAR(10), ;
                        Job        CHAR(20), ;
                        Dept       CHAR(15), ;
                        Hiredate   DATE, ;
                        Salary     DECIMAL(6,0) )
* This command, a WordTech extension, accesses SQL.
SET DATASERVER ON
* Open the Employee table.
USE Employee
STORE .F. TO done
* A loop that allows the user to enter data for the Employee table into memory
* variables. The loop continues until the user leaves all variables blank.
DO WHILE .NOT. done
    * CLEAR AUTOMEM is a WordTech extension. In standard dBASE, you need
    * to RELEASE from memory and initialize variables one by one.
    CLEAR AUTOMEM
    CLEAR
    @ 5, 5 SAY "Employee's Social Security Number: " GET m->soc_sec_no;
      PICTURE "999-99-9999"
    @ 7, 5 SAY "Employee's last name: " GET m->lastname
    @ 7,50 SAY "First name: " GET m->firstname
    @ 10, 5 SAY "Job Title: " GET m->job
    @ 10,50 SAY "Department: " GET m->dept
    @ 12, 5 SAY "Date Hired: " GET m->hiredate
    @ 12,50 SAY "Current Salary: " GET m->salary
    READ
    * If the user entered data, check for a Social Security number and name.
    * If the user did not enter data, exit the loop.
    IF READKEY() > 255
        IF EMPTY(m->soc_sec_no) .OR. EMPTY(m->lastname)
            * The Soc_sec_no and Lastname columns must be non-NULL
            @ 20,5 SAY "You must enter a name and Social Security Number " +;
               "for each employee. Press any key to return to editing."
            WAIT
        ELSE
            * Add a row to Employee with the new values, then clear the
            * variables for the next time.
            INSERT INTO Employee (Soc_sec_no, Lastname, Firstname, Job, ;
                Dept, Hiredate, Salary) ;
                VALUES (:soc_sec_no, :lastname, :firstname, :job, ;
                :dept, :hiredate, :salary)
        ENDIF
    ELSE
        done = .T.
    ENDIF
```

```
ENDDO
USE
SET DATASERVER OFF
```

Sample Program 2

```
    * Initialize memory variables for user name and password.
    STORE SPACE(8) TO username, password
    @ 3,5 say "Enter your user name: " GET username
    READ
    @ 5,5 SAY "Enter your password: "
    * Change the display color for GET areas to hide the user's password.
    SET COLOR TO N/N, N/N
    @ 5,27 GET password
    READ
    SET COLOR TO
    @ 7,5 say "Enter database name: " GET dbname
    READ
    * Following command, to select the SQLBase server, is a WordTech extension.
    SET DATASERVER TO SQLBASE
    * Log onto the SQL data server.
    CONNECT &dbname/&username/&password
    * This command, a WordTech extension, accesses SQL.
    SET DATASERVER ON
    * Use a cursor to process the rows of the Employee table. Each salesperson
    * who has worked for the company for more than six months and who earns $20,000
    * or less is given a 10 percent raise. Each salesperson who earns $40,000 or
    * more takes a 10 percent pay cut.
    DECLARE Personnel CURSOR FOR ;
        SELECT Hiredate, Salary FROM Employee;
            WHERE Dept = 'Sales';
        FOR UPDATE OF Salary
    OPEN Personnel
    FETCH Personnel INTO hiredate, salary
    * FETCHing the last row sets SQLCODE() to 1.
    DO WHILE .NOT. SQLCODE() = 1
        IF m->salary <= 20000 .AND. DATE() - m->hiredate >= 180
            UPDATE Employee SET Salary = Salary + (Salary * .10) ;
                WHERE CURRENT OF Personnel
        ELSE
            IF m->salary >= 40000
                UPDATE Employee SET Salary = Salary - (Salary * .10) ;
                    WHERE CURRENT OF Personnel
            ENDIF
        ENDIF
        * FETCH the next row and store its values into the memory variables.
        FETCH Personnel INTO hiredate, salary
    ENDDO
    CLOSE Personnel
    SET DATASERVER OFF
```

APPENDIX F

Reserved Keywords

Some words have a special meaning in SQL and therefore cannot be used as names of tables, views, columns, indexes, or users. These words are reserved for use by the system. Every implementation of SQL has its own list of reserved keywords, but these lists overlap. The following list, which contains the words reserved in SQLBase, is representative.

ABORT	DELETE
ADD	DESC
ALL	DISTINCT
ALTER	DOUBLE
AND	DROP
ANY	EXISTS
AS	FLOAT
ASC	FOR
AVG	FROM
BETWEEN	GRANT
BY	GROUP
CHAR	HAVING
CHECK	HOUR[S]
COLUMN	IDENTIFIED
COMMENT	IN
COMMIT	INDEX
CONNECT	INSERT
COUNT	INT
CREATE	INTEGER
CURRENT	INTO
DATE	IS
DATETIME	LIKE
DAY[S]	LONG
DBA	MAX
DEC	MICROSECOND
DECIMAL	MIN

MINUTE[S]	SELECT
MODIFY	SET
MONTH[S]	SMALLINT
NOT	SUM
NULL	SYNONYM
NUMBER	SYSDATE
OF	SYSDATETIME
ON	SYSTIME
OPTION	SYSTIMEZONE
OR	TABLE
ORDER	TO
PASSWORD	UNION
POST	UNIQUE
PRECISION	UPDATE
PUBLIC	USER
REAL	VALUES
RENAME	VARCHAR
RESOURCE	VIEW
REVOKE	WAIT
ROLLBACK	WHERE
ROWCOUNT	WITH
ROWID	YEAR[S]

Glossary

Aggregate function. A type of function that computes a single value from an entire column of data.

Argument. A value—column name, constant, or arithmetic expression—used in a function.

Authority level. Granted by SYSADM; determines the types of operations a user can perform in a database.

Back end. The database engine, as opposed to an interface.

Before image log. A file, maintained by the system, that keeps a backup image of the original version of any records changed by a user in the course of a transaction. The images are kept until the transaction is rolled back or committed.

Binding variables. The operation of associating each bind variable in a SQL statement with a particular input buffer so that the engine knows where to look for the data to use for that variable.

Clause. A major syntactical unit of a SQL statement. For example, a query might contain all of the following: a SELECT clause, a FROM clause, a WHERE clause, a GROUP BY clause, a HAVING clause, and an ORDER BY clause.

Column. A named field for data of a specified type.

Column name. The name of a column; one type of expression that can appear in a query or other SQL statement.

Compile. The first of the three major phases in the processing of SQL statements, the others being execute and fetch.

Compiler. A program that translates source code into lower-level code.

Composite primary key. A primary key based on two or more columns of a table.

Concatenated index. An index created on several columns jointly.

Concurrency. The degree to which a system can be shared among users.

Connection. An active relationship of a user to a database, analogous to being logged on; the assignment of a cursor to a user's authorization ID.

Connectivity. The degree to which the interface, or front end, of a database system can be successfully used with the engine, or back end, of a different SQL implementation.

Constant. A value, either string, numeric, or date/time, that takes no arguments and does not vary, that is, is the same for any row.

Correlated subquery. A subquery that requires information from the rows of an outer query and so must be run and correlated with each row of the outer query.

Correlation names. Abbreviated, temporary table names assigned in the FROM list of a query and used as a shorthand whenever an ambiguous reference makes it necessary to prefix a column name with the name of its originating table.

Cursor. Mechanism used to pick out a particular row position in a result set; the cursor represents where the engine is in the set, for purposes of row-at-a-time fetching.

Data-control statements. SQL statements that create other users or determine authority levels and privileges on tables and views in the database.

Data-definition statements. SQL statements that define or change the structure of the database.

Data-manipulation statements. SQL statements that change the data in a database by inserting new data, updating existing data, or deleting rows.

Data type. Any of the kinds of data recognized by SQL; all data in a given column is of one and the same of these specific data types.

Delimited identifiers. Identifiers (that is, names) that, because they consist of reserved keywords or contain spaces or other special characters, must be set off in double quotes.

Equijoin. A join embodying a join condition based on an equality.

Execute. Second of three major phases in the processing of SQL statements. The others are compile and fetch.

Expression. A syntactic structure that yields a value. Examples are column names, which, used as expressions, yield the value of the column at successive rows; expressions built around arithmetic operators (for example, +, −), which yield the result of performing the operations; and functions, which yield the value of the function for its arguments.

Fetch. Third of three major phases in the processing of SQL statements. The operation that takes rows from a query result one at a time.

Field. Another term for *column*; any place in a row that can contain a value.

Foreign key. Column based on a primary key column: every value in a foreign key should either be null or match some value in the primary key from which the foreign key column derives.

Front end. An interface to a database system; as distinct from the back end, or engine.

Function. A type of expression that can be used with constants, column names, and arithmetic expressions to manipulate data and return other expressions. The two basic kinds of function are aggregate and nonaggregate functions.

Function calls. Implementation-specific commands that can be used in application programming for performing the component operations of processing SQL statements; for example, to connect to a database or compile a statement.

Handle. A connection ID that identifies the connection to the engine.

Host structure. A group of host variables used collectively in a precompiler application as the source or destination for a set of selected values—for example, as a set of values to be inserted into or selected from the columns of a row.

Host variables. A species of program variable, namely, program variables that occur in SQL statements.

Identifier. The name of a user, column, table, or index.

Index. Database object created by a user on one or more columns of a table and subsequently applied and maintained by the system; catalogs rows so that the system can look up their location in the index instead of having to read the entire table.

Index key. The column or columns in an index.

Input buffer. Memory variable for binding to program data that is to be substituted for program variables in a SQL statement.

Interpreter. A program that, unlike a compiler, translates a line of higher-level language source code into lower-level executable code and runs the line immediately.

Isolation level. A level or order of stringency in the locking scheme.

Join. A query that draws data from several tables at once by using a join condition in the WHERE clause to join or merge rows from two tables on a similar column from each table.

Join condition. A search condition differing from ordinary search conditions in that the expressions related in the join condition refer to more than one table.

Journaling. A type of commonly implemented extension of SQL that enables data to be recovered when a media failure has destroyed some or all of a database.

Keyword. Any of the words having a special meaning in SQL (for example, "SELECT") such that the word is reserved and is not allowed to be used as an identifier without being delimited by quotation marks.

Label. Correlation name.

Length attribute. Component of a column definition when any of certain data types requiring a length attribute are declared to be the data type of the column; specifies how many characters or digits a column's values can have.

Lock. Mechanism for restricting access to database records to prevent simultaneous updates that might result in inconsistent data.

Nonaggregate function. A type of function that returns a value for each row.

Output buffer. Memory variable provided for, or set, in an application program as a place to put data returned by the engine in the fetch phase of a query.

Parse. Operation, performed by database engine, of checking a SQL statement for syntactical validity and to be sure that all columns, tables, users, and so forth that a statement refers to exist.

Portability. Degree to which one and the same application can run on a variety of machines.

Precision. The first of two components of the length attribute of certain numerical data types; specifies the overall maximum number of digits accepted by a column.

Precompiler. A program for analyzing another program and replacing higher-level source code with lower-level source code for a particular system.

Predicate. An element consisting of a relational operator followed by an expression; used to complete a search condition in a WHERE or HAVING clause.

Primary key. The column or group of columns in a table that allow the table's rows to be differentiated. The primary key should contain no nulls, and no two rows in the primary key may be duplicates.

Privileges. Warrants to perform various operations on tables and views.

Program variables. Placeholders in a SQL statement, representing the actual program data to be bound to the statement before it is executed.

Qualified identifier. A name explicitly qualified with a prefix—for example, "GUESTS.NAME".

Query. SQL statement used to retrieve data from the tables in a database. Queries are also called SELECT statements, after the operative keyword ("SELECT") in a query.

Referential integrity. The special relationship between primary key and foreign key columns.

Relational operator. Any of the operators used to form predicates comparing one value with another: specifically, =, !=, < >, >, !>, <, !<, < =, > =, BETWEEN, IS NULL, LIKE, EXISTS, IN.

Result table. Data matching the specifications of a query, that is, data that meets the conditions or has undergone the operations specified in the query. Only a query generates a result table.

Roll-forward journal. A file that logs any changes committed to the database while the journaling utility is set on. The file records any data-manipulation, data-definition, or data-control statements; it does not log queries, as these do not change data.

Row. A horizontal line of data in a table, containing the values of one or more columns.

Scale. The second of two components of the length attribute of certain numerical data types; indicates how many of the digits specified in the precision component are to the right of the decimal point.

Scroll cursor. A special kind of cursor that permits scrolling, allowing the application to range freely through the result set, forward or backward, and fetch any specified row instead of always having to fetch the *next* row.

Search condition. Consisting of an expression followed by a predicate, search conditions appear in the WHERE clause of DELETE and UPDATE statements and in the WHERE and HAVING clause of queries. They state a requirement that a row must meet if that row is to be included in the scope of operation of the statement containing the search condition. Multiple search conditions are linked by the operators AND and OR.

Statement. In the context of SQL, a directive built around a SQL keyword and addressed to the database to retrieve data or effect a change.

Subquery. A query nested in another SELECT statement.

Subselect. A query nested in another statement that may or may not be a SELECT statement.

Synonym. A user's private name for a table or view; used to make it unnecessary to qualify table-name references with the table owner's identifier.

System catalog. A group of tables maintained by the system, that automatically keeps track of information about the database.

System table. Any of the tables in the system catalog.

Table. The structure, consisting of a two dimensional arrangement of columns and rows, in which data is stored and returned in a relational system.

Transaction. Any consecutive series of interactions with a database begun with either a new database connection or with a SQL (or SQL-extension) statement issued after a commit. A transaction ends with either a commit or a rollback.

Transaction ID. An identification attached by the system to any statement or command issued during a transaction.

Unique index. An index created by adding the keyword UNIQUE in the CREATE INDEX statement; ensures that in the column or columns indexed all rows are unique, that is, that none are duplicates. Used to prevent operations that would create duplicate rows in the column or group of columns indexed.

View. The result table of a query, preserved with the CREATE VIEW statement.

Index

"
  enclosing words containing spaces, 20-21
  items in ASCII format files enclosed by, 154
% wild card used with LIKE operator, 40
&
  macro-substitution variables prefixed with, 228
  passing address rather than value of variable, 177
,
  in character string, 25, 34, 110
  numeric data types do not require, 26, 37
( ) to enclose column definitions, 21
*
  DOS wild card, 31, 40
  selecting columns in a program for the precompiler, 207
  selecting from all columns of a single table, 206
  wild card in functions, 52
+ marking columns that lack matching rows in outer joins, 83
, separating column definitions, 21
/ terminating SQL statements, 20, 166
: preceding host variables, 205, 217
; terminating SQL statements, 20
? DOS wild card, 40
@ prefixing nonaggregate SQLBase functions, 54
\
  terminating SQL statement and preceding data, 166
  disabling pattern-matching and treating character as literal, 40
|| representing the concatenate operator, 57
  representing space within names, 20
  wild card used with LIKE operator, 40

A

aggregate functions. *See* functions, aggregate
American National Standards Institute (ANSI), 2
arithmetic operators, 45-50
  * multiplication, 46
  + addition, 46
  − subtraction, 46
  / division, 46
ASCII format files, 154
attributes, table, 8-9
  length, 21
    precision of, 22
    scale of, 22
authority levels, 138
  CONNECT, 139-140, 143, 149
  DBA, 139, 143, 146, 149
  listing, 142
  RESOURCE, 139, 143
  SYSADM, 139, 143
authority, revoking, 148-150

B

before image log, 158
binding, 169-170, 181-182

book organization, 2-3
Boyce, R. F., 250
buffers
  binding data to, 169-170, 182
  data, 181
  defined, 169
  input, 169, 181
  output (SELECT), 169, 183-184

C

C programming language for programming with function call interface, 174, 203
Cartesian product, 79
catalog. *See* system catalog
Chamberlain, D. D., 250
COBOL
  host structures, 218-219
  portability of, 203
  precompiler written with, 204. *See also* precompiler (preprocessor)
  SQLBase function call interface for, 201
Codd, E. F., 250
column definitions enclosed in parentheses and separated by commas, 21
column names, operators and functions used with, 45
columns, database table, 8
  adding, 120-121
  grouping, 63
    numeric, 72
    primary, 64
    restricting, 70-72
  modifying, 121
  NOT NULL, 21, 91, 120-121
  order of, 12-13
  outer join to join on different length, 82
  renaming, 122
  selecting data from, 12-14
  UPDATE privilege for selected, 144
  updating multiple, 116
commands, dBASE-language
  @...SAY...GET, 226
  COPY, 225
  LIST, 224
  SELECT, 225
  SET DATASERVER, 225
  SET RELATION, 225
command, dBXL SET DATASERVER, 226
commands, SQL, 15-16
commands, SQLTalk
  APPLY JOURNAL, 157
  LOAD, 153
    ASCII format, 154
    DIF format, 154-155
    SQL format, 154
  REORGANIZE, 153, 156
  SET JOURNAL ON, 157
  UNLOAD, 133, 153, 155-156

295

UNLOAD ALL, 156
UNLOAD DATABASE, 156
constants
    operators used with, 45
    selecting, 59-61
    types
        date or time, 59
        numeric, 59
        string, 59
constants, SQLBase
    DAYS[S], 50
    HOUR[S], 50
    MICROSECOND[S], 50
    MINUTES[S], 50
    MONTH[S], 50
    SECOND[S], 50
    YEAR[S], 50
correlation names (labels) of temporary tables, 87
cursor(s)
    in embedded SQL, 172
    multiple, 208
    operations in dBASE interface, 228-230
    scroll, 238-240

D

data
    case of, 25, 34-35
    changing, 115-118
    duplicate values
        in columns other than primary key, 236
        key fields and, 9-10
    inserting
        in a table, 24-27
        in a view, 109
    integrity, 103, 111-112
    redundancy, minimizing, 7
    security using views, 108-109
    storage in tables for relational DBMS, 7
    string
        case sensitivity of, 26
    unambiguous column references to, 89
data dictionary. *See* system catalog
data type
    CHAR (character), 21-23
    DATE, 22-23
    DECIMAL, 21, 23, 47, 120
    DOUBLE PRECISION, 21
    FLOAT, 21, 23
    INTEGER, 21, 23, 47, 121
    LONG VARCHAR (LONG), 22-23, 181, 184
        manipulating columns of type, 187-190
        queries, 188-189
        writing, 189-190
    NUMERIC, 21, 23
    REAL, 21
    SMALLINT, 21, 23
    TIME, 22-23
    TIMESTAMP, 22-23, 213
    VARCHAR, 22-23, 47, 91, 121

database
    access cycle, 163
    automatic recovery of, 157-158
    development of a SQL-based, 250
    fragmentation, 156
    loading data from external file to, 154
    logging on (connecting) to, 19
    modular, 13
    purpose, 1
    restoring, 157
    undoing changes to, 118
    utilities to overcome SQL deficiencies, 153
database management system (DBMS)
    nonrelational, use of tables in, 7
    relational
        features, 1
        overview, 7-17
data-control statements as category of SQL statement, 15
data-definition statements as category of SQL statement, 15
data-manipulation statements as category of SQL statement, 15
date formats (table), 24
DB2
    keywords in, 49
    locking scheme, 193
    multiple connections and multiple databases not supported by, 207
    OS/2 Extended Edition compatibility with mainframe, 253
    SQL precompiler
        DCLGEN declaration generator program, 220
        fields, 212-213
        origins, 251
        syntax, 202-203
dBIII Compiler (Wordtech), 222
dBASE IV (Ashton-Tate), 221, 230
dBASE-language interface, 173, 221-230
    interpreter, 222
    macro-substitution feature in, 228
    precompiler stage skipped with, 223
    SQL applications written in, 222
dBXL (WordTech), 221, 223, 249
    DBTOSQL utility for converting databases to SQL tables, 226
    embedded SQL interface of, 223, 225-228
    filter conditions, 224
    invisible SQL interface of, 223-225
declaration generator, 220
DIF (Data Interchange Format) file format, 154-155
dynamic SQL feature, 203

E

entity
    information in table rows for individual, 9
    primary key and, 9-12
equijoins, 79-82
error conditions of API functions, 177-178
error handling, 166
expression(s)
    arithmetic operations as, 31
    arithmetic operators in, 50

column names as, 31
defined, 31
evaluating, 31
functions as, 31
ordering a sort by, 74

F

fetch phase, 165, 171, 184-185
file
   .dbf, 227
   error.sql, 176
   errsql.h, 176
   fragmentation, 156
   LONGTEXT, 189
   roll-forward journal, 157
   sql.h, 176, 179
function call interface, 173-186
   error conditions, 177-178
   origins, 251
   sample code for, 175-178
function calls, 173, 201-202
   to C available in Quicksilver and dBASE IV, 230
   incompatibilities among SQL implementations for, 254
functions and function calls, SQLBase API (Application Programming Interface), 249
   selbuf, 185
   selitem, 181
   sqlblo, 181
   sqlbnd, 182
   sqlcmt, 184-185
   sqldes, 184
   sqldis, 185
   sqlfet, 184, 202
   sqlnbv, 177
   sqlrbk, 185
   sqlrlo, 188-189
   sqlssb, 183, 188
   sqlwlo, 189
functions, SQLBase, 51-58
   aggregate, 45
      AVG(argument), 51, 107
      COUNT(argument), 51-52, 68
      GROUP BY clause and, 65-66, 69-70
      MAX(argument), 51, 70
      MIN(argument), 51
      nested, 53
      in search conditions, 53
      to specify replacement values in views, 117
      SUM(argument), 51
      WHERE clause and, 106-107
   arithmetic operators used with, 46
   nonaggregate, 45
      @DAY, 57
      @HOUR, 58
      @LEFT, 54-55
      @LENGTH, 55
      @MINUTE, 58
      @MONTH, 58
      @MONTHBEG, 58
      @PROPER, 54

@QUARTER, 58
@QUARTERBEG, 58
@SECOND, 58
@VALUE, 56
@WEEKBEG, 58
@WEEKDAY, 58
@YEAR, 58
@YEARBEG, 58
   ordering a sort by, 74
   types of nonaggregate
   date or time, 57-58
   string, 54-57

H

handle(s) (connection ID), 172, 176
   multiple, 190-191
host structures, 218-210

I

IBM Research Laboratory, 250
identifier
   delimited, 21
   as name for user, column, table, or index, 20, 79
   qualified, 79
indexes, 125-130
   accepting duplicates in, 137
   concatenated (composite), 126, 128-129
   defined, 16
   dropping, 122, 129
   on multiple columns, 137
   speeding query execution, 127
   speeding searches, 126
   unique, 126, 128
   uses of, 127
      concatenated, 128-129
      unique, 128
INGRES (Relational Technologies), 250-251

J

join condition
   for complex queries, 88-89
   defined, 78-79
   equijoin, 79-82
   non-equijoins, 88
   outer joins, 82-85
   self-joins, 85-87
   on views, 107-108
journaling, 157

K

key(s)
   composite or composite primary, 10
   foreign, 237
      delete rule, 237
      update rule, 237
   primary, 9-12, 236-237
   referential integrity of, 237

keywords, ANSI-standard SQL
    ABSOLUTE, 239
    FIRST, 239
    LAST, 239
    NEXT, 239
    PRIMARY KEY, 236
    PRIOR, 239
    RELATIVE, 239
    UNIQUE, 236
keywords, Oracle
    LEVEL, 243
    PRIOR, 242
keywords, SQLBase, 46
    ALL, 34, 52, 142, 156
    ASC, 73
    AUTOMEM, 229
    CASCADE, 238
    CURRENT DATE, 49
    CURRENT DATETIME, 49
    CURRENT TIME, 49
    CURRENT TIMESTAMP, 49
    DATA, 155-156
    DATE, 70
    DESC, 73
    DISTINCT, 32-34, 52, 72, 110, 209
    FROM, 29, 31, 109
    HAVING, 63, 71-72, 95, 110, 209
    IN, 95
    INTO, 213, 228
    KEEP, 227
    MONTHS, 50
    NOT, 41
    NULL, 26-27
    PUBLIC, 142, 146
    SYSDATE, 49, 59
    SYSDATETIME, 49-50
    SYSTIME, 49-50, 61
    UNION, 91-94, 104, 209
    UNIQUE, 126
    WHERE, 34-43, 50, 65, 166, 216, 228

L

locks
    level of isolation of, 194
        Cursor Stability (CS), 195-196
        Read Only (RO), 196
        Read Repeatability (RR), 195
    on pages, 193
    rollbacks causing, 196-197
    on rows or records, 193-194
        exclusive (X-locks), 194, 196
        shared (S-locks), 194-196

M

multiuser systems
    concurrency in, 194-195
    deadlocks in, 196
    ensuring data consistency in, 193-196
    record and page locks in. *See* locks

N

nonaggregate functions. *See* functions, nonaggregate
non-equijoins, 88
Novell, dBASE interface for, 221
null value, 21, 26, 30, 64
    replaced with DEFAULT clause, 233-234

O

objects, SQL
    indexes as, 16
    synonyms as, 16
    system catalog as, 16
    views as, 16
operators
    AND, 42-43, 98, 112
    concatenate, 57, 60-61
    NOT, 41, 97
    OR, 42-43
Oracle
    dBASE interface for, 221
    forms interface for, 251
    function call interface, 251
    keywords in, 49
OS/2 Extended Edition, 253
outer joins, 82-85

P

passwords
    changing, 150
    listing, 142-143
precompiler (preprocessor)
    advantages, 201-203
    COBOL SQL, 205-220
        delimited statements, 206
        multiple connections with, 207-208
        statement syntax, 205-207
    defined, 199
    dynamic SQL feature, 203
    interface, 173-174
    limitations, 203-204
    origins, 251
    program portability aided by, 202-203, 251
    purpose, 200
privileges
    dropping, 122
    listing users', 143
    required for updates to rows, 110
    revoking, 140, 148-150
    types
        ALTER, 140
        DELETE, 110, 140-141
        INDEX, 127, 140
        INSERT, 110, 140-141
        SELECT, 110, 140-141, 145
        UPDATE, 110, 140-141, 144

Q

QUEL relational language, 250
query(ies), 29-43
   basic elements, 29-34
   as category of SQL statement, 15
   complex
      joins in, 88-89
      replaced with simpler ones, 103-105
   fetch phase for, 165, 171, 184-185, 215-216
   inserting data with, 101-102
   manipulating data with, 45-61
   of multiple tables, 77-89
   narrowing, 34-43
   nested
      compound, 98-99
      simple, 94-98
   results
      arranging, 63-76
      grouped in sets, 63-70
      restricting focus of, 70-72
      sorting order of, 72-75
   subquery(ies)
      correlated, 99-101
      precedence of, 94
      queries containing multiple, 98
      as query within, 87, 91
      views examined with CHECK option cannot contain, 112
   unions of, 91-94
   views required by some, 106-107
Quicksilver, 249
   C function calls available with, 230
   DBTOSQL utility to convert databases to SQL tables, 226
   interface, 221

R

referential integrity, 237
relational operators
   other
      BETWEEN, 88
      BETWEEN...AND, 38-39
      EXISTS, 38-39, 95-97, 99
      IN, 38, 41
      IS NULL, 38-39
      LIKE, 38-41
   simple, 95
      !< is not less than, 36
      != is not equal to, 36
      !> is not greater than, 36
      < is less than, 36
      <= is less than or equal to, 36
      <> is not equal to, 36
      = is equal to, 35-36
      > is greater than, 36
      >= is greater than or equal to, 36
relational predicates
   connecting, 42-43
   other, 38-42
   simple, 35-38

result. *See also* table(s), result
   set for LONG VARCHAR operations
      operations, 191-192
   uses, 192
result set mode, 192
rollbacks, 118, 123
   explicit, 158
   implicit, 158
   locking out other users with, 196-197
   preventing deadlocks, 196
rows, database table, 8-9
   deleting, 117
   fetching, 165, 167, 171, 184-185, 213-214
   join for retrieving, 14
   SELECT statements to return multiple, 208-214
   selecting data from, 12-14, 29
   suppressing duplicate, 33, 67-68, 72, 92
   tree-structured order for retrieving, 242
   updating data in, 116-117

S

scroll cursors defined, 191
search conditions, 34
SELECT statements. *See* queries
self joins, 85-87
SEQUEL/2 language, 250
spooling, 30
spreadsheet programs, loading data into SQL databases from, 154
SQL Communication Area (SQLCA), 210
   defining, 211
   error conditions, 212
   fields composing, 212-213
   header string, 212
   length, 212
   return code, 212
   warning
      for adjusted date or TIMESTAMP value, 213
      for data truncation, 212
      for disregarded null values, 212
      for lack of WHERE clause, 213
      for unequal number of host variables, 213
      for unused character string, 213
      for warning flags, 212
SQLBase, 2
   CHECK option enhanced to allow subqueries in, 112
   development of, 252
   outer joins in, 82-85
   table and view update features, 118-119
SQLBase API (Application Programming Interface), 174-175
   database access cycle, 178-179
      bind data, 181-182
      commit, 185
      compile, 180-181
      connect, 179-180
      disconnect, 185-186
      execute, 184
      fetch, 184-185
      set output buffers, 183-184
   differences between other function call interfaces and, 252-253

error conditions, 177-178
files, 176
LONG VARCHAR operations, 187-197
    for data consistency and multiple users, 193-196
    manipulating columns for, 187-190
    multiple handles for, 190-191
    result set operations for, 191-192
SQL/DS, 251
SQLTalk, 2, 163. *See also* commands, SQLTalk
statements,
    access path for, 168
    ADD, 119-121
    ALTER, 197
    ALTER PASSWORD, 150
    ALTER TABLE, 15, 118-120
    CLOSE, 172, 208
    COMMENT ON, 134-135
    COMMIT, 118, 123, 157-158, 181, 185, 196, 214
    CONNECT TO, 207
    CREATE, 196-197
    CREATE INDEX, 15, 126, 154-155
    CREATE SYNONYM, 145-146
    CREATE TABLE, 15, 19-21, 24, 70, 104-155, 180-181, 234-236, 238
    CREATE VIEW, 15, 104, 109, 136, 234
    DECLARE, 172, 219-220
    DECLARE CURSOR, 208-209, 213
    DECLARE TABLE, 220
    DELETE, 15, 46, 115-117, 190, 213-214, 229
        CURRENT OF cursor phrase, 213-214
    DROP, 109, 119, 122-123, 196
    DROP INDEX, 127
    DROP SYNONYM, 147
    DROP VIEW, 109
    END-EXEC, 201, 206
    EXEC SQL, 201, 206
    EXECUTE, 204
    FETCH, 172, 208, 213-214, 229
    FETCH INTO, 215
    GRANT, 196-197
    GRANT (Database Authority), 15, 139, 142, 150
    GRANT (Table Privileges), 15, 140-141
    GROUP BY, 53, 63-72, 74-75, 89, 92, 110, 209, 244-245
    INSERT, 15, 25-27, 91, 101, 115, 154, 165, 180-181, 184, 187, 217
    MODIFY, 119, 121
    OPEN, 172
    ORDER BY, 63, 72-75, 92, 104, 209
    parsing, 168
    PERFORM, 203-204
    phases of processing, 167
        compile, 167-169
        execute, 167, 169-170
        fetch, 165, 167, 171
    precompiling, 169
    PREPARE, 203-204, 213
    RENAME, 119, 122
    RENAME TABLE, 119, 122
    REVOKE (Database Authority), 139, 148-149
    REVOKE (Table Privileges), 140, 148-149
    ROLLBACK, 118, 123, 158, 214
    security check on, 168

    SELECT, 15, 29, 34, 45-46, 50, 59-60, 66-68, 74, 89, 91-92, 102, 104, 110, 136, 181-184, 187, 190-191, 208-214, 225
        FOR UPDATE OF clause in, 209
        SAVE TO clause in, 227, 228
    SELECT INTO, 215-217, 226, 228
    SET, 166
    SET DEFAULT, 238
    SET NULL, 238
    UNION, 92-93
    UPDATE, 15, 46, 115-117, 166, 184, 187, 190-191, 213-214, 229
        CURRENT OF cursor phrase, 213-214
    WHENEVER, 210-211
string digits, 47-48
Structured Query Language (SQL)
    connectivity between environments, 252
    dialects, 252
    drivers (translators or routers), 254
    embedded, 2
        connecting and disconnecting to, 172-173
        cursors in, 172
        dBXL product for, 223-224, 226-228
        error handling with, 166-167
        function call interface for, 173-174
        precompiler (preprocessor) interface, 173-174, 199-204
        programming, 163
            options, 173-174
        reasons to use, 163-167
        results and, 30
        row-at-a-time processing with, 164-165
        setting orientation of, 165
        substituting for variables with, 165-166
    extensions, 2, 233-248
        COMPUTE, 233
        CONNECT BY, 233
    hierarchical relationships in, 240-242
    incompatibilities between implementations of, 252
    interactive, 2, 164
        results and, 30
        termination marks for, 20
    invisible, 223-225
    new features
        CHECK constraint, 234-235
        COMPUTE clause, 243-247
        CONNECT BY clause, 240-243
        DEFAULT clause, 233-234
        FOREIGN KEY clause for referential integrity, 237
        integrity constraints, 236
        START WITH clause, 242
    origins, 250-252
    predictions and trends for, 254−255
    as standard for managing relational DBMS, 1-2
    standardization, 253-254
    statement types, 15
    syntax, 15
    universal (portable), 252-253, 255
subselect, 91
Sybase Inc., 245
synonyms
    creating, 145-146

defined, 16
dropping, 122
system administrator (SYSADM)
    actions performed on system tables, 147
    authorization ID, 133
    granting levels of authority, 138-139
    as owner of all tables, 133, 138
    password display restricted to, 143
    passwords changed by, 150
    synonyms for tables or views created by, 146
system catalog, 131-151
    defined, 16
    granting access to, 147-148
    selective views to restrict access to, 147-148
    system administrator actions on, 147
    system administrator as owner of, 133
    tables, SQLBase
        SYSCOLAUTH, 131, 144
        SYSCOLUMNS, 131, 134-135
        SYSCOMMANDS, 131-132
        SYSINDEXES, 131, 137
        SYSKEYS, 131, 138
        SYSSYNONYMS, 131, 146
        SYSTABAUTH, 131, 143-144
        SYSTABLES (SYSCATALOG), 131-134
        SYSUSERAUTH, 131, 142-143
        SYSVIEWS, 131, 135-137
System R (IBM) prototype, 250

T

table(s)
    changing structure of, 118-119
    constructing, 19-27
    definitions, 219-220
    destination, 102
    dropping, 118, 122-123
    join, 14, 77-89
        based on an equality, 79-82
        on columns with unequal numbers of rows, 82-85
        to the same table, 85-87
    owner
        name as prefix to name of, 145
        synonyms created by, 146
    renaming, 122
    result, 15, 29, 60
    sample
        GUESTS, 8-10, 12, 20, 25, 77-89, 92, 96, 99, 101, 104, 111-112, 128
        GUEST—ROSTER, 10-11, 19-20, 25, 30-32, 46-50, 56, 60, 77-89, 92, 96-97, 99-101, 108, 116-117, 119-122, 125, 127, 129, 141, 143, 237-238
        GUEST—WT, 70-75, 106, 143
        MALE—GUESTS, 134
        ROOMS, 79-80
        WEIGHT—CHART, 80-81, 104, 126, 128-129
    storing and displaying data in, 7
    synonym names for. *See* synonyms
    system. *See* system catalog
    temporary, 87
    unloading data from, 133

updating selected columns of, 144
virtual. *See* views
time formats (table), 24
transaction defined, 118
transaction ID, 158

U

UFI (User Friendly Interface), 250

V

variables
    host, 205
        assignment rules for, 218
        data conversions and, 218
        defined, 205
        as the destination of data retrieved, 216
        host structures for, 219
        retrieving columns into, 215
        in a search condition, 216
        as the source of data entered, 217
        unequal number of SQL and table or view, 213
    for information about SQL statement, 176
    passing address of, 177
    program, 165-166, 171, 181
    substituting for, 165-166, 171
views, 103-113
    aggregate functions in, 53
    CHECK option, 234-235
        to create, 136
        to ensure data integrity in, 103, 111-112
    definitions for, 219-220
    dropping, 118, 123
    joins on, 107-108
    queries that require, 106-107
    security using selective access to data in, 108-109
    synonyms for, 145-146
    UPDATE privilege for selected columns of, 144
    updateable
        fully, 110
        partially, 110
        removing rows from, 117

W

wild cards
    %, 40
    *, 31, 40
    —, 40
    ?, 40

More Computer Knowledge from Que

LOTUS SOFTWARE TITLES

1-2-3 QueCards	21.95
1-2-3 QuickStart	21.95
1-2-3 Quick Reference	6.95
1-2-3 for Business, 2nd Edition	22.95
1-2-3 Command Language	21.95
1-2-3 Macro Library, 2nd Edition	21.95
1-2-3 Tips, Tricks, and Traps, 2nd Edition	21.95
Using 1-2-3, Special Edition	24.95
Using 1-2-3 Workbook and Disk, 2nd Edition	29.95
Using Symphony, 2nd Edition	26.95

DATABASE TITLES

dBASE III Plus Handbook, 2nd Edition	22.95
dBASE IV Handbook, 3rd Edition	23.95
dBASE IV Tips, Tricks, and Traps, 2nd Edition	21.95
dBASE IV QueCards	21.95
dBASE IV Quick Reference	6.95
dBASE IV QuickStart	21.95
dBXL and Quicksilver Programming: Beyond dBASE	24.95
R:BASE Solutions: Applications and Resources	19.95
R:BASE User's Guide, 3rd Edition	19.95
Using Clipper	24.95
Using Reflex	19.95
Using Paradox, 2nd Edition	22.95
Using Q & A, 2nd Edition	21.95

MACINTOSH AND APPLE II TITLES

HyperCard QuickStart: A Graphics Approach	21.95
Using AppleWorks, 2nd Edition	21.95
Using dBASE Mac	19.95
Using Dollars and Sense	19.95
Using Excel	21.95
Using HyperCard: From Home to HyperTalk	24.95
Using Microsoft Word: Macintosh Version	21.95
Using Microsoft Works	19.95
Using WordPerfect: Macintosh Version	19.95

APPLICATIONS SOFTWARE TITLES

CAD and Desktop Publishing Guide	24.95
Smart Tips, Tricks, and Traps	23.95
Using AutoCAD	29.95
Using DacEasy	21.95
Using Dollars and Sense: IBM Version, 2nd Edition	19.95
Using Enable/OA	23.95
Using Excel: IBM Version	24.95
Using Managing Your Money	19.95
Using Quattro	21.95
Using Smart	22.95
Using SuperCalc4	21.95

HARDWARE AND SYSTEMS TITLES

DOS Programmer's Reference	24.95
DOS QueCards	21.95
DOS Tips, Tricks, and Traps	22.95
DOS Workbook and Disk	29.95
IBM PS/2 Handbook	21.95
Managing Your Hard Disk, 2nd Edition	22.95
MS-DOS Quick Reference	6.95
MS-DOS QuickStart	21.95
MS-DOS User's Guide, 3rd Edition	22.95
Networking IBM PCs, 2nd Edition	19.95
Programming with Windows	22.95
Understanding UNIX: A Conceptual Guide, 2nd Edition	21.95
Upgrading and Repairing PCs	24.95
Using Microsoft Windows	19.95
Using OS/2	22.95
Using PC DOS, 2nd Edition	22.95

WORD-PROCESSING AND DESKTOP PUBLISHING TITLES

Microsoft Word Techniques and Applications	19.95
Microsoft Word Tips, Tricks, and Traps	19.95
Using DisplayWrite 4	19.95
Using Microsoft Word, 2nd Edition	21.95
Using MultiMate Advantage, 2nd Edition	19.95
Using PageMaker IBM Version, 2nd Edition	24.95
Using PFS: First Publisher	22.95
Using Sprint	21.95
Using Ventura Publisher, 2nd Edition	24.95
Using WordPerfect, 3rd Edition	21.95
Using WordPerfect 5	24.95
Using WordPerfect 5 Workbook and Disk	29.95
Using WordStar, 2nd Edition	21.95
WordPerfect Macro Library	21.95
WordPerfect QueCards	21.95
WordPerfect Quick Reference	6.95
WordPerfect QuickStart	21.95
WordPerfect Tips, Tricks, and Traps, 2nd Edition	21.95
WordPerfect 5 Workbook and Disk	29.95
Ventura Publisher Tips, Tricks, and Traps	24.95
Ventura Publisher Techniques and Applications	22.95

PROGRAMMING AND TECHNICAL TITLES

Assembly Language Quick Reference	6.95
C Programming Guide, 3rd Edition	24.95
C Quick Reference	6.95
DOS and BIOS Functions Quick Reference	6.95
QuickBASIC Quick Reference	6.95
Turbo Pascal Quick Reference	6.95
Turbo Pascal Tips, Tricks, and Traps	19.95
Using Assembly Language	24.95
Using QuickBASIC 4	19.95
Using Turbo Pascal	21.95
AutoCAD Quick Reference	6.95

Que Order Line: **1-800-428-5331**

All prices subject to change without notice. Prices and charges are for domestic orders only.
Non-U.S. prices might be higher.

SELECT QUE BOOKS TO INCREASE YOUR PERSONAL COMPUTER PRODUCTIVITY

R:BASE User's Guide, 3rd Edition

by Allen G. Taylor

If you use R:BASE for DOS or R:BASE for OS/2, *R:BASE User's Guide*, 3rd Edition, is the book for you. This well-written text serves as both a tutorial and a lasting reference to Microrim's powerful database management system, taking you step-by-step from database basics to advanced R:BASE features and applications. This new edition features information on R:BASE's new SQL commands and includes an expanded troubleshooting section. Make R:BASE work for you with Que's new *R:BASE User's Guide*, 3rd Edition!

DOS Programmer's Reference

by Terry Dettmann

Intermediate and advanced programmers will find a wealth of information in Que's *DOS Programmer's Reference*. Designed for serious applications programmers, this "nuts and bolts" guide contains sections on DOS functions and their use; IBM-specific programs; expanded and extended memory; and the use of DOS with various languages, such as C, BASIC, and assembly language. A combination of tutorial and reference, this text helps you gain a greater understanding of what your operating system has to offer. Choose *DOS Programmer's Reference*, the definitive guide to DOS applications programming.

C Programming Guide, 3rd Edition

by Jack Purdum, Ph.D.

A completely new edition of a Que classic. Rewritten to reflect C's ongoing development—including the new ANSI standard—this text contains many programming tips that let readers benefit from the author's practical programming experience. Also included are a complete keyword reference guide, a host of program examples, and a tear-out quick reference card. This is the perfect guide for beginning programmers in the C language.

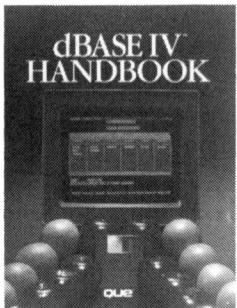

dBASE IV Handbook, 3rd Edition

by George T. Chou, Ph.D.

Learn dBASE IV quickly with Que's new *dBASE IV Handbook*, 3rd Edition! dBASE expert George Chou leads you step-by-step from basic database concepts to advanced dBASE features, using a series of Quick Start tutorials. Experienced dBASE users will appreciate the extensive information on the new features of dBASE IV, including the new user interface, the query-by-example mode, and the SQL module. Complete with comprehensive command and function reference sections, *dBASE IV Handbook*, 3rd Edition, is an exhaustive guide to dBASE IV!

R881—SQL Programmer's Guide

REGISTRATION CARD

Register your copy of *SQL Programmer's Guide* and receive information about Que's newest products. Complete this registration card and return it to Que Corporation, P.O. Box 90, Carmel, IN 46032.

Name _____ Phone _____

Company _____ Title _____

Address _____

City _____ State _____ ZIP _____

Please check the appropriate answers:

Where did you buy *SQL Programmer's Guide*?
- ☐ Bookstore (name: _____)
- ☐ Computer store (name: _____)
- ☐ Catalog (name: _____)
- ☐ Direct from Que _____
- ☐ Other: _____

How many computer books do you buy a year?
- ☐ 1 or less   ☐ 6-10
- ☐ 2-5   ☐ More than 10

How many Que books do you own?
- ☐ 1   ☐ 6-10
- ☐ 2-5   ☐ More than 10

How long have you been using SQL?
- ☐ Less than 6 months
- ☐ 6 months to 1 year
- ☐ 1-3 years
- ☐ More than 3 years

What influenced your purchase of *SQL Programmer's Guide*?
- ☐ Personal recommendation
- ☐ Advertisement   ☐ Que catalog
- ☐ In-store display ☐ Que mailing
- ☐ Price   ☐ Que's reputation
- ☐ Other: _____

How would you rate the overall content of *SQL Programmer's Guide*?
- ☐ Very good   ☐ Satisfactory
- ☐ Good   ☐ Poor

How would you rate *the sample programs*?
- ☐ Very good   ☐ Satisfactory
- ☐ Good   ☐ Poor

How would you rate *Chapter 4: Using Queries To Manipulate Data*?
- ☐ Very good   ☐ Satisfactory
- ☐ Good   ☐ Poor

How would you rate *Chapter 13: SQL Programming Concepts*?
- ☐ Very good   ☐ Satisfactory
- ☐ Good   ☐ Poor

What do you like *best* about *SQL Programmer's Guide*?

What do you like *least* about *SQL Programmer's Guide*?

How do you use *SQL Programmer's Guide*?

What other Que products do you own?

For what other programs would a Que book be helpful?

Please feel free to list any other comments you may have about *SQL Programmer's Guide*.

_____
_____
_____
_____

FOLD HERE

Place
Stamp
Here

Que Corporation
P.O. Box 90
Carmel, IN 46032

Free Catalog!

Mail us this registration form today, and we'll send you a free catalog featuring Que's complete line of best-selling books.

Name of Book _____
Name _____
Title _____
Phone (___) _____
Company _____
Address _____
City _____
State _____ ZIP _____

Please check the appropriate answers:

1. Where did you buy your Que book?
   - ☐ Bookstore (name: _____)
   - ☐ Computer store (name: _____)
   - ☐ Catalog (name: _____)
   - ☐ Direct from Que
   - ☐ Other: _____

2. How many computer books do you buy a year?
   - ☐ 1 or less
   - ☐ 2-5
   - ☐ 6-10
   - ☐ More than 10

3. How many Que books do you own?
   - ☐ 1
   - ☐ 2-5
   - ☐ 6-10
   - ☐ More than 10

4. How long have you been using this software?
   - ☐ Less than 6 months
   - ☐ 6 months to 1 year
   - ☐ 1-3 years
   - ☐ More than 3 years

5. What influenced your purchase of this Que book?
   - ☐ Personal recommendation
   - ☐ Advertisement
   - ☐ In-store display
   - ☐ Price
   - ☐ Que catalog
   - ☐ Que mailing
   - ☐ Que's reputation
   - ☐ Other: _____

6. How would you rate the overall content of the book?
   - ☐ Very good
   - ☐ Good
   - ☐ Satisfactory
   - ☐ Poor

7. What do you like *best* about this Que book?
   _____
   _____

8. What do you like *least* about this Que book?
   _____
   _____

9. Did you buy this book with your personal funds?
   ☐ Yes   ☐ No

10. Please feel free to list any other comments you may have about this Que book.
    _____
    _____
    _____

Que

Order Your Que Books Today!

Name _____
Title _____
Company _____
City _____
State _____ ZIP _____
Phone No. (___) _____

Method of Payment:

Check ☐   (Please enclose in envelope.)
Charge My: VISA ☐   MasterCard ☐
American Express ☐

Charge # _____
Expiration Date _____

Order No.	Title	Qty.	Price	Total

You can **FAX** your order to 1-317-573-2583. Or call 1-800-428-5331, ext. ORDR to order direct.
Please add $2.50 per title for shipping and handling.

Subtotal _____
Shipping & Handling _____
Total _____

Que

NO POSTAGE
NECESSARY
IF MAILED
IN THE
UNITED STATES

BUSINESS REPLY MAIL
First Class Permit No. 9918   Indianapolis, IN

Postage will be paid by addressee

que®

11711 N. College
Carmel, IN 46032

NO POSTAGE
NECESSARY
IF MAILED
IN THE
UNITED STATES

BUSINESS REPLY MAIL
First Class Permit No. 9918   Indianapolis, IN

Postage will be paid by addressee

que®

11711 N. College
Carmel, IN 46032